Rediscovering a Nation

Other Books by Michael Wayne Santos

Caught in Irons: North Atlantic Fishermen in the Last Days of Sail

A Beacon through the Years: A History of Lynchburg College, 1903–2003

United States Foreign Policy 1945–1968: The Bomb, Spies, Stories, and Lies

Clouds of White Sail: Fishermen, Racing, and the End of an Era

A Radical Proposal to Reinvigorate the Teaching of the Liberal Arts

Rediscovering a Nation

Will the Real America Please Stand Up?

Michael Wayne Santos

Rowman & Littlefield
Lanham • Boulder • New York • London

Published by Rowman & Littlefield
An imprint of The Rowman & Littlefield Publishing Group, Inc.
4501 Forbes Boulevard, Suite 200, Lanham, Maryland 20706
www.rowman.com

86-90 Paul Street, London EC2A 4NE

British Library Cataloguing in Publication Information Available

Library of Congress Cataloging-in-Publication Data

Names: Santos, Michael Wayne, author.
Title: Rediscovering a nation : will the real America please stand up? /
    Michael Wayne Santos.
Description: Lanham, Maryland : Rowman & Littlefield, 2022. | Includes
    bibliographical references and index. | Summary: "Many Americans wonder
    how our politics became dysfunctional—and what it will take to fix it.
    Michael Wayne Santos takes readers on a journey to the heart of the
    American nation and the values that have allowed us to overcome previous
    challenges, sometimes in spite of ourselves"— Provided by publisher.
Identifiers: LCCN 2022001237 (print) | LCCN 2022001238 (ebook) | ISBN
    9781538169216 (cloth) | ISBN 9781538169223 (epub)
Subjects: LCSH: Political culture—United States. | Political
    ethics—United States. | Civics. | United States—Politics and
    government—Moral and ethical aspects.
Classification: LCC JK1726 .S324 2022 (print) | LCC JK1726 (ebook) | DDC
    306.20973—dc23/eng/20220215
LC record available at https://lccn.loc.gov/2022001237
LC ebook record available at https://lccn.loc.gov/2022001238

For the Two Things I Love Most in Life:
My Wife, Mary Colin,
and
My Country;
and
For the Memory of Daisy

CONTENTS

PREFACE

This book began as I tried to make sense of what was happening to my country after the 2016 presidential election. I was clearly not alone in this. Most sane Americans watched first in disbelief, then frustration, then anger, and even despair. To view the news was to simultaneously rage and weep at what Donald Trump and his administration were doing to the nation I love. Just when I thought things could not get worse, when the president and his minions could not go any lower, they found new bottoms and continued to drill down. As I joked with my wife, when they reached what seemed to be bedrock, they looked for a shovel. When that wasn't good enough, out came the jackhammer. Then the backhoe, etc., etc., ad nauseam.

I'm lucky to have a venue in which to sort out my feelings, because I teach history to college students. Together, we sought to understand how we had gotten to this place and time. Clearly there were unresolved issues like systemic racism that had gone largely ignored since the founding of the Republic, which allowed Trump's hate-filled agenda to find traction. There were also new complicating factors, like the creation of news silos that, despite the information superhighway created by the internet, made us more isolated and insular.

There was, however, something else in the American story that was being forgotten in the twenty-four-hour-a-day news coverage that fixated on Mr. Trump's buffoonery. He represented a very real part of America that has always lurked in the shadows—that is true. Still, he did not represent the heart of the nation.

He and his enablers did not understand the foundational principles that allowed the country that he failed to lead and sought to destroy to move from a loose, vulnerable collection of thirteen states pressed up against the Eastern Seaboard to the world's dominant superpower. To look at that history was to stand humbly in awe of the birthright that previous generations had bequeathed to us.

As I spoke to my students, I found myself, more than ever, harkening back to the lessons of the past that allowed us to overcome the odds, to the ideals that kept us honest, sometimes despite ourselves. I found myself talking about the heroes and heroines who challenged us to be better versions of ourselves. In short, I began reflecting on what I have always asked my students to do: think in terms of the legacies of the past for an understanding of the present.

The results were enlightening, and they ultimately restored some hope for me, for my students, and for my family and friends when they were discussed and shared. That is what this book seeks to do—to share some of the reflections that a crisis of faith about the nation I love have led me to. What are the legacies of this country, handed down to us by the Founders? What have previous generations done to keep the principles on which the Republic rests alive and to advance their implications for more and more people? Where were the fault lines that put the American experiment at risk, and how have we overcome them? And when we have failed to overcome them, what possible lessons are there for understanding what America is and can become?

A belief in self-evident truths about human rights and dignity provide us a high bar to reach for, but then again, as Robert Browning once said, "A man's reach should exceed his grasp, or what's a heaven for?" And here, as with the words from the Declaration of Independence, may lie a central truth about the American Republic: its emphasis on our very humanity. With all our flaws as human beings, we seek to be better, to reach for more, and that is only possible when we are free.

There have and always will be obstacles to making the ideals that Thomas Jefferson penned in the Declaration of Independence real. In fact, it may fairly be said that the miracle of America is that it has survived and become the nation it has. After all, its founding concept—liberty—is by its very nature antithetical to the existence of a country, which requires union to exist, let alone thrive.

If human beings are even partially free to be themselves, the tendency is to fragment. Yet without unity, there can be no guarantee of liberty (or anything else). Finding and constantly recalibrating the balance point where liberty and union can coexist in dynamic tension with each other and allow for the nation to progress was, and is, a remarkable achievement and an unending challenge. But without the inherent give-and-take born of liberty that leads to conflict, the nation would likely not have been able to move forward or to endure.

For the enterprise to work, though, citizens must be resilient, tolerant of dissent, and able to agree to disagree. We've had a few close calls. We have indulged our darker impulses. But despite everything, the nation has been able to absorb change, be open to those who bring with them different cultures and points of view, and create a uniquely human (and, by extension, American) amalgam. As the grandchild of working-class Portuguese immigrants who arrived on these shores at the turn of the twentieth century, I can personally attest to what the "American Dream" looks like.

It has been a dream with national and international implications. And because it is a human dream, transcendent in many ways, it is always in the process of becoming. Perfection is not possible on this plane of existence. The striving for it has inspired both the best and the worst in us. That fact has had ramifications both at home and abroad.

Still, at the end of the day, average citizens have done extraordinary things because they had the character to use liberty responsibly. They had the audacity to dream and to ask a different set of questions. Bobby Kennedy was fond of saying, "Some men see things as they are, and ask why. I dream of things that never were, and ask why not." That approach to life has shaped American character from the beginning.

Put in the starkest terms, if the nation forgets what it is, where it came from, and what it stands for, it is at risk of losing its soul. This book seeks only to remind Americans of these very basic things.

A word about the "Suggested Readings": These are a collection of works that I've cited in the text or that I feel those who want to learn more about America's challenges might find interesting or helpful. It is by no means comprehensive but may provide readers with a place to begin their own quests for an understanding of this nation.

My students deserve special thanks for challenging me and inspiring me to ask tough questions, because they ask tough questions. Likewise, my friends and colleagues push me to think about issues in new ways.

Most especially, I have to single out my dear friend and my brother by another mother, Phil Stump. Our conversations always stimulate new insights and perspectives. The same can be said of my son, Nathaniel.

I would be remiss if I did not point out the invaluable contribution of my nonhuman support system—namely, our dog, Daisy. She was my muse as she snuggled up against me while I wrote, reminding me of what good there is in the simple things in life if we only take the time to appreciate them. Unfortunately, she did not live to see the end of this project because of cancer, but her spirit somehow lives on in the book and in so many other ways.

Of all the people in my life, my wife, Mary Colin, deserves special recognition. She was the first to read the manuscript and offer insightful comments and suggestions. She is a first-class editor but also, and more important, my best friend and lifelong love.

A book is only as good as its publisher, and, as always, I count myself very lucky to be able to work with the folks at Rowman & Littlefield, who not only take what they do very seriously but also do it so well. Jon Sisk and Sarah Sichina provided help and guidance through the whole process. Julie Kirsch was there every step of the way, making my experience a good one.

Of course, it goes without saying that any errors are mine alone.

CHAPTER ONE
WE HOLD THESE TRUTHS . . .

A tall, thin, rather shy thirty-three-year-old redhead from Virginia sat on a Windsor chair in front of a writing desk he had had specially made. His lodgings were a furnished parlor and bedroom on the second floor he had rented from the owners of a fairly new three-story brick house on the corner of Seventh and High Streets in Philadelphia. It was the summer of 1776, and he found himself searching for the right words to, as he would later recall,

> place before mankind the common sense of the subject . . . terms so plain and firm, as to command their assent, and to justify ourselves in the independant [*sic*] stand we [were] compelled to take. [N]either aiming at originality of principle [n]or sentiment, nor yet copied from any particular and previous writing, it was intended to be an expression of the [A]merican mind, and to give to that expression the proper tone and spirit called for by the occasion. [A]ll it's [*sic*] authority rests then on the harmonising [*sic*] sentiments of the day, whether expressed, in convers[atio]ns in letters, printed essays or in the elementary books of public right, as Aristotle, Cicero, Locke, Sidney E°c. [*sic*].[1]

Following a resolution proposed by Richard Henry Lee on June 7 calling for the thirteen British colonies in America to sever their connection to the Crown, the young Virginian, Thomas Jefferson, was named to a committee of five individuals made up of himself, John Adams of Massachusetts, Roger Sherman of Connecticut, Benjamin Franklin of Pennsylvania, and Robert R. Livingston of New York, to draft a formal statement explaining why. The other four chose Jefferson to draft the document because he was a talented writer. Working alone, he would solicit input from Adams and Franklin before he submitted what would be known as the Declaration of Independence to Congress on July 2.

Lee's resolution was approved that day, but it took two more before Jefferson's handiwork was ratified. It would be a landmark document, not only in the history of the soon-to-be United States but also in world history. In clear terms, Jefferson captured political theory dating back to the Greeks and Romans and articulated some eighty-six years earlier by John Locke in his *Second Treatise on Government*.[2] As Jefferson explained, it spoke to the way the "American mind" understood reality. More significantly, since then, because of the universality of its language, it has framed the agenda of others around the globe who aspire to freedom.[3]

The words Jefferson penned were once standard fare for American students of a certain age to memorize as part of their education in civics: "We hold these truths to be self-evident, that all men are created equal, that they are endowed by their Creator with certain unalienable Rights, that among these are Life, Liberty and the pursuit of Happiness."[4]

But how "self-evident" are these truths if, around the world, so many people have and continue to suffer under totalitarian regimes? Or if the history of the nation that first sought to make what had been little more than political theory a reality is littered with so many examples of oppression? The answer to these questions is simple and complicated at the same time and speaks to the often-contradictory aspects of human nature. The more we can come to appreciate that fact, the closer we might be able to approach what has always been at the heart of what Jefferson understood to be the "American mind." If, in turn, we can understand that, perhaps we can make the truths on which the Republic stands just a bit more self-evident.

This is a tall enough order for anyone seeking to understand the state of America, and this book makes no pretensions to have found all the answers. It certainly makes no effort to wrestle with the wider implications of the issues it examines for nations beyond the water's edge, except as it applies to the lessons that the history of US foreign policy may have to teach. But given what has been a struggle for the soul of the United States from its founding, and perhaps most existentially since 2016, some historical perspective seems especially valuable.

Let Freedom Ring

On Saturday, November 7, 2020, at 11:25 a.m., the Associated Press officially called the 2020 presidential election for Joe Biden and Kamala Harris. The major news networks quickly followed suit. Even Fox News, which had for all intents and purposes become an arm of Donald Trump's propaganda machine, declared the results at 11:40 a.m. EST.[5] The pent-up frustration of four years of borderline Fascist behavior from the Trump administration triggered mass celebration across the United States and the globe.

People all around America, in cities and small towns, spilled into the streets in spontaneous celebrations that lasted well into the evening. This while the nation was still reeling from an uncontrolled COVID-19 pandemic that saw the numbers of cases rising (and, with them, deaths) in no small measure because of the blatant and unrelenting denial of science and the promotion of reckless behavior by the president of the United States.

Unlike those who attended Trump's rallies, though, the citizens who gathered to celebrate his defeat, even if not always socially distanced as per COVID health protocols, were generally masked. More important, they were overjoyed. Bri Gills of Washington, DC, told a reporter, "I think it's going to be so nice to wake up every morning and not worry about what the president is tweeting. I'm so excited for Madam Vice President Kamala Harris. She's the reason I voted for this ticket."[6]

Large crowds gathered in Lafayette Park, across from the White House. Among the signs they carried: "You're Fired!" (a reference to the former reality star turned commander in chief's catchphrase on his TV show, *The Apprentice*). It was no small irony that the celebration converged at the site of Trump's use of force against peaceful protestors demonstrating against police brutality and systemic racism only months earlier just so the president could indulge in a photo op holding a Bible in front of St. John's Episcopal Church.[7]

The scenes and the sentiments expressed at Lafayette Park were repeated across the nation. In Philadelphia, Ron Kolla said, "I'm thrilled, I'm thrilled. As soon as I heard the result I rushed out to the city. I wanted to be here for this historic moment. This is the most important election in our lifetimes. After four years of craziness from Donald Trump, I am thrilled to have Joe Biden and Kamala Harris in the White House." Alice McCourt declared, "Amazing things happen in Philadelphia. I'm so proud that Philadelphia was the one to seal the deal to make Vice President Joe Biden our new president. I'm so excited."[8]

McCourt was referring to the fact that Pennsylvania—and heavy pro-Biden support from Philadelphia—put the Democratic nominee over the top in the Electoral College. Her statement spoke to a thread connecting 2020 to 1776.

On July 8, 1776, four days after the Continental Congress ratified Jefferson's masterpiece, the bell atop the tower of the Pennsylvania State House rang out, calling citizens to the first public reading of the Declaration. That bell would become the famous Liberty Bell, with its crack and inspiring inscription, "Proclaim Liberty Throughout All the Land Unto All the Inhabitants thereof."[9]

Fittingly, on November 7, 2020, bells rang out not only across the nation but also across the world. People around the globe poured out of their homes and joined Americans in celebration.[10] The mayor of Paris probably spoke for many when she tweeted, "Welcome Back, America!"[11] The United States was taking its first steps toward returning to the path it had charted for the world in 1776 and had, over the previous four years, forgotten.

Somehow, the values Jefferson had articulated that placed "before mankind the common sense of the subject"—specifically, about the cause of liberty—had the power they always possessed. To inspire, to speak to something deep within not only the "American mind" and heart but also the human mind and heart. It was fitting that the mayor of Paris should welcome the United States back, since the French had helped the country achieve its independence in the first place, and the American Revolution had inspired the French to cast off the oppression of monarchy in 1789. The Declaration of Independence even inspired the French Declaration of the Rights of Man and of the Citizen.[12]

Watching Americans reclaim the self-evident truths "that all men are created equal, that they are endowed by their Creator with certain unalienable Rights" was a vivid reminder of the power of liberty and why the truths are self-evident. Put simply, the words Jefferson penned have the ability to inspire great change, making the so-called American Dream the human dream. They are why the bells that "Proclaim Liberty" rang out on November 7, 2020.

Martin Luther King Jr. knew their enduring truth when he delivered his "I Have a Dream Speech" on the steps of the Lincoln Memorial on August 28, 1963.

> And so let freedom ring from the prodigious hilltops of New Hampshire.
> Let freedom ring from the mighty mountains of New York.
> Let freedom ring from the heightening Alleghenies of Pennsylvania.
> Let freedom ring from the snow-capped Rockies of Colorado.
> Let freedom ring from the curvaceous slopes of California.

But not only that:
Let freedom ring from Stone Mountain of Georgia.
Let freedom ring from Lookout Mountain of Tennessee.
Let freedom ring from every hill and molehill of Mississippi.
From every mountainside, let freedom ring.[13]

Such rhetoric, born of the words penned by Jefferson during that summer in 1776, not only inspired the civil rights movement but also spoke to those who took to the streets in 1989 in Eastern Europe demanding their freedom and who helped bring down the Berlin Wall that same year.[14] In words and scenes similar to those in America on November 7, 2020, the events in those heady days as the Cold War drew to an end was, as some German novelists remembered, "a source of energy we lived off for years."[15] They also inspired the pro-democracy student movement that occupied Beijing's Tiananmen Square in the spring of 1989 and that sustained the push for freedom in China, and especially in Hong Kong, thereafter.[16]

In 1990, the same thing happened in Chile after seventeen years of dictatorship under strongman General Augusto Pinochet.[17] In 2010, the power of the people, along with the release of energy, was on display again—this time in the Middle East during the so-called Arab Spring.[18] As people celebrated their pushback against authoritarianism, their actions were documented by the news media and appeared little different from what occurred in East Germany, China, Chile, or the United States.

All of this is but the tip of the iceberg, for history is littered with similar scenes inspired by the power of the ideas that were first brought to life by the United States during its fight for independence. That the nation has not always lived up to its principles is beside the point. That revolutions in the name of freedom have been crushed or turned against the ideals that first inspired them does not matter either.

What does matter is that ideas challenge and inspire people of all races, colors, creeds, and sexual orientation, regardless of time and place, to seek change—to try to, as Martin Luther King put it, "live out the true meaning of . . . [Jefferson's] creed: 'We hold these truths to be self-evident: that all men are created equal.'"[19]

American Exceptionalism and Human Resilience

When that occurs, it is because people actually remember what that creed is and are committed to it, even as they may disagree as to the means of realizing it. Consider one of the inspirations Jefferson cited for the Declaration of Independence, the great Roman statesman Cicero, who posed the following hypothetical in his discourse on whether there was such a thing as natural law:

> It is justice, beyond all question, neither to commit murder nor robbery. What then would . . . [a] just man do, if in a case of shipwreck he saw a weaker man than himself get possession of a plank? Would he thrust him off, get hold of the timber himself, and escape by his exertions, especially as no human witness could be present in the mid-sea. If he acted like a wise man of the world, he would certainly do so; for to act in any other way would cost him his life. If on the other hand he prefers death to inflicting unjustifiable injury on his neighbor, he will be an eminently honorable and just man, but not the less a fool, because he saved another's life at the expense of his own.[20]

The fledging United States, like Cicero's sailor, had a choice. But it opted for a third alternative. The delegates at the Second Continental Congress knew, as Benjamin Franklin allegedly put it, "We must all hang together, or, most assuredly, we shall all hang separately." Even if apocryphal, the statement aptly described a fundamental reality.

So as Jefferson searched for the words that would "be an expression of the [A]merican mind, and to give to that expression the proper tone and spirit called for by the occasion," he inadvertently framed an answer to Cicero's dilemma as well. Without the board, any talk of natural law or rights was moot. Likewise, without a country, Jefferson's words were no more than platitudes. A nation that theoretically made room for all to exercise their rights required finding a way to accommodate all comers. In other words, they needed to figure out a way to coexist and share the board.

It was a uniquely American answer that was at the same time transcendent and human, that spoke to the universal aspirations, hopes, and dreams of people regardless of time and place. One could say that Jefferson's words represented a leap of faith about what was possible when the focus was on our shared humanity, and thus on what was best about the human spirit. Such an approach made all things achievable "if only . . ." And is that not the very definition of faith: "the substance of things hoped for, the evidence of things not seen"?[21]

Certainly the founding of the American Republic was just that—a leap of faith. For it to work, there had to be some consensus on the ends, an optimism about the future, and a belief that all things were ultimately possible, regardless of the odds. This shared belief was the way around Cicero's conundrum. It was possible for both castaways to share the board together and not only survive but even make it to shore and thrive. In seeking to give voice to the fledgling American nation, Jefferson also instilled it (and the world) with a moral compass that nuanced Cicero's dilemma by expanding the alternatives beyond either/or.

The essence of the American Dream, of the human dream, hangs on such alternatives, as well as on the self-evident truth that all people are entitled by birth to the same rights. Which is why the Declaration of Independence was framed in terms of John Locke's understanding of reality.

Jefferson may well have been ahead of his time as he applied Locke's logic to an understanding of the unique aspects of America. So, too, though, was the United States ahead of its time, which is why Jefferson's ideas resonated so well in its particular cultural context. Put simply, the United States started from a very different place than her European counterparts and has used the ideals espoused by Jefferson that were at the heart of her very nature as a sort of national conscience ever since.

Although there can be no sugarcoating the inequalities that were part and parcel of life in the British colonies and then in the United States, when compared to Europe, relative equality was a given, in no small part because land was available in sufficient abundance that many men could acquire enough property to vote at a time when property was a requirement of citizenship. In Concord, Massachusetts, for example, where minutemen gathered at the North Bridge on April 19, 1775, to face off against the British, 70 percent of males over the age of twenty-one had enough property to qualify them for the franchise.[22]

Such equality was reinforced by the fact that most Americans were farmers and lived in small, close-knit communities where they saw their neighbors as equals. In the northeast, that translated into the purest form of democracy since ancient Athens—the New England town meeting. Overlay that with the religious traditions of Congregationalism and Quakerism, along with the First Great Awakening that spread Christian revivalism through the colonies between the late 1720s and 1740s. The socioeconomic realities that already tended to encourage people to see one another as fellow citizens simply grew exponentially as they came to acknowledge each other as children of God.[23]

Even in cities, the infrastructure and the economic system fostered a degree of common purpose that was unheard of in the great European capitals. There were only five real cities in colonial America at the time—Boston, Massachusetts; Newport, Rhode Island; Philadelphia, Pennsylvania; New York, New York; and Charleston, South Carolina.

As Jefferson sat writing in his rooms on the corner of Seventh and High Streets, the city around him was bustling. With people packed in cheek by jowl, they experienced a common community life. Shopkeepers were often skilled artisans who shared their home and shop with both their immediate family and the apprentices and journeymen who became members of the household as they learned a trade. Social life focused on taverns, where a cross-class of individuals met to socialize and gossip.[24]

Since Philadelphia was typical of her sister cities, it was small wonder that when the British began to restrict the rights of the American colonists, the topic of conversation at the bar was often English taxes. Which goes a long way toward explaining the ability of the Sons of Liberty to mobilize support for a movement against the Crown. It was likely no coincidence that many a plan was hatched at the Green Dragon Tavern in Boston, including the infamous Tea Party.[25]

That America clearly no longer exists. But the ideals that gave birth to it persist. Although they have sometimes been forgotten or ignored, the fundamental truths Jefferson sought to capture found new expression and meaning with each new generation of Americans. It should come as no great surprise that this fact has been especially true with those who were disenfranchised and marginalized.

The words Jefferson penned speak of hope to such people because that is how the colonists saw themselves in the face of British tyranny. If these truths really are "self-evident," then they are "self-evident" especially to those who find themselves denied what is by birth their God-given unalienable rights.

That the founding ideals of America were framed in universalist language may make sense for another reason as well. They spoke to what has always been a "nation of immigrants." Indeed, it was the reality of the ideas that Jefferson gave voice to that drew—and continues to draw—people to US shores. Americans (except for Native Americans) have always been, by definition, people from somewhere else or whose ancestors were from somewhere else. American culture is the result of a polyglot of humanity, which goes a long way toward explaining the universal appeal of ideas that were first framed and tried in the United States.

Viewing the "American Story" as a microcosm of the "Human Story" can help to understand why the principles of the nation have managed to inspire those seeking freedom around the world, beginning with the French in 1789. Herein may lie the source of the unique genius of both the man Jefferson and the nation he helped to birth. It may even be what frames America's so-called exceptionalism.

When that truth is humbly owned, when focus is on the fundamental national optimism that grew in no small measure from immigrants who dreamed of better, the nation has moved forward. When that has occurred, the possibilities have seemed endless.

Consider the essence of John Locke thinking in this light and why it so perfectly informed what Jefferson wrote in the Declaration of Independence. Locke argued that people had the capacity to reason, to see that they share a common humanity with their fellows. This, he said, "obliges every one," and it also taught "all mankind . . . that being all *equal and independent*, no one ought to harm another in his life, health, liberty, or possessions."[26] Or, as Jefferson paraphrased it in the Declaration of Independence, we are all "endowed by . . . [our] Creator with certain unalienable Rights, that among these are Life, Liberty and the pursuit of Happiness."

The Darker Side of Our Nature

Common sense and appeal to divinity and reason have their limits, however, and Locke acknowledged as much when he added the caveat that reason makes all this plain to anyone "who will but consult it."[27] Unfortunately, given human nature, that is not always the case and, depending on who one consults, not even usually so.

Certainly Thomas Paine, whose famous work *Common Sense* reflected in its title what one needed to understand about liberty, knew that "equality could . . . be destroyed by some subsequent circumstance [such as] the distinctions of rich and poor."[28]

CHAPTER ONE

So humans, unwilling to apply reason, and/or enamored of the privilege conferred by wealth or other things, like race and gender, have and continue to be the biggest obstacle to operationalizing Jefferson's self-evident truths.

There is really nothing new here. The wisdom of John Locke and Thomas Jefferson rested on insights dating back to the Romans and individuals like Cicero, as well as the Greeks of fifth-century BCE Athens. Indeed, perhaps no one described the challenge of being human more succinctly than Plato, Aristotle's teacher, whom Jefferson credited with being one of his muses in drafting the Declaration of Independence. Writing in *The Republic*, Plato observed, "And . . . there . . . [are] many . . . cases in which we observe that when a man's desires violently prevail over his reason, he reviles himself, and is angry at the violence within him."[29]

The lesson to be learned is something parents have taught their children for millennia: think before you act. Unfortunately, people all too often forget that good advice and, as a result, both individually and collectively, spend a lot of time reviling themselves and/or others.

The reason may come down to the observations of John Locke's contemporary, Thomas Hobbes. Clearly a man who was the product of his life experiences, he had a rather dour view of human nature. Born prematurely on April 5, 1588, when his mother heard about the threatened invasion of England by the Spanish Armada, Hobbes would later reportedly say, "My mother gave birth to twins: myself and fear."[30] Or, as he poetically described his entry into the world,

IN Fifteen hundred eighty eight, Old Style,
When that Armada did invade our Isle, . . .
April the fifth (though now with Age outworn)
I'th' early Spring, I, a poor worm, was born.[31]

Things only went downhill from there. Hobbes's father was an alcoholic minister who got into a fight with another clergyman outside his church. In disgrace, he fled to London, leaving his family to

12

the care of his brother. Later in life, Thomas witnessed the upheaval that tore England apart during the Civil War of 1642–1648, largely from exile in Paris, where he had fled when he feared that his political writings had put him at risk.

One does not have to be schooled in psychology to draw the logical connections between Hobbes's life experiences and his political philosophy. Even so, as the old joke goes, just because someone is paranoid does not mean others are not out to get him or her. By the same logic, just because Hobbes had reason to be bitter does not mean that what he observed about human behavior was not true. Certainly, history is strewn with enough evidence that, as Hobbes believed, humans can be selfish, love only *their* liberty, and, left to their own devices, will seek to exert power and dominance over others.[32]

When that occurs, Jean-Jacques Rousseau's opening line in his *Social Contract* rings especially true: "Man is born free and everywhere he is in chains."[33] Chains that have nothing to do with character, justice, or the natural state that all the Enlightenment philosophers of the seventeenth and eighteenth centuries agreed on, even if they all did not see it as a positive—specifically, that all humanity is born heir to liberty and equality. Unfortunately, as Rousseau and Thomas Paine pointed out, society can and does create artificial situations that give certain individuals advantage over others simply because they were born into the right social group.

Part of that is a function of economics, but hardly all, since gender and race, to say nothing of religion, play a role in setting people apart, giving some privilege and arbitrarily denying equity to others. This has been a part of the social order probably for as long as there has been a social order among humans. Put another way, every society comes with its "preexisting conditions" that are built into the system, which is why they manifest as systemic racism, sexism, and classism.

Be that as it may, that certainty was not in the best interest of a people who aspired to reach their true and full potential. As Jefferson would explain to John Adams:

> [T]here is a natural aristocracy among men. [T]he grounds of this are virtue & talents . . . there is also an artificial aristocracy founded on wealth and birth, without either virtue or talents. . . . [M]ay we not even say that that form of government is the best which provides the most effectually for a pure selection of these natural aristoi [aristocrats] into the offices of government?[34]

Forging a new approach to governance, men like Jefferson sought to put the old world of privilege which defined the European experience behind them. A new nation needed to be formed, not from old bloodlines but from provincials, yeoman farmers, and shopkeepers. People with dreams and aspirations who had the opportunity to develop their "virtue and talents."

Such individuals could do anything because they were so fundamentally different from those born wealthy, who were, in Jefferson's view, "without either virtue or talents." From such reasoning grew the hopes embodied in what would later be called the American Dream. The United States would become a place where a man like Abraham Lincoln, born in a log cabin on the frontier, could rise to become president. Where a poor immigrant like Andrew Carnegie could arrive in the United States in 1848 and rise from being a bobbin boy in a textile mill in Pittsburgh to the richest man in the world. Where countless unnamed people rose, if not from rags to riches, then at least from rags to respectability (even if over several generations).

Despite such truths, and the optimism that it has inspired, the fact remains that America was not carved from a pristine wilderness where all began life as equals. And therein lies the primary challenge of living into the so-called self-evident truths that Jefferson wrote about. Regardless of European assumptions, America was not a New World. It was peopled by millions of individuals with diverse cultures and lifestyles.[35] These peoples were slowly and systematically removed from their land, and they often were the victims of unintended biological warfare, as Europeans brought a host of diseases with them to which Native Americans had no immunities.[36]

The laws of supply and demand being what they are, a labor shortage in America set in motion not only an influx of Europeans who were often willing to sell themselves into indentured servitude to get a new start in the New World but also the importation of Africans as slaves to feed—after John Rolfe discovered the marketability of Virginia tobacco—a growing plantation economy. In these developments lay the origins of systemic racism and class exploitation, as real as the aspirations that informed the hopes and dreams of the white Europeans who came to America, and with which it existed in dynamic tension.[37]

Of course, these socioeconomic realties, transplanted to America as a result of the development of empire in the seventeenth and eighteenth centuries, were only part of the "preexisting conditions" that implicitly restricted Jefferson's soaring rhetoric. With the addition of the unwritten caveats of race and wealth, what he wrote was quite literally true in the minds of most eighteenth-century Americans: the terminology that ostensibly spoke to all huMANity, in the context of 1776, meant only white males who had enough assets to qualify them to vote.

Fortunately for the United States, such distinctions have evolved over time, and the universalist truths espoused by the logic of the Enlightenment that inspired Jefferson have become more inclusive. Perhaps that speaks to the fact that the "American mind" that Jefferson sought to inspire and encapsulate was already ahead of the rest of the world when it came to the fundamental equalitarianism necessary for a functioning republic.

The Power of Choice versus the Choice of Power

During the Peloponnesian War, the little island of Melos was invaded by Athens, which was then engaged in a struggle with Sparta for control of the Greek peninsula. The Melians knew well enough that if they were sucked into the conflict, they would be destroyed. According to Greek historian Thucydides's telling, they appealed to honor and justice, refusing Athenian demands that they choose sides. The Athenian answer was brutal and honest: "[Y]ou and we should say what we really think, and aim only at what is possible, for we both alike know that into the discussion of human affairs the question of justice only enters where the pressure of necessity is equal, and that the powerful exact what they can, and the weak grant what they must."[38]

Hobbes would have seen nothing shocking or unexpected in such a retort. After all, it was human nature to deal in power and seek dominance over others. But there was something disturbing about the answer the Athenians allegedly gave, for they prided themselves on being a democracy. After all, just fifteen years earlier, Pericles, the city's leader, had extolled the virtues of a system that set Athens apart:

> Our form of government does not enter into rivalry with the institutions of others. Our government does not copy our neighbors', but is an example to them. It is true that we are called a democracy, for the administration is in the hands of the many and not of the few. But while there exists equal justice to all and alike in their private disputes, the claim of excellence is also recognized; and when a citizen is in any way distinguished, he is preferred to the public service, not as a matter of privilege, but as the reward of merit.[39]

The words could just have easily been spoken by any American politician. Certainly, Jefferson had penned similar sentiments when he wrote to John Adams. As with Pericles's oration, holes could be poked into the eloquent defense of a reality that seems to exist only in people's minds, on the pages of arcane books about political theory, and in the rhetoric used to justify sacrifice for the nation (Pericles's agenda) or to inspire people to mobilize for change.

The middle two of these provide reason enough for cynicism about the whole prospect of democracy, particularly the great

American experiment to make the ideals of Athens and the Roman Republic real on a size and scale heretofore untried and unheard of. However, the first and last of these is where the power of Jefferson's words—and that of any other defender of freedom and democracy—finds its traction. In people's minds, in their imagination, where they can dream of possibilities that seem impossible, that is where these ideas take root. Their real force, however, is ignited only when they are channeled into action and foster meaningful positive change.

That was the truth behind Jefferson's words that summer in Philadelphia. It was what pushed abolitionists and feminists forward in the antebellum period. It was what mobilized countless thousands to believe in the possibility of the dream articulated by Martin Luther King. It was what brought protestors to the streets demanding police reform and asserting the very self-evident truth that Black Lives Matter. It was what informed the spontaneous eruptions of pure joy when Donald Trump was defeated for a second term.

Unfortunately, the words lie dormant unless people choose to live by them, to fight for them, and, as the Declaration of Independence concluded, "mutually pledge to each other . . . [their] Lives . . . Fortunes, and . . . sacred Honor."[40] There is no great surprise here, for those with the power always choose in their own interest.

Thus, Martin Luther King observed, "freedom is never voluntarily given by the oppressor; it must be demanded by the oppressed."[41] That is *the* fundamental takeaway from American history, starting with the Revolution and moving forward. The oppressed have believed in their power to affect change and have chosen to act on the belief that as humans, they were by nature entitled to be free.

Again, Jefferson understood the dynamics at play. As he explained it:

> The mass of mankind . . . [in a republic] enjoys a precious degree of liberty and happiness. It has it's [*sic*] evils too: the principal of which is the turbulence to which it is subject. But weigh this against . . . oppressions . . . and it becomes nothing. . . . Even this

evil is productive of good. It prevents the degeneracy of government, and nourishes a general attention to the public affairs. I hold it that a little rebellion now and then is a good thing, and as necessary in the political world as storms in the physical.[42]

Indeed, protest, rebellion, or (at the minimum) conflict is built into the nature of a republic whose foundation is liberty. After all, liberty encourages the full range of human diversity, including regarding opinions over the means of making it applicable and real. As long as consensus over that end informs the struggles around the means to achieve and advance liberty, the republic can function and thrive. When that consensus dissolves, however, all that remains is conflict and invective.

So, the choices of citizens matter. It is a tall order to put one's life, fortune, and honor on the line to claim liberty as a birthright, but one that the Founders took seriously and, in doing so, passed down as a sacred trust to future generations of Americans to live into and make ever more real because they are both American and human. The challenge remains unaltered despite the passage of time. It boils down to the fact that for the American Republic not only to survive but also to thrive and progress, its citizens must choose to make it so.

CHAPTER TWO

THE DELICATE BALANCE

I magine reading that a large, heavily armed crowd had marched on a government building, preventing "the sitting of the court, and the orderly administration of justice."[1] There are also reports that "authorities declared a riot . . . when protesters breached a fence surrounding the city's . . . courthouse" and were warning that the incident was causing a "grave risk of public alarm."[2] Finally, and perhaps most disturbingly, there is this editorial:

> This attempt to subvert the Government of the United States by a handful of crazy families may seem ridiculous, and hardly worthy of serious attention for a moment. But there is another light in which the matter is to be viewed and one that presents a more alarming aspect. This outbreak is only the beginning—the foreshadowing of more serious troubles. That an extensive organization exists in various States to overthrow the Government by means of general . . . insurrection there can no longer be doubt.[3]

Care to venture a guess as to when these stories made the news? During the tumultuous year that was 2020? Perhaps on the eve of the Civil War? Early in the history of the country? Yes, yes, and yes, but which story is about which period?

The first story was written almost three years after the official end of the American Revolution in 1783. It came from a report on an uprising in Western Massachusetts that came to be known as Shays's Rebellion. The second story was out of Portland, Oregon, in the summer of 2020, during protests over police brutality. The last was an analysis of the state of the nation in the aftermath of John Brown's raid on the armory at Harper's Ferry, Virginia, in 1859.[4]

So, what is the point? America has endured many upheavals that have threatened to tear it apart, to destroy the hope of liberty, to pull the Republic asunder, to make union impossible. Still, it persevered, even emerging stronger after each crisis. Not, though, by magic, but because enough people committed themselves to making it so.

The realties that led to Shays's Rebellion speak to what happens when equity does not exist.[5] Veterans of the American Revolution had been poorly compensated for their patriotism and returned home to farms that barely allowed them to squeeze out a living. Circumstances were especially difficult in Massachusetts.

That fact meant little to creditors, who demanded payment for what they were owed. Cash-strapped since paper money was fundamentally worthless and not having gold or silver, farmers found themselves over a barrel. Meanwhile, state taxes were onerous, making what had been paid to the British Crown seem like chicken feed. Unsympathetic, officials in Boston arrested farmers for delinquent debt and failure to pay their taxes. Family farms were foreclosed on. The situation was proving a replay of the causes of the American Revolution, only instead of tyrants three thousand miles away, they were only fifty miles away.

When the farmers' efforts to resolve the issues peacefully failed, many took matters into their own hands. Courthouses were prevented from conducting business. As the situation deteriorated, violence escalated. In January 1787, the governor hired his own army, privately funded by Boston businessmen, to put down what had become an insurrection. Daniel Shays and other movement leaders continued to resist. It was not until the summer that an uneasy peace was restored. Newly elected governor John Hancock granted pardons to many of the rebels, and the legislature declared a moratorium on debts and cut taxes.

Still, the events shook the new country to its core. Henry Knox, who had served as George Washington's artillery commander during the Revolution, wrote to his former boss:

> Our political machine constituted of thirteen independent sovereignties, have been constantly operating against each other, and against the federal head, ever since the peace—The powers of Congress are utterly inadequate to preserve the balance between the respective States, and oblige them to do those things which are essential to their own welfare, and for the general good. . . . Our government must be braced, changed, or altered to secure our lives and property. We . . . [must] establish a government which shall have the power to protect [our] lawful pursuits, and which will be efficient in all cases of internal commotions or foreign invasions.[6]

Knox's logic informed the motivations of the delegates who went to Philadelphia and spent the summer of 1787 drafting a new Constitution for the United States.[7] Clearly, if Shays's Rebellion was any indication, the states were not up to the task of sustaining a country. As Knox pointed out and the framers of the Constitution knew, that problem had international implications. If the nation could not handle its "internal commotions," it was likewise incapable of fending off "foreign invasions."

A stronger central government was necessary, but how strong? Clearly, moneyed interests were behind the desire to create a more powerful regime, but at what cost to liberty? Left to run amok, either the elites or the mob could imperil the domestic tranquility needed for liberty to thrive, and yet too much government threatened the very existence of the freedom that allowed for dissent.

And therein lay the enduring challenge. Americans then, and since, have been divided on how to make government work in such a way that it protects the nation and fairly balance the rights of all its citizens. The problem was made more difficult not only by economics but also by other "preexisting conditions," like race, gender, ethnicity, and sexual orientation, that denied certain individuals or groups their rights for no other reason than societal prejudice. That made the relative equality necessary to make democracy work difficult to come by, especially when these were viewed from the narrow lens of self, which reinforced both prejudice and individual interests.

Still, the universal nature of the founding principles, and the commitment of people to their particular understanding of them, has defined their evolution. It is probably fair to say that the realties confronting the nation at its founding never went away. In fact, they have been exacerbated over time. However, each challenge has contained within it the opportunity to create anew, to move closer to the ideals that gave birth to the American experiment. People's agendas may be complex and often contradictory, but the issue always seems to turn on the question of how to balance the need for stability and economic prosperity with the rights of the citizenry to exercise their God-given unalienable rights.

Shays's Rebellion illustrated that point clearly. The farmers who rose up in anger were calling for justice and a stronger voice in the policies that impacted their lives. Their creditors feared mob rule because the masses, as Henry Knox put it, "feel at once their own poverty . . . and their own force."[8] In some form or other, this has been the framework within which nearly every domestic policy debate in the nation's history has been framed. At its heart is the very nature of liberty and the best form of government to preserve it. That means that the American story needs to be understood in light of the long-term, often agonizing process born of the ideals on which the nation was founded and the realities that artificially and arbitrarily divide the country's citizens.

Put simply, Barry McGuire's protest song from the 1960s, "Eve of Destruction," got it right. "Handful of Senators don't pass legislation,"[9] he sang. There can be little doubt that laws, by themselves, can bring about lasting change. However, new mores need to be established, and that takes longer to accomplish. Still, the basis for those mores has deep roots, grounded in what John Locke and Thomas Jefferson knew—namely, that a shared humanity requires all people to respect one another's rights. It is simultaneously a tall order and a non-negotiable challenge.

For a country to exist (let alone liberty itself), citizens needed to identify with each other as members of the *United* States. Indeed, the words "E Pluribus Unum" (Out of Many, One)—first proposed by Thomas Jefferson, John Adams, and Benjamin Franklin for the country's Great Seal in 1776 and approved by Congress in 1782— were meaningless, as was the concept of the nation itself, until that identification occurred.[10]

At the beginning and since, that process required not only laws but also leadership and a belief in and willingness to fight and sacrifice for the ideals of republicanism. Perhaps most significant, these principles have always been premised on the assumption of "human respect." And whether one agrees with their methods or not, that was the through line linking Shays's farmers, John Brown's vehement antislavery movement, the Portland protestors, and anyone else who ever challenged the inequities of the system.

Law, Order, and Liberty

At the outset of the American experiment, there was no model to follow beyond the political musings of Greek, Roman, and Enlightenment thinkers, lessons from ancient history, and the lived experience of most Americans, which included the wisdom of the only real federated system to exist before the United States—the Iroquois Confederacy.

The way the nation was founded, and how it moved forward, has been a function of this fundamental truth. Fortunately, Americans have long been pragmatists, maybe because they had to be. They understood the basic tenets of liberty and self-government even when they vehemently disagreed on how to make it work or how inclusive liberty was supposed to be.

Until the Trump presidency, when a cult of personality developed like a cancer on the body politic, most Americans would have agreed with John Adams's clear explanation of what characterized a republic. In one of a series of letters published in the *Boston Gazette* during the winter of 1774–1775, in response to fellow Massachusetts lawyer Daniel Leonard's defense of English policies, Adams famously explained that a republic is "a government of laws and not of men." He went on to say that "If this definition be just, the British constitution is nothing more nor less than a republic, in which the king is first magistrate."

That office, moreover, even if hereditary and imbued with "ample and splendid prerogatives," was "bound by strict laws which the people have a voice in making and a right to defend." The alternative was an empire, which "is a despotism, and an emperor a despot, bound by no law or limitation but his own will." Such a situation constituted "a stretch of tyranny beyond absolute monarchy," for even an absolutist king required that his edicts be "registered by parliaments."[11]

Adams and the other Founders knew the danger of power in the hands of a despot or would-be autocrat. They revered the English constitution and understood that liberty could only be preserved by what a constitution was—a social contract among the people of a nation whereby citizens had both "a voice in making and a right to defend" the laws under which they lived.

That their rights as free Englishmen had been abused despite the theoretical limits of English constitutional law was reason enough to push back and, when repeatedly ignored, "to dissolve the political bands" that connected them to the British government and "to assume among the powers of the earth, the separate and equal station to which the Laws of Nature and of Nature's God entitle them."[12]

No American could rightly call him- or herself a patriot, either at the founding or since, who would tolerate any would-be tyrant undermining this fundamental tenet of government, nor would they stand idly by while either a fellow citizen or a foreign adversary sought to do so. The price paid for freedom was simply too high to even entertain the concept.

To their credit, the Founders had a clear-eyed realism that helped them to "baby-proof" the system enough that it has survived many a trauma. That has included not only a civil war but also the actions of a president who, in refusing to concede the 2020 election, sought to encourage what was nothing short of a coup.

Perhaps most important, the system has remained flexible enough to accommodate the voices of the marginalized, even if belatedly and painfully. In assessing this tortured history, one must recognize that the Founders were products of the eighteenth century. They could not create a perfect system for their own time, much less anticipate every contingency that might arise in the future. Still, their wisdom and insights into the human condition allowed room for growth and change. It fell to each succeeding generation to rise to the challenges facing them and, to borrow from the Preamble to the Constitution, create "a more perfect Union."

The simple but profound lesson is that freedom, rights, and republicanism cannot be taken for granted. There are always those who would subvert the system. They appear in many guises: as a king and parliament more than three thousand miles away; as creditors and government officials closer by; as those who would deny fellow citizens their rights on the basis of race, color, creed, gender, ethnicity, national origin, or sexual orientation; or as a wannabe dictator enabled by Republicans who forgot the meaning of their party's name.

The cure for all of these has proven to be a belief in the rule of law, in its power and efficacy, and in the right of the people to make and defend it. The framers of the Constitution knew that when they wrote the Preamble to Constitution:

> We the People of the United States, in Order to form a more per-
> fect Union, establish Justice, insure domestic Tranquility, provide

for the common defence, promote the general Welfare, and secure the Blessings of Liberty to ourselves and our Posterity, do ordain and establish this Constitution for the United States of America.[13]

These fifty-two words contained the mission statement for the nation, the framework under which the laws of the country would be established. They were an important step forward in defining the nature of the United States and what it meant to be an American. Indeed, "We the People" spoke of something profound. Creating unity while premising union on the notion of liberty has been an ongoing and herculean task. The glue that has always held the system together has been respect for the law—and the liberty it is designed to protect.

A Matter of Leadership

The movement toward such law and the notion of a shared investment by all citizens takes trial and error, to say nothing of effort, as evidenced by the fact that the Constitution was the second social contract the United States had in its first decade-plus of existence, along with the fact that its ideals have never fully been realized. To appreciate the significance of this situation, we must return to the beginning.

As the American War of Independence heated up, the practical matter of governance had to be addressed. That moved the notion of creating a social contract out of the realm of theory and into reality. The results were the Articles of Confederation.[14] This first law of the land began with the less-than-stirring words "To all to whom these Presents shall come, we, the undersigned Delegates of the States affixed to our Names send greeting."[15]

In fairness, the members of Congress had a lot on their minds, like how to win the nation's freedom from the world's most powerful country. Truth be told, the American government had little substantive power to conduct such a war.

George Washington, commander in chief of the Continental Army, often wrote of his difficulties in retaining an army and of procuring supplies.[16] On December 27, 1776, almost six months after the country had declared independence, Americans had been driven out of three of the five largest cities in the fledgling United States—Boston, Newport, and New York—and nothing stood between the British and Philadelphia except an exhausted Continental Army that had just achieved a surprise victory over the Hessians at Trenton.

Though fighting for liberty, Congress realized it would have to grant the commander in chief extraordinary powers if he was to be able to prosecute the war. For the next six months, Washington was authorized to directly raise troops and supplies from the states, appoint officers and administer the military, and arrest anyone who would not accept Continental currency or was otherwise found to be disloyal to the cause.

A lesser man would have seen an opportunity to seize power for himself. Fortunately for the United States, like the other American patriots who had pledged their "Lives . . . Fortunes, and . . . sacred Honor"[17] to the cause of liberty, Washington understood what was at stake. In accepting the authority, he wrote:

> The confidence which Congress has honored me with these proceedings, has a claim to my warmest acknowledgements. At the same time, I beg leave to assure them, that all my faculties shall be employed to direct properly the powers they have been pleased to visit me with and to advance those objects and only those, which gave rise to this honorable mark of distinction.[18]

The spirit with which George Washington accepted Congress's grant of power set a tone for his later presidency, and it defined the ideal to which most American leaders have aspired ever since. There was a seamlessness between Washington's battlefield persona in 1776 and his graceful exit from power as president in 1796. As he prepared to leave office, he felt bound to tell the American people why he would "decline being considered" for re-election.

"A strict regard to all the considerations appertaining to the relation which binds a dutiful citizen to his country" demanded nothing less. Having put the country first in all his considerations, he had hoped to serve only one term as president, but circumstances demanded he stay on. Now, at last, he could in good conscience, despite "whatever partiality may be retained for my services," retire.

As he left office, he acknowledged the "debt of gratitude" he owed to his "beloved country for the many honors it has conferred" on him. He then reminded Americans to remember that they were

> Citizens, by birth or choice, of a common country, that country has a right to concentrate your affections. The name of American, which belongs to you in your national capacity, must always exalt the just pride of patriotism more than any appellation derived from local discriminations. With slight shades of difference, you have the same religion, manners, habits, and political principles. You have in a common cause fought and triumphed together; the independence and liberty you possess are the work of joint counsels, and joint efforts of common dangers, sufferings, and successes.[19]

American leaders, whether presidents or, when presidents forgot—as with Richard Nixon and Donald Trump—members of Congress, the courts, or those at the state and federal level, individuals who refused to bow to political pressure, all have appreciated the *gravitas* of exercising power within the context of this wisdom.

So, beyond law, a republic needs principled and effective governance. That involves a combination of what has come to be known as transactional and transformational leadership.[20] Put simply, the first involves trade-offs—exchanges of one thing for another. Since compromise is the business of functioning politics, the key to success in that realm is the ability to affect a transaction, to close a deal that is acceptable to all the parties involved.

For transactional leadership to work for the greater good, however, it must be informed by principles beyond the immediacy of the deal, which moves leadership to the transformational level. That may involve placing country ahead of party or self-interest, as has been the norm with countless public servants over the history of the nation. It may be evidenced with those who demand that systemic problems be addressed when what is legislated by a "handful of senators" is not enough.

In either case, the sort of leaders demanded by a republic must have a sense of duty to the country and to the people they serve. They must carry within them a moral imperative that informs their agendas. This was true of Washington and the other Founders, and it has remained so with real leaders, both inside and outside of government, ever since.

Still, it requires more than reliance on the good will of honorable people for the system to work. As James Madison explained:

> It is in vain to say that enlightened statesmen will be able to adjust these clashing interests, and render them all subservient to the public good. Enlightened statesmen will not always be at the helm. Nor, in many cases, can such an adjustment be made at all without taking into view indirect and remote considerations, which will rarely prevail over the immediate interest which one party may find in disregarding the rights of another or the good of the whole.[21]

The simple truth is that although God may have imbued humans with the reason to create government as an arbiter of differences among them, neither divinity nor rationality are adequate checks on human egocentricity. Again, Madison understood this fact when he wrote, "If . . . impulse and . . . opportunity . . . coincide . . . neither moral nor religious motives can be relied on as an adequate control."[22]

The reason is simple:

> As long as the reason of man continues fallible, and he is at liberty to exercise it, different opinions will be formed. As long as

the connection subsists between his reason and his self-love, his opinions and his passions will have a reciprocal influence on each other; and the former will be objects to which the latter will attach themselves.[23]

Compromise and the Search for a More Perfect Union

What America was to be was not at all clear when she declared her independence from Great Britain in 1776. Indeed, there was no guarantee that she would even survive. By the fall of 1777, Congress was forced to evacuate Philadelphia ahead of advancing British forces. That winter, General Washington and his men would spend a cold, brutal winter at Valley Forge, some thirty-five miles from their country's now-occupied capital. Meanwhile, Congress tried to conduct business from exile eighty-plus miles to the west in York, Pennsylvania.

What exactly was being fought for beyond a vague notion of liberty was not always clear. The Articles of Confederation established that the delegates who created them were "of the United States of America in Congress assembled," and Article I did make it clear that "this confederacy shall be, 'The United States of America.'"[24]

That was hardly a guarantee that what they had in mind was a truly unified nation-state. Given their experience with the English, there was good reason to fear centralized power. To ensure that liberty was preserved, Article II declared, "Each state retains its sovereignty, freedom and independence, and every Power, Jurisdiction and right, which is not by this confederation expressly delegated to the United States, in Congress assembled."[25]

This new government was, for all intents and purposes, a mutual defense pact among thirteen separate and independent republics. Achieving even that much consensus on what should bind the new nation together required compromise. It took six drafts to get something the Continental Congress could agree on in 1777. The first three went nowhere. The fourth, submitted by John Dickinson of Pennsylvania in June 1776, was revised in committee and discussed by the Congress during the next two months. The result was significantly revised again after much debate over the coming year. Finally, in November 1777, Congress submitted its handiwork to the states.

It took another two years for twelve of the thirteen to ratify the Articles. The thirteenth, Maryland, held out because of growing conflict over claims to western lands. Virginia, North and South Carolina, Georgia, Connecticut, and Massachusetts asserted that their territory extended either to the "South Sea" or to the Mississippi River. The charters of Maryland, Pennsylvania, New Jersey, Delaware, and Rhode Island, meanwhile, limited their claims to several hundred miles from the Eastern Seaboard. Land speculators in Maryland and elsewhere argued that the West belonged to the United States, and, as such, their claims (and not those of states with broad western ambitions) should be honored. Maryland in particular sided with the speculators out of fear of what would happen if the assertions of their larger neighbor, Virginia, ruled the day. Forget the fact that the lands in question were occupied by Native Americans.

The impasse ended when Thomas Jefferson convinced his state to abandon its western claims provided that the speculators' demands would be ignored and that any new states that might join the Union from the West would enter on an equal footing with the original thirteen. With that promise, Maryland ratified the Articles, and they became the law of the land on March 1, 1781.

There are some instructive takeaways from this story, the first being that it was by no means preordained that there would be a *United* States of America. While fighting a revolution for their freedom, Americans were preoccupied with protecting their parochial interests. In light of that fact, in addition to the miracle of defeating the most powerful empire on the planet, there was the equal and just as important one of forging a nation from what amounted to thirteen independent ones.

The foresight of Jefferson and the willingness of his fellow Virginians to compromise for the greater good speak to what would be necessary not only to create a country but also to sustain it. In working out the nature of their government, Americans were evolving a sense of themselves as a new people, an enterprise they undertook without a clear script or a certain destination save for their commitment to liberty. This was the sort of pragmatism that would set the tone for the Republic throughout its history.

Pragmatism and the compromise it engenders often make for very convoluted solutions to complex problems. That is, in some sense, the nature of the beast, and in this case, the beast can be equated to a camel, which, as the old joke has it, is a horse designed by committee. It may be ugly and clumsy looking, but somehow it works because it is perfectly suited to its environment. An American ecosystem that thrived on liberty, which inevitably allows and even encourages people to disagree, was just the right environment for governmental camels.

When the first governmental system proved unworkable, evolution dictated creation of another, and so the Constitution, no less a product of compromise than the Articles of Confederation, would be born. There are many ways to analyze that document, but perhaps the simplest is to view it as a Camel 2.0. Consider the most fundamental issue in a republic: representation. Few would probably disagree with the statement that

> In the representative branch . . . several important considerations must be attended to. It must possess abilities to discern the situation of the people and of public affairs, a disposition to sympathize with the people, and a capacity and inclination to make laws congenial to their circumstances and condition. It must afford security against interest combinations, corruption and influence. It must possess the confidence, and have the voluntary support of the people.[26]

Nor would they find fault with the assertion that "Congressional representation should not be a political blood sport that protects incumbents, disenfranchises legitimate interests, and allows people to achieve with surgical reappointment what they couldn't do honestly at the ballot box."[27] Most Americans would even likely concur that

> If we want a better politics, it's not enough just to change a congressman or change a senator or even change a President. We have to change the system to reflect our better selves . . . to end the practice of drawing our congressional districts so that politicians can pick their voters, and not the other way around.[28]

The first statement was made in 1787 by an opponent to the new Constitution. The second and third were articulated in 2014 and 2016, in reaction to the policy of gerrymandering, which gives one political party advantage over another and effectively disenfranchises voters.

Gerrymandering is a tradition that dates back a long way. In fact, Elbridge Gerry, governor of Massachusetts and one of the Founders of the Republic, unintentionally lent his name to the practice when, in 1812, he signed a law that created a voting district shaped like a salamander in order to help his party. Despite being used by both parties, gerrymandering has long been widely condemned by politicians and citizens alike. Yet still it persists because it is a logical outgrowth of partisanship (or what James Madison would have termed the evils of faction).

Consider that comments from 2014 and 2016 were made by Democrats in response to Republican efforts to apportion voting to benefit themselves and suppress the franchise among people of color. For their part, Republicans have expressed similar concerns, but for different reasons. No less a GOP icon than Ronald Reagan stated in 1987 that "all we're asking for [is] an end to the antidemocratic and un-American practice of gerrymandering congressional districts."[29]

Even an arch-conservative and Republican power broker like former Speaker of the House Newt Gingrich said, "We've been drawing lines for political reasons all the way back to 1812. But I think it's wrong. I think it leads to bad government."[30]

How could such practices be allowed under Article I of the Constitution, especially if a representative democracy was the goal? The short answer is that representation, like everything else created at the Constitutional Convention during the summer of 1787, was the result of compromise.

The framers came up with a bicameral system, with a popularly elected House of Representatives apportioned according to population, along with a Senate, which provided for equal representation of each state, only after painstaking debate and negotiation. The product was the result of transactional leadership, pure and simple. If the object was creating a union, issues of equity would have to be sacrificed to win approval of the Constitution, and so the tone was set for future struggles.

Certainly, the issue of fair representation in the House was a sticking point from the get-go. Under Article I, Section 2, the number of representatives would not "exceed one for every thirty Thousand," and each state would have at least one. For the purposes of taxation and representation, there would be a census taken every ten years to determine each state's "respective Numbers," which was to be calculated "by adding to the whole Number of free Persons, including those bound to Service for a Term of Years, and excluding Indians not taxed, three fifths of all other Persons."[31]

Clearly this calculation left out African Americans, who were counted three-fifths of a person because they were "bound to Service for a Term of Years" (a polite way of saying they were slaves). Likewise, "Indians," who were explicitly excluded because they were not taxed. Women were not mentioned, and given the attitudes pertaining at the time, they did not have rights either.

Despite such glaring efforts at what would later be called voter suppression, the framers were not completely oblivious to the issues of race and gender. They simply acknowledged the political economics of the challenges they were confronting if they wanted to achieve any sort of consensus on creation of a new central government.

This recognition is clear from the debates over representation. Many of the framers, even those who owned slaves, were uncomfortable with its existence in a republic ostensibly dedicated to liberty. But they had to accommodate the interests of their compatriots whose livelihood depended on it if they hoped to get enough support to ratify the Constitution.

As for women, their rights were recognized by the only other republic on the planet at the time: the Iroquois Confederacy.[32] But Native Americans were not seen as equals, and in the only other mention of them in the unamended Constitution, they were viewed in terms of trade, which, along with "commerce with foreign Nations, and among the several States," Congress was authorized to regulate.[33] In short, the Founders were not predisposed to follow the example of people many of them considered "savages."

Still, women did enter the conversation at the Philadelphia Convention—specifically, on June 11, 1787, during the contentious arguments over representation in the House of Representatives. James Wilson of Pennsylvania rose to suggest that

> the rights of suffrage in the 1st branch of the National Legislature ought not to be according to the rule established in the articles of confederation but according to some equitable ratio of representation, namely, in proportion to the whole number of white & other free citizens and inhabitants of every age sex & condition including those bound to servitude for a term of years and three fifths of all other persons not comprehended in the foregoing description, except Indians paying taxes, in each State.[34]

There was more here than the origins of the infamous three-fifths compromise. Granted that Wilson's proposal pretty much ended any discussion of gender, and when the final language of

Article I was crafted, references to race, age, and sex were deleted. However, as one historian explains:

> Once representation was shifted off the ground of property and onto that of persons, there was no longer any obvious rationale for excluding women. It would have been quite easy to use the word "men," but the delegates chose instead the more inclusive "persons," and in their debates, if not the final, edited version of the Constitution, they made it clear that "persons" included women.[35]

This makes sense not only in terms of the political theory governing much of the thinking of the framers but also, and more important, perhaps, for the principles that undergirded the document that future generations would build on. The Declaration of Independence and the Constitution are foundational documents for a reason.

It is no coincidence, for example, that the women who gathered in 1848 at Seneca Falls, New York, demanding their rights as equal citizens took the Declaration of Independence as their template.[36] The Declaration of Sentiments produced by the Seneca Falls Convention read in part:

> We hold these truths to be self-evident: that all men and women are created equal; that they are endowed by their Creator with certain inalienable rights; that among these are life, liberty, and the pursuit of happiness; that to secure these rights governments are instituted, deriving their just powers from the consent of the governed.

Pointing to "a history of repeated injuries and usurpations on the part of man toward woman, having in direct object the establishment of an absolute tyranny over her," the Declaration noted that men had denied women the ability "to exercise . . . [their] inalienable right to the elective franchise" while forcing them "to submit to laws, in the formation of which . . . [they] had no voice." Without the vote, women were "without representation in the halls of legislation," leaving them "oppressed . . . on all sides."[37]

Moving forward from there, in 1866, Elizabeth Cady Stanton and Susan B. Anthony headed up a petition signed by several suffragists asking Congress for universal suffrage. Pointing out that they constituted "fifteen million people—one half of the entire population of the country," they stood "outside the pale of political recognition." Moreover, "the Constitution," they argued, "classes us as 'free people,' and counts us as *whole* persons in the basis for representation, and yet are we governed without our consent, compelled to pay taxes without appeal, and punished for violation of law without choice of judge or juror." Herein was the implicit logic of the framers of the Constitution made explicit.

The women went on: The lessons of history, to say nothing of the recently concluded Civil War, "prove the uncertain tenure of life, liberty, and property so long as the ballot—the only weapon of self-protection—is not in the hands of every citizen." Since the Constitution was being amended "in harmony with advancing civilization, placing new safeguards round the individual rights of four millions of emancipated slaves," women should likewise be granted the vote, for they were "the only remaining class of disenfranchised citizens." To do so would be to fulfill the "Constitutional obligation to 'Guarantee to every State in the Union a Republican form of Government.'" Finally, since "partial application of Republican principles must ever breed a complicated legislation as well as discontented people," it was imperative "to simplify the machinery of government and ensure domestic tranquility" by granting universal suffrage.[38]

Several points need to be made here. First, the rights of women and African Americans have been intimately linked since the early days of the abolition movement—and for good reason. Both women and blacks have found themselves oppressed by white males, especially white male property owners, for a long time.

Second, women were not "the only remaining class of disenfranchised citizens" after the Fourteenth Amendment granted citizenship to "All persons born or naturalized in the United States" and the Fifteenth ensured that "The right of citizens . . . to vote shall not be denied or abridged by the United States or by any State on account of race, color, or previous condition of servitude."[39] It took the Snyder Act of 1924 to grant Native Americans full US citizenship. That was four years after the Nineteenth Amendment granted women suffrage.

Even with all this, everything from Jim Crow laws to gerrymandering have persisted in helping to disenfranchise people of color. Yet, despite that negative history, the fight has continued because the ideals debated in 1787 stood the test of time and served as a sort of national conscience to keep the country striving to become a "more perfect Union."

It behooves us, then, to appreciate that America has always been a "work in progress," especially where it involves non-white and non-male individuals. That seems especially important as demographic trends project that by the middle of the twenty-first century, Caucasians will be a plurality, but not a majority, of the country's population.[40] And of course, women will always make up half of the population.

The parameters of the debates on these issues, like so much else that has preoccupied the United States since its founding, were anticipated in one form or another by the disputes between Federalists and Anti-Federalists during the Constitution's ratification process. Consider just a few of these questions.

Was an executive branch too powerful and a clear and present danger to liberty? In light of the creation of what some have called the "imperial presidency," there have been many over the years who have echoed the concerns first articulated by the Anti-Federalists on that issue.[41]

Then there is the matter of the inefficacies created by having co-equal branches of government. Yet, without this clumsy and often arcane system, there would be no check on the potential abuse of power by the chief executive. To cite but two examples, Congress's impeachment power helped to rein in the abuses perpetuated by the Nixon administration, forcing the president to resign in disgrace rather than be removed from office. Even when Congress's two impeachments of Donald Trump failed to hold him accountable for abuses of office because of the craven sycophancy of certain members of both houses, the courts (including the Supreme Court with a conservative majority) stepped in, squashing frivolous lawsuits aimed at subverting democracy by overturning the results of the 2020 election.

The tension among branches of government is likewise built into the relationship between federal and state power, for much the same reason. Thus Article VI of the Constitution, the so-called Supremacy Clause, declares that "this Constitution, and the Laws of the United States which shall be made in Pursuance thereof . . . shall be the supreme Law of the Land."[42] Meanwhile, the Tenth Amendment asserts that "The powers not delegated to the United States by the Constitution, nor prohibited by it to the States, are reserved to the States respectively, or to the people."[43] Which is it?

It depends on who one asks and when one asks the question. The debate over "states' rights" that surrounded much of the political upheaval that eventually exploded in the Civil War grew from the logic of the Tenth Amendment. Likewise, efforts to block civil rights during the twentieth and twenty-first centuries were framed in similar terms.

However, for a time during the all-too-short Reconstruction after the Civil War, the Supremacy Clause not only reigned supreme but also did so while adding three new amendments to the Constitution that moved the nation closer to its ideals. The Thirteenth Amendment abolished slavery, while the Fourteenth defined citizenship. The Fifteenth established the right to vote as sacrosanct (at least for men).[44]

A bit later on, under the guise of Theodore Roosevelt's Square Deal and Woodrow Wilson's New Freedom, the government expanded its role to address the inequities brought on by industrialization. During the Great Depression, Franklin Roosevelt's New Deal made the federal government responsible for the so-called forgotten man. In the 1960s, Lyndon Johnson committed the nation to becoming a "Great Society" where poverty and racism would become a thing of the past. All this and more were the result of accepting the notion that to guarantee the rights of *all* Americans, the Supremacy Clause must be enforced.

Still, the federal government cannot always be trusted to do the right thing, and in such cases, states and localities have actually served as bastions of liberty, as when states, counties, and cities have declared themselves sanctuaries, refusing to cooperate with draconian anti-immigrant policies. Or when state officials from both parties refused to cave into pressure from President Trump or his supporters to subvert the results of the 2020 election. So, as with everything else surrounding the Constitution, the Founders created a dynamic and often contradictory set of rules that have provided a multiplicity of safeguards on the abuse of power, even if they are sometimes slow to work.

Add to these the Bill of Rights, the first ten amendments to the Constitution, which exist courtesy of the Anti-Federalists and reflect the same level of concern for liberty. Everything from freedom of speech, religion, assembly, and the press to a person's right against unreasonable searches and seizures and self-incrimination is spelled out. And just to make sure, the Ninth Amendment asserts "the enumeration in the Constitution, of certain rights, shall not be construed to deny or disparage others retained by the people."[45] So armed, Americans, mindful of their God-given unalienable rights, have been able to work out their destiny, even if at times painfully and at great sacrifice and peril.

The Power of Principle and Pragmatism

The beauty of the American system is that it unleashes humans to be fully human. That can be dangerous given all the species' flaws. However, it can also be empowering in a way that no other system allows. People are pragmatic creatures. They have to be given how little they can actually control, despite their pretensions to the contrary.

That point is obvious from living life, but it was explained clearly by economist Herbert Simon, who coined the term "satisficing." According to Simon, people tend to make decisions in light of short-term realities. That is, they usually cannot foresee outcomes or accurately assess probabilities, rarely can or do evaluate all possible situations with precision, and suffer from fallible memories. When operating in a group, they tend to look for the solution on which everyone can agree. In short, people tend to make decisions based on circumstances, usually choosing an option that seems to best address the immediate problem.[46]

Constantly satisficing, we can never fully understand or appreciate the consequences of our actions and decisions for the future. After all, decisions are based on short-term considerations. Even when premised on long-term thinking, we are limited by the impossibility of having perfect information or of knowing or anticipating all possible contingencies. That is simply a function of the universe in which we live.

What better form of government could there be than one that not only was the product of satisficing but also allows for it in every aspect of its structure? It was the Founders' wisdom that created competing dialectics that acted to check the human impulse to indulge self-love while simultaneously enshrining laws to save us from ourselves. They also established the ideals that allow people not only to be themselves but also to be the best version of themselves. When that is not immediately possible, those same principles inspire individuals and groups to fight like hell to make it so.

CHAPTER THREE

A REPUBLIC . . . IF YOU CAN KEEP IT

On September 18, 1787, James McHenry, a representative from Maryland and the secretary of the Constitutional Convention, began his diary entry, "A lady asked Dr. Franklin . . ." It almost sounds like the set-up for a joke. What followed, though, was anything but. The lady, we learn in a footnote to McHenry's diary entry, was prominent Philadelphia socialite Elizabeth Willing Powel, who was a close personal friend to many of the nation's movers and shakers. She regularly hosted gatherings where a veritable "who's who" indulged in fine food and stimulating conversation about the political and social events of the day.

While the details of the story have been embellished and Mrs. Powel's role sometimes forgotten over the years, the essence of the exchange with Franklin has not. "A lady asked Dr. Franklin, 'Well Doctor what have we got a republic or a monarchy?' 'A republic,' replied the Doctor, 'if you can keep it.'"[1]

And with that simple statement, the challenge that would face America was succinctly and clearly laid out. How can you keep a republic? Certainly, the choices are stark, and they do not always seem to favor a system based on freedom. The astute French observer of American democracy, Alexis de Tocqueville, pointed out:

That nothing is more prodigal of wonders than the art of being free is a truth that cannot be repeated too often. But nothing is harder than the apprenticeship of liberty. This is not true of despotism. Despotism often presents itself as the remedy for all ills suffered in the past. It is the upholder of justice, the champion of the oppressed, and the founder of order. Nations are lulled to sleep by the temporary prosperity to which it gives rise, and when they are awake, they are miserable. Liberty, in contrast, is usually born in stormy times. It struggles to establish itself amid civil discord, and its benefits can be appreciated only when it is old.[2]

There is much insight in this statement. Like Benjamin Franklin's retort to Mrs. Powel, it serves as a reminder of how fragile republicanism truly is. There can be little doubt that monarchy or despotism is easier because the delicate balancing of competing interests is eliminated by a powerful sovereign or a dictator who commands without consultation or consent.

Republicanism offers no easy answers and, by its very nature, encourages discord because people are allowed to disagree, often quite vehemently. It is tempting, especially in times of crisis or discontent, to conclude, as Benito Mussolini did, that "Democracy is beautiful in theory; in practice it is a fallacy."[3]

That temptation accounts for what historian Richard Hofstadter characterized as America's "paranoid style" of politics. In illustrating his case, he traced examples of the phenomenon back to fear of the so-called illuminati, which first appeared in 1798. Since then, the country has witnessed various manifestations of essentially the same thing from individuals of all political persuasions. There was the anti-Masonic movement of the 1820s and 1830s, as well as the nativist and anti-Catholic movement that dominated politics off and on through the nineteenth and twentieth centuries.

Likewise, even "certain spokesmen of abolitionism" during the antebellum period fell prey to the disease, believing that the nation was being held hostage by "a slaveholders' conspiracy." There were Populists who spun stories of cabals of international bankers and munitions makers and saw the nefarious manifestations of their manipulation in the outbreak of World War I. Racial politics brought out similar ideas, from both White Citizens' Councils and members of the Nation of Islam. And, of course, there was Joseph McCarthy's witch hunt for Communists during the early years of the Cold War, along with the extreme paranoia evidenced by the John Birch Society.

"The idea of the paranoid style as a force in politics," argued Hofstadter, "would have little contemporary relevance or historical value if it were applied only to men with profoundly disturbed minds. It is the use of paranoid modes of expression by more or less normal people that makes the phenomenon significant." Although this approach to politics had "greater affinity for bad causes than good . . . nothing really prevents a sound program or demand from being advocated in the paranoid style. Style has more to do with the way in which ideas are believed than with the truth or falsity of their content."[4]

What Hofstadter described is not unique to America. Every nation is susceptible to what the ancient Greeks called demagoguery, because no system of government is perfect, and because every country is made up of fragile human beings who crave the security that a theoretically perfect system would afford. That leaves two choices: (1) as Tocqueville put it, despots who offer "the remedy for all ills suffered in the past" while portraying themselves as "the upholder of justice, the champion of the oppressed, and the founder of order"; or (2) as civil rights icon and congressman John Lewis called us to do, "Get in good trouble, necessary trouble."[5] The second option is clearly in keeping with American values at their best.

After all, the Founders were about getting into the kind of "good trouble" that gave birth to a nation premised on the ideals of freedom. Recall that Thomas Jefferson believed that "a little rebellion now and then is a good thing, and as necessary in the political world as storms in the physical."[6] That is because, as every patriot has known, and as John Lewis so eloquently expressed, "Freedom is not a state; it is an act. It is not some enchanted garden perched high on a distant plateau where we can finally sit down and rest. Freedom is the continuous action we all must take, and each generation must do its part to create an even more fair, more just society."[7]

This process takes constant work, struggle, and effort. Ceding responsibility to someone who promises to have answers, who claims they have the keys to the "enchanted garden," is much easier but far more dangerous. It results in the hangover effect that Tocqueville so neatly described when he wrote that when citizens "awake, they are miserable." And by then, it is often too late. One need only reflect on the end of Fascism in Italy and of Nazism in Germany, and the consequences that went well beyond either nation's borders courtesy of World War II.

So what, besides laziness, accounts for the all-too-human penchant to cede control of one's destiny and one's life to a demagogue or despot? A study done in the early 1950s by self-educated longshoreman Eric Hoffer offers some valuable insights. Demagogues need followers, who, in Hoffer's words, are true believers both in their leader and in their cause. It is, in essence, the logic of cultism transferred to the political arena.

Such individuals "see their lives as irremediably spoiled. . . . Their innermost craving is for a new life—a rebirth—or failing this, a chance to acquire new elements of pride, confidence, hope, sense of purpose and worth by an identification with a holy cause."[8] That makes skewed views of an idealized past an important part of policy creation. According to Hoffer, "This preoccupation with the past stems not only from a desire to demonstrate the legitimacy of the movement and the illegitimacy of the old order, but also to show up the present as a mere interlude between past and future."[9]

Of course, no movement can be complete without ideology and leadership, no matter how insane. As Hoffer so clearly explained:

> For men to plunge headlong into an undertaking of vast change, they must be intensely discontented yet not destitute, and they must have the feeling that by the possession of some potent

doctrine, infallible leader or some new technique they have access to a source of irresistible power. They must also have an extravagant conception of the prospects and potentialities of the future. Finally they must be wholly ignorant of the difficulties involved in their vast undertaking. Experience is a handicap.[10]

A lack of experience may be a handicap for those intent on subverting the system, but it also poses a real problem for running one. After all, with expertise comes a sense of ethics, a code of conduct, and principles. Historian Timothy Snyder puts it this way:

> If members of professions think of themselves as groups with common interests, with norms and rules that oblige them at all times, then they can gain confidence and indeed a certain kind of power. Professional ethics must guide us precisely when we are told that the situation is exceptional. Then there is no such thing as "just following orders." If members of the professions confuse their specific ethics with the emotions of the moment, however, they can find themselves saying and doing things that they might previously have thought unimaginable.[11]

This situation gets us into the realm of something that cannot be legislated, quantified, or even easily measured, but is essential for keeping a republic. There must be some baseline consensus on the fundamental values that inform the way the society functions. There must be an agreed-on safe space where people can passionately agree to disagree, knowing that the long-term benefits outweigh any short-term conflicts or hardships. This creates the invisible glue that unites, eliminating any need for the heavy hand of a tyrant to ensure unity through conformity, intimidation, and fear.

Factionalism and the Fringe

As long as most people are in the middle, with some leaning a bit to the left and some leaning a bit to the right, a republic can function. The logic here is straightforward: If the majority of citizens are somewhere in the middle, there is room for compromise and accommodation. Put another way, compromise is the means by which a republic conducts its business. That is why the Founders were so concerned about the evils of faction.

If a nation becomes too factionalized, it opens the door for tyranny. All it takes, in fact, is for a well-organized fringe group to garner a plurality and subvert the will of the people. After all, if citizens become too divided, they leave the path clear for anyone who can effectively organize and agitate for their particular cause. It is a simple matter of divide and conquer. As George Washington warned:

> All obstructions to the execution of the laws, all combinations and associations, under whatever plausible character, with the real design to direct, control, counteract, or awe the regular deliberation and action of the constituted authorities . . . serve to organize faction, to give it an artificial and extraordinary force; to put, in the place of the delegated will of the nation the will of a party, often a small but artful and enterprising minority of the community . . . [who] make the public administration the mirror of the ill-concerted and incongruous projects of faction. . . .
>
> [The result] . . . is itself a frightful despotism . . . [and] leads at length to a more formal and permanent despotism. The disorders and miseries which result gradually incline the minds of men to seek security and repose in the absolute power of an individual; and sooner or later the chief of some prevailing faction, more able or more fortunate than his competitors, turns this disposition to the purposes of his own elevation, on the ruins of public liberty.[12]

His point anticipated Tocqueville's analysis that despotism is the all-too-easily-reached-for solution to the conflicts, the "stormy times," and the "civil discord" for which liberty allows. The truth of such statements, when overlaid by the insights of Eric Hoffer and Timothy Snyder, explains what happened to the Weimar Republic in the 1930s.

Germany had to deal with a harsh peace after the end of World War I. The Weimar Republic, which had become the official government of the country when Kaiser Wilhelm II abdicated only a few days before the end of the war, was resented by many Germans. After all, it had signed the Versailles Peace Treaty that limited German sovereignty and imposed crushing war reparations on the country. The nation factionalized as extreme left- and right-wing organizations (often supported by paramilitary wings) battled each other. Average Germans, meanwhile, dealt with hyperinflation.

Things stabilized in 1924, but only for a few short years. Then the Great Depression hit in 1929. With hard times came the return of political, social, and economic chaos. In March 1932, the head of the Nazi Party, Adolf Hitler, ran for president against Paul von Hindenburg and Ernst Thälmann. The popular Hindenburg won handily, polling 53 percent of the vote. Hitler came in second with 36.8 percent, and Thälmann, a Communist, garnered 10.2 percent.

Four months later, elections for the Reichstag (the German legislature) were held. Nazi popularity had changed little from the presidential election. They won 37.3 percent of the popular vote. However, this was an increase of some 19 percent from the previous Reichstag election in 1932, and it gave them a plurality and thus control of that body. With that, the party chose Hermann Göring as president of the Reichstag. Pressure was applied to Hindenburg to appoint Adolf Hitler chancellor. He refused. Meanwhile, political violence continued and Göring pushed for draconian legislation to punish the perpetrators, in large part because Communists had been responsible for the deaths of several Nazi Party members.

Another election was held in November 1932, in which the Nazis lost thirty-five seats but retained control of the Reichstag. Through a series of backroom negotiations, Hindenburg finally named Hitler chancellor. It did not take long for the Nazis to orchestrate events, including the burning of the Reichstag in February 1933, so that Hitler could use the laws Göring had forced through earlier to seize power and persecute his enemies. The following month, the

Reichstag passed the Enabling Act, granting the new chancellor absolute authority to govern for four years. With that, the Weimar Republic breathed its last.[13]

There are those who may argue, as did Francis Tasbrough in Sinclair Lewis's cautionary tale from 1935, "No, no! Couldn't happen here!"[14] The truth is, it could because Americans are human, like everyone else, with all the foibles that make people susceptible to the blandishments of factionalism and extremism. It was this recognition that led the Founders to build in all the checks and balances that they did.

Still, not every contingency can be anticipated, so the risk of subversion is always present. The survival of the Republic is thus never guaranteed and requires, as Benjamin Franklin told Mrs. Powel, our willingness to keep it. Despite the nation's long history of "stormy times" and "civil discord," there have been, remarkably, only two occasions when the Republic was almost lost because Americans forgot that fact and put factional interest above the common good. One was during the Civil War; the other, when Donald Trump and his allies sought to overturn the results of the 2020 election.

A Nation Torn Asunder

In the first case, the factionalism that manifested during the 1860 election had been building for a while. Four major candidates, and a slew of minor ones, ran for president, suggesting the degree of fragmentation gripping the nation.

The Republicans put up Abraham Lincoln. Their platform left little doubt that they took their name seriously. It argued that "maintenance of the principles promulgated in the Declaration of Independence and embodied in the Federal Constitution . . . is essential to the preservation of our Republican institutions." As such, they abhorred "all schemes for disunion, come from whatever source they may," and condemned "the threats of disunion so often made by Democratic members [of Congress], without rebuke and with applause from their political associates." This, the Republicans believed, was "an avowal of contemplated treason, which it is the imperative duty of an indignant people sternly to rebuke and forever silence."

Although they emphatically stood for "the rights of the states, and especially the right of each state to order and control its own domestic institutions," Republicans believed "the new dogma that the Constitution, of its own force, carries slavery into any or all of the territories of the United States is a dangerous political heresy." The truth, they asserted, was "that the normal condition of all the territory of the United States is that of freedom." Moreover, "the recent reopening of the African slave trade" was "a crime against humanity and a burning shame to our country and age."

Finally, on the matter of immigration, Republicans were unequivocally "opposed to any change in our naturalization laws or any state legislation by which the rights of citizens hitherto accorded to immigrants from foreign lands shall be abridged or impaired." Additionally, they favored "giving a full and efficient protection to the rights of all classes of citizens, whether native or naturalized, both at home and abroad."[15]

The Democrats, for their part, were divided. Two conventions in two months produced nothing but strife. When the party finally nominated Stephen A. Douglas, Southern delegates bolted and put up their own candidate, John Breckenridge, a pro-slavery senator from Kentucky and the vice president under President James Buchanan.

That left what became the Northern Democrats to come up with a rather nondescript platform. Believing that "Democratic principles are unchangeable in their nature," they declared their "affirmance of the resolutions unanimously adopted and declared as a platform of principles by the Democratic Convention at Cincinnati, in the year 1856." Like the Republicans, they avowed support for the rights of all citizens, "whether at home or abroad, and whether native or foreign born."

Acknowledging their inability to agree on the powers of the territorial governments versus that of Congress on the issue of slavery, they decided to "abide by the decision of the Supreme Court of the United States upon these questions of Constitutional law." The party was firm, however, in its condemnation of "enactments of the State Legislatures to defeat the faithful execution of the Fugitive Slave Law." Such actions, they contended, were "hostile in character, subversive of the Constitution, and revolutionary in their effect."[16]

That was hardly enough to appease the Southern Democrats, even though in almost every other respect their platform was identical to their Northern compatriots. The one significant difference was when it came to admission of new states into the Union. The state, they argued, "ought to be admitted into the Federal Union, whether its Constitution prohibits or recognizes the institution of slavery."[17]

Finally, there was the Constitutional Union Party, which put up former Tennessee senator John Bell. Bell and his supporters were vehemently anti-immigrant but argued for the "Union and the Constitution as it is." According to their platform, "it is both the part of patriotism and of duty to recognize no political principle other than THE CONSTITUTION OF THE COUNTRY, THE UNION OF THE STATES, AND THE ENFORCEMENT OF THE LAWS." As such, the party was committed "to maintain, protect, and defend, separately and unitedly, these great principles of public liberty and national safety, against all enemies, at home and abroad."[18]

In the general election, Lincoln won 39.8 percent of the popular vote, Douglas 29.5 percent, Breckenridge 18.1 percent, and Bell 12.6 percent. In the Electoral College, Lincoln garnered 59.4 percent of the vote, Breckenridge 23.8 percent, Bell 12.9 percent, and Douglas 3.9 percent. All of Lincoln's support was in the North and in the new states of California and Oregon. Breckenridge took the Deep South; Bell won Kentucky, Virginia, and Tennessee.

What does this all mean? The vast majority of Americans seemed to favor a moderate or even a progressive position, based on Douglas's (who was a moderate on the issue of slavery) and Lincoln's combined 69.3 percent of the popular vote. If the Constitutional Union Party is factored in, another 12.6 percent wanted simply to maintain the status quo. By that measure, almost 82 percent of Americans supported either some reform or more of the same.

Although 18.1 percent of the population, confined to a particular geographic region, supported protection of slaveholders' rights in the Western territories, far fewer supported secession. John Breckenridge certainly did not, and he was the standard-bearer for the Southern Democrats. Dissolving the Union, put bluntly, was not something the overwhelming majority of Americans wanted, even in the South.[19]

So if less than 20 percent of the population voted for a pro-slavery agenda, and far fewer favored the end of the Republic, how did the nation end up in a state of civil war? The answer involves the power of propaganda, or agitating a base of support to convince people that a cause has more power and validity than it does in truth. Adolf Hitler explained it this way:

> [I]n the big lie there is always a certain force of credibility; because the broad masses of a nation are always more easily corrupted . . . and thus in the primitive simplicity of their minds they more readily fall victims to the big lie than the small lie, since they themselves often tell small lies in little matters but would be ashamed to resort to large-scale falsehoods.
>
> It would never come into their heads to fabricate colossal untruths, and they would not believe that others could have the impudence to distort the truth so infamously. Even though the facts which prove this to be so may be brought clearly to their minds, they will still doubt and waver and will continue to think that there may be some other explanation. For the grossly impudent lie always leaves traces behind it, even after it has been nailed down.[20]

Such insights not only explain why mass movements and cults work but also speak to something universal about the human experience that both predates and postdates Hitler. According to the assertion often attributed to P. T. Barnum, "there's a sucker born every minute." All con artists and hucksters instinctively operate from this assumption. Indeed, they count on it as a fact. It is why they so openly flaunt the "grossly impudent lie," the one tool that, as Hitler explained, is "known to all expert liars in this world and to all who conspire together in the art of lying."[21] Whether true believer or not, the art of stirring people to do what they might not otherwise do involves polarization and the nuances that have been mastered by the practitioners of the art of paranoid politics for time immemorial.

As the nation waited for what would happen after the election of Lincoln, those who spoke for so few went about the work of ending the Union. How much they believed their own rhetoric is beside the point. In fact, many probably did, for lies become truth in the minds of those who hear and articulate them if they are repeated strongly and frequently enough. And the so-called fire-eaters, who agitated for Southern secession after the 1860 election, had been at it for at least a decade.

Between June 3 and 11, 1850, delegates from nine states met in Nashville, Tennessee, to discuss what they should do if Congress banned slavery in the new territories recently won in the Mexican-American War. The answer: secession. The threat was enough to force the Compromise of 1850, which placed some of the land claimed by Texas under federal control; organized two new territories, New Mexico and Utah, which would be permitted to choose for themselves whether they would be free or slave; admitted California as a free state; abolished the slave trade in the District of Columbia; and mandated a strict Fugitive Slave Law. It also served to embolden those who put their interests in expanding slavery ahead of love of country.

During the election of 1856, fire-eaters again used threats of secession as they actively campaigned for James Buchanan. Their concern: the Republican candidate James C. Fremont, who, as a Free Soiler, opposed all expansion of slavery into the Western territories. The third candidate, Millard Fillmore, was the standard-bearer for the No-Nothing Party, known for its vehement anti-immigrant positions. The contest was a dry run for 1860. Fremont carried the majority of the electoral votes from the free states and finished second in the popular vote. Buchanan won all the slave states except Maryland, which went for Fillmore.

Still, the fault lines were clear. Even as the vast majority of Americans wanted to keep the Union intact, the secessionists were a force to be reckoned with. When the 1860 election rolled around, the fire-eaters demonized the Republicans and Abraham Lincoln. When that strategy failed to influence the vote, they took their fight to the states, starting with South Carolina, whose legislature was convinced to pass an Ordinance of Secession in December 1860.

The rhetoric of one of the most outspoken advocates for the extreme Southern cause is sufficient to capture the essence of the message. Edmund Ruffin, a native of Virginia, found himself in Charleston, lobbying for the cause. Speaking to a crowd of supporters, he first congratulated the South Carolina legislature for its prompt action in meeting to address the crisis and pointed with gratification to the movements in Georgia, Florida, Mississippi, Alabama, and North Carolina to do the same. He then focused his vitriol on his home state.

[I]f Virginia remains in the Union, under the domination of this infamous, low, vulgar tyranny of Black Republicanism, and there is one other State in the Union that has bravely thrown off the yoke, I will seek my domicil [sic] in that State and abandon Virginia forever. If Virginia will not act as South Carolina, I have no longer a home, and I am a banished man . . . I will say, there is not one of you, young and ardent as most of you are, that has this cause more at heart than I have, or would make greater sacrifices to secure its success.[22]

To his credit (such as it was), Ruffin was true to his word. Years later, with the Confederacy defeated, he wrote in his diary:

> I here declare my unmitigated hatred to Yankee rule—to all political, social and business connection with the Yankees and to the Yankee race. Would that I could impress these sentiments, in their full force, on every living Southerner and bequeath them to every one yet to be born! May such sentiments be held universally in the outraged and downtrodden South, though in silence and stillness, until the now far-distant day shall arrive for just retribution for Yankee usurpation, oppression and atrocious outrages, and for deliverance and vengeance for the now ruined, subjugated and enslaved Southern States! . . . And now with my latest writing and utterance, and with what will be near my latest breath, I here repeat and would willingly proclaim my unmitigated hatred to Yankee rule—to all political, social and business connections with Yankees, and the perfidious, malignant and vile Yankee race.[23]

He then shot himself. The date was June 18, 1865. Unfortunately, he got his wish. His sentiments would be bequeathed to "living Southerner[s]" and those "yet to be born." They would also drive the logic of those who chose to nurse grievances, wallow in hate, and instigate violence in the name of their supposedly righteous cause.

Unresolved Issues

One need only fast forward to the years between 2016 and 2020 to see the spirit of Ruffin very much alive and well, with the same polarizing effects and existential threat to the Republic. Not surprisingly, as with the build-up to the Civil War, the rise of what became Trumpism was a long time coming and was grounded in the same sort of logic and manipulation.

Indeed, to fully appreciate that, we must go back to 1968. Knowing that they could not directly promote racism and white supremacy like the fire-eaters, leaders of Richard Nixon's presidential campaign took a more subtle approach. Using terms like "law and order" and "states' rights," Nixon appealed to white Southerners who were increasing dissatisfied with the progressive direction of the Democratic Party.

The plan worked. Ironically, though (and something that was lost on right-wing strategists and those Republicans who would later totally capitulate to Donald Trump's hijacking of their party), Nixon actually promoted further desegregation.[24] But that was beside the point. His divide-and-conquer strategy won elections, and that was what mattered.

A decade after Nixon, the Moral Majority's outrage over abortion rights, gays, and the loss of so-called family values served pretty much the same function of rallying a base of the disaffected as had Nixon's Southern Strategy. However, the Moral Majority's agenda was more than a cynical election strategy to capture the presidency. It mobilized a core of true believers around a coherent agenda fixated on conservative reform and grievance.

The Moral Majority was just the beginning. Organizations like the Council for National Policy, the Leadership Institute, the Salem Media Group, Fox News, and Breitbart News Network (to name but a few) provided the infrastructure, capital, and media know-how to organize a movement.[25] When Donald Trump ran in 2016 as a Washington outsider committed to "draining the swamp" and rooting out the imaginary deep state, it was a sign that the festering problem had bubbled to the surface, much as the 1856 election had been the manifestation of long-standing Southern elite grievance and a precursor to the 1860 election.

Its final incarnation came when many members of the Republican Party abetted a coup attempt by Trump after the 2020 election. Remaining silent or actively supporting the president's efforts, their actions were both dangerous and reckless. Orchestrated by Trump and his aides, the resulting circus featured bizarre conspiracy theories and overt attacks by Trump on state Republicans who certified election results that were not in his favor. Some sixty frivolous lawsuits were filed by the president and his associates to overturn the election.[26]

Typical was the case brought by Attorney General Kenneth Paxton of Texas, who, facing charges of bribery and abuse of office, sued Georgia, Pennsylvania, Michigan, and Wisconsin to have their certified election results overturned. Trump lawyers, along with the attorneys general of eighteen other states, filed amicus briefs in support of the suit. One hundred twenty-six House Republicans did the same, including Minority Leader Kevin McCarthy, House Minority Whip Steve Scalise, and Republican Policy Committee Chairman Gary Palmer. As with other cases thrown out by other courts as specious, the Supreme Court refused to hear the case.[27]

When the legal maneuverings fell flat, efforts were made to encourage state legislatures to authorize "faithless electors," who would not honor the vote of their states when the Electoral College met on December 14, 2020.[28] That, too, went nowhere.

Then there was Michael Flynn, Trump's convicted former chief of national security. Pardoned by the president, despite having twice pleaded guilty to lying to the FBI about his contacts with Russia, Flynn went on the ultra-right-wing cable television network Newsmax to call for martial law, saying Trump "could take military capabilities and basically rerun an election . . . in . . . [each of the swing] states."[29]

It was a doubling down of an earlier statement he had made on December 1, when he retweeted a message from a right-wing group in Ohio that called on Trump to "suspend the Constitution" and have the military hold a "national re-vote." With few exceptions, Republicans were quiet about Flynn's call to end American democracy. In fact, many praised the president for pardoning the former national security chief for his crimes of collusion with a foreign power.[30]

No law or tradition was sacred. The Electoral Count Act of 1887, for example, requires the vice president to preside over the validation of Electoral College votes in a largely ceremonial capacity and to affirm the winner of the presidential election. On December 27, Republican Representative Louie Gohmert of Texas joined a group of Arizona Republicans who sued Vice President Mike Pence. They argued that not only was the 133-year-old law unconstitutional, but Pence should also be authorized to appoint pro-Trump electors on January 6, 2021, at the pro forma joint meeting of Congress to count the Electoral College votes and certify the election. Like all the other suits, the case was thrown out of court.[31]

Undeterred, Trump loyalists in Congress, led by Senators Ted Cruz of Texas and Josh Hawley of Missouri, announced that they would object to the electoral votes of several of the swing states that the president had lost. They were joined by eleven senators who went on record saying that they would do the same. Meanwhile, some 140 Republican members of the House made a similar pledge.[32]

Cruz, Hawley, and their cronies called for a commission to investigate the repeatedly debunked claims of voting irregularities, citing the 1877 Electoral Commission as precedent. In addition to the disingenuous nature of their argument, their choice of the Commission (and, by implicit extension, the resulting Compromise of the same year) spoke volumes. It was sadly appropriate that the final defense of Trumpism would be framed in terms of the legacies of the white grievance agenda from which it sprang. So little seemed to have been learned from the nation's history with such thinking, which included the Civil War, Jim Crow, the pushback against civil rights, and Nixon's Southern Strategy.

The Commission had been the result of the hotly contested election of 1876 between Democrat Samuel Tilden and Republican Rutherford B. Hayes. Tilden won the popular vote and was one electoral vote shy of clinching the presidency with four states still to be counted. In Florida, Louisiana, and South Carolina, Republican-controlled canvassing boards had disenfranchised Democratic voters. Democrats in those states convened their own boards and certified a second Electoral College vote and sued the Republicans. In Oregon, Governor La Fayette Grover, a Democrat, disqualified

Republican elector John W. Watts on the grounds that his appoint-
ment as assistant postmaster violated the constitutional prohibition
against electors holding federal office.

When Congress met to certify the result of the election in 1877,
it faced the problem of which slate of electors from these four states
to accept. The prospect of armed conflict loomed as Tilden supporters called for mobilizing the National Guard and Republicans
threatened to use federal troops to maintain order. Thus was born
the Electoral Commission. Through the month of February, it
labored to resolve the disputes. They eventually agreed that all four
states had gone in favor of Hayes.

Their work finished, the commissioners turned their results over
to Congress. The Democrats were livid and threatened to filibuster.
Tilden supporters again made noise about taking up arms. Leaders
of both parties met to find a solution—the infamous Compromise
of 1877.

The Democrats accepted the results in favor of Hayes in exchange
for Republicans agreeing to remove federal troops from Louisiana,
South Carolina, and Florida, the only remaining Confederate states
where they were still present. Additionally, Southern states would
be allowed to deal with their African American citizens as they saw
fit without federal interference, a second intercontinental railroad
would be built, Hayes would name at least one Southern Democrat
to his cabinet, and Congress would pass legislation to help build the
South's economic infrastructure. With that, Reconstruction ended
and systemic racism went on about its merry way, reinforced by Jim
Crow laws that disenfranchised African Americans and condemned
them to the equivalency of debt peonage.[33]

It would not be until the 1950s that a second effort at righting
the wrongs that were the legacy of slavery was undertaken with the
push for civil rights. The ensuing reforms fell short in no small measure because white politicians either denied the problem or turned
what gains that had been made for people of color into a rationale
for stoking white grievance. With Trumpism the logical next step

in a process begun during Reconstruction, it was no wonder that congressional defenders of the president harkened back to such an infamous chapter in American history.

Even if meant as nothing more than political theater by feckless Republicans trying to appeal to Trump's base, the issue was serious and called into question everything from the ethics and patriotism of its perpetrators to the very security of the nation. On January 6, 2021, the price for the wanton immaturity, gutlessness, and enabling of the majority of Republicans came crashing in on them, their Democratic colleagues, and the country.

Trump had spent much of December stirring up his supporters, saying January 6 would be "a day of reckoning" to "save America" and "stop the steal." Pushing a slew of increasingly bizarre conspiracy theories that "proved" he had won the 2020 election in a "landslide," the delusional chief executive kept up a steady stream of tweets. Typical was the one on December 19, in which he wrote, "Big protest in DC on January 6th. Be there, will be wild!"[34]

January 6 began with a rally at which Trump's personal attorney, Rudy Giuliani, spoke, pushing his conspiracy-laden false claims of voter fraud. In the midst of his tirade, he suddenly shouted, "Let's have trial by combat!"[35] Representative Mo Brooks of Alabama echoed the theme, telling the crowd:

> America does not need and cannot stand—cannot tolerate—any more weakling, cowering, wimpy Republican congressmen and senators who covet power and the prestige the swamp has to offer while groveling at the feet of the special interest masters. Today's the day American patriots start taking down names and kicking ass.[36]

The president's son, Don Jr., delivered an expletive-filled rant laced with threats to Republican lawmakers. "To those Republicans, many of which may be voting on things in the coming hours: You have an opportunity today," he said. "You can be a hero, or you can be a zero. And the choice is yours. But we are all watching. The whole world is watching, folks. Choose wisely." He went on to suggest that if they did not do his father's bidding, they could expect him to campaign against them. "[G]uess what?" he menaced. "I'm going to be in your backyard in a couple of months!"

In perhaps the only bit of honesty spoken at the rally, Donald Jr. blustered that "This gathering should send a message [to all the Republicans who have not sided with the president]: This isn't their Republican Party anymore! This is Donald Trump's Republican Party!"[37]

His father kept up the invective in a rambling, incoherent, nearly seventy-five-minute speech. In rhetoric that would have done a Southern fire-eater on the eve of the Civil War proud, Trump told an increasingly agitated crowd:

> Our country has had enough. We will not take it anymore and that's what this is all about. To use a favorite term that all of you people really came up with, we will stop the steal. . . . States want to revolt. The States got defrauded. They were given false information. They voted on it. Now they want to recertify. They want it back. . . .
>
> After this, we're going to walk down and I'll be there with you. We're going to walk down. . . . We're going to walk down to the Capitol, and we're going to cheer on our brave senators, and congressmen and women. We're probably not going to be cheering so much for some of them because you'll never take back our country with weakness. You have to show strength, and you have to be strong.[38]

After the rally, Trump and his motorcade returned to the safety of the White House. The emboldened mob, meanwhile, stormed the Capitol grounds.

Before they arrived en masse, Senator Hawley entered the Capitol. Looking smug, he turned to a crowd of protestors who were already assembled on the Hill and gave them a clinched fist salute. Later, when the building was under siege, he tweeted his thanks to the police for their efforts in defending the Capitol, called for peace and the prosecution of those who had violated the law, and noted that Congress needed to get back to business.[39]

As vandals roamed the halls of Congress, an organization working to raise funds for Hawley sent out the following message: "Hi, it's Josh Hawley. I'm leading the charge to fight for free and fair elections. We need to ensure that everyone has their voice heard at the ballot box. That's why I'm asking you to join me today!"[40] Hawley's cynical exploitation of the situation made the Compromise of 1877 (and his use of it) look tame.

With dry runs having occurred during the weeks before at the state level, the Washington rally quickly turned into open insurrection and sparked similar actions at several state capitals. Sedition-addled rabble broke windows and desecrated the hallowed halls of Congress. Among other things, there was an armed standoff outside the House floor, bombs were found on Capitol grounds, hooligans seized and vandalized offices, and one yahoo paraded a Confederate flag through the rotunda.

Self-righteous thugs took selfies and bragged about the havoc they were wreaking. Gallows were set up and angry looters chanted, "Hang Mike Pence!" One self-styled revolutionary stole a letter from House Speaker Nancy Pelosi's office and bragged of leaving her a profanity-laced threat. Another posed for pictures while sitting on the Senate Dais that had recently been occupied by the vice president.[41]

Such cavalier behavior belied the fact that the violence was deadly. It could have been much worse, though. Indications were that some of the groups that stormed the Capitol fully intended to take congressional leaders hostage and execute both the vice president and House Speaker Nancy Pelosi, the number two and three heads of the government. Had things proceeded according to that plan, the end result would have decapitated one of the three co-equal branches of government—the legislature, which is where the voice of the people most clearly has its say. If that had occurred, the Republic would have perished.

Meanwhile, at the other end of Pennsylvania Avenue, the president remained hunkered down watching the news coverage of the chaos and, by some accounts, was borderline ecstatic. After resisting the urging of aides to tell the terrorists at Capitol Hill to stand down, Trump finally went to the Rose Garden and tweeted a video saying, "I know your pain. I know you're hurt. We had an election that was stolen from us. It was a landslide election and everyone knows it, especially the other side, but you have to go home now. We have to have peace. We have to have law and order."[42]

Later, he walked back even that half-hearted call for an end to the violence. He tweeted, "These are the things and events that happen when a sacred landslide election victory is so unceremoniously & viciously stripped away from great patriots who have been badly & unfairly treated for so long. Go home with love & peace. Remember this day forever!"[43] Twitter and Facebook would later suspend Trump's accounts for continuing to incite insurrection.

After order was restored, Congress reconvened to do its job. It took them until 3:40 a.m. on January 7 to complete what should have been a ceremonial function and certify the election of President-elect Joe Biden and Vice President–elect Kamala Harris. The reason it took so long: despite the horrific day's events, and the clear fallacy of the case being put forth, some 60 percent of Republicans from both houses stuck by their pledge to challenge the votes.[44]

Although several of Trump's enablers over the four years of his presidency began to distance themselves from the president, it was a case of locking the barn door after the horse had escaped. More disturbing was the reaction of the unrepentant. Alabama Representative Brooks was typical. Taking to Twitter, he condemned the violence, only later to advise, "Please, don't be like #FakeNewsMedia, don't rush to judgment on assault on Capitol. Wait for investigation. All may not be (and likely is not) what appears. Evidence growing that fascist ANTIFA orchestrated Capitol attack with clever mob control tactics."[45]

One wonders why someone who helped to incite the violence and spoke to the Trump revolutionaries would suddenly think that those he had addressed were members of ANTIFA. Then again, expecting intellectual consistency, moral integrity, or rationality from individuals like Mo Brooks was like asking fire-eater Edmund Ruffin to tone down his racist rhetoric. And for good reason. Both were cut from the same cloth.

To his credit, Brooks did get one thing correct, even if inadvertently in his stilted, illogical Twitter rhetoric: The assault on the Capitol was carried out by Fascists, who by definition are right-wing authoritarians. Loosely organized groups that exist under the umbrella term ANTIFA (for Anti-Fascist) have a diametrically opposed mission: to aggressively confront authoritarian movements and groups in the belief that the Nazis would not have seized power in Germany had they been more forcefully resisted. With many of the groups rooted in anarchist ideology, the very notion of a tight-knit movement with the degree of organization ascribed to it by the likes of Mo Brooks was on its face ridiculous.[46]

Still, there was no small irony that the 2020–2021 incarnation of the fire-eaters were members of the party that 161 years earlier had gone on record chastising Democrats for allowing "threats of disunion" to pass "without rebuke and with applause from their political associates," asserting that such conduct was "an avowal of contemplated treason, which it is the imperative duty of an indignant people sternly to rebuke and forever silence."

So, it fell to others to state the obvious. The president-elect condemned the insurrection, as did former government officials. Discussion of impeaching Trump or invoking the Fourteenth and/or Twenty-Fifth Amendments swirled in the immediate aftermath of January 6 and led to the unprecedented: Donald Trump became the first president to be impeached twice. Postmortems preoccupied government officials and media pundits.

Consideration of using the Fourteenth Amendment focused on Section 3, which prohibits anyone from holding office who, having sworn an oath to the Constitution, "shall have engaged in insurrection or rebellion against the same, or given aid or comfort to the enemies thereof."[47] The clause was in direct response to those who had caused the Civil War. That invoking it would be suggested to deal with their modern-day compatriots seemed as fitting as the use of the 1877 Electoral Commission precedent by the insurgents.

Meanwhile, as cabinet secretaries and members of his staff resigned, Trump posted a video grudgingly promising a peaceful transition and acknowledging that a new administration would be inaugurated on January 20. It was a futile attempt to avoid impeachment. In fact, that video was the only thing Trump would claim to regret after all the turmoil he had unleashed.

When the president made his first public appearance after the uprising some six days later, he defiantly justified his actions and attacked those who sought to hold him accountable. At the urging of his advisors, who hoped to mitigate some of his legal exposure, another video was issued later, but, like the one he regretted making earlier, its tenor and tone rang hollow.

In that sense, even his farewell video on January 19, 2021, was significant for what it did not include—any reference to his successor. His real focus on the last day of his presidency was working, with the help of his daughter Ivanka, on a slew of questionable pardons. To his credit, such as it was, he did listen to suggestions and refrained from issuing any to himself or his family.

If nothing else, Donald Trump was consistent to the end. In keeping with his strongman dictatorial aspirations, he had hoped to depart Washington on the morning of Inauguration Day standing on a red carpet, a military band playing, jets flying overhead, and a twenty-one-gun salute punctuating the air. Instead, a small crowd at Joint Base Andrews listened to a self-congratulatory speech, which included a few lines from First Lady Melania Trump.

There was a twenty-one-gun salute and a red carpet, but the music was piped in, featuring Laura Branigan's "Gloria" and the Village People's "YMCA." As Air Force One took off, Frank Sinatra's

"My Way" played. It seemed more a scaled-down version of one of Trump's "Make America Great Again" rallies than something befitting the departure of an American president. Then again, for an administration that did nothing remotely normal, and was always obsessed with theatrics over substance, it was an appropriate way to go out.

For its part, the extreme right saw nothing untoward in any of this theater, continuing its rationalizations and defense of the president. More ominously, threats of violence persisted against Washington and all fifty state capitals in the days leading up to Inauguration Day. Fortunately, they proved to be more smoke than fire.[48]

The end of 2020 and the beginning of 2021 was in many ways a national reckoning, bringing into clear focus what can happen when issues are left to fester unresolved and, perhaps more significant, when enough people are duped into forgetting what the values of the nation really mean. Despite that, the most important thing was that, at the end of the day, a peaceful transition of power occurred on the steps of the recently besieged Capitol building.[49] The nation moved forward from there, beginning the long process of healing because the vast majority of Americans still remained committed to keeping the Republic.

The Middle Ground

Make no mistake about it, though: the consequences of the botched coup were real, just as were the legacies of the Civil War. Meaningful progress required that the nation honestly confront what had led it to the events of January 6, 2021. Although some sought to do that, there were still those who, as during Reconstruction and with the Compromise of 1877, just wanted to move on.

Trump's second impeachment failed to yield a conviction because Republicans remained hopelessly wedded to the fear of what standing against his base would mean for their re-election.[50] In what seemed like a replay of the South's implementation of Jim Crow laws after Reconstruction, by mid-February 2021, just a month after President Biden's inauguration, forty-three state legislatures were considering 253 bills to restrict voter access to the polls.

The good news was that, at the same time, there were some 704 bills in a different set of forty-three states that were designed to increase voter participation.[51] Additionally, Democrats in Congress pushed legislation to expand voting rights, institute campaign finance reform, and establish guidelines to end gerrymandering. Unfortunately, Republicans stood unified in their opposition, motivating President Biden to sign an executive order to expand voter access.[52]

That he had do to so, or that there could be such resistance to what was essentially a fundamental tenet of American democracy, especially in the aftermath of the 2020 election fiasco and the January 6 insurrection, seemed unfathomable. However, when considered against the larger backdrop of US history, there was, unfortunately, nothing really shocking or new here. As detailed in the previous chapter, gerrymandering and voter suppression have had a long history even as the country's ideals speak against their logic.

Still, the struggle to move the country forward so that it can better live into its ideals is, for good and for ill, part of its ongoing narrative. After all, in a system in which people are at liberty to be what they are, to believe what they will, and to act accordingly, they will do so. Sometimes that is to their and their nation's credit. Sometimes, however, it is to their everlasting infamy and their country's shame.

Put simply, when Americans cannot agree on the fundamentals of their shared narrative, the results sometimes devolve into a theater of the absurd. Such was the case when hard-core Trump supporters and followers of QAnon, the ultra-right wing internet conspiracy group, concocted a new reason to believe that the ex-president would be re-inaugurated on March 4, 2021.

In a bit of twisted logic that only true believers could follow, the argument ran that since the old date for inaugurating presidents was March 4, Trump would be sworn in on that date. Pointing to an obscure 1871 law that established the government of the City of Washington, QAnon devotees reasoned (incorrectly) that it had dissolved the United States government and turned it into a corporation. As such, every law, amendment, and president after 1871 was illegitimate. When the hoped-for return of Trump occurred on March 4, he would become the nineteenth president of the United States.[53]

Needless to say, the fantasy did not become reality, but new ones soon arose to take its place. Such was the depth of the continuing challenges confronting the nation. As after the Civil War, an ongoing struggle for the soul of America was underway with no guarantees as to the outcome.

Certainly, though there were reasons for hope, there were also serious reasons for concern. Indeed, to dismiss QAnon-style conspiracy theories as out-of-hand is to ignore that unreconstructed Southerners were able to successfully hijack the narrative surrounding the Civil War and Reconstruction, contending that the Confederate rebellion had been a "Glorious Lost Cause," heroic, moral, and just in all its aspects, an interpretation that opponents to civil rights have clung to furiously ever since.[54]

For a republic to function, it needs consensus on the soundness of its institutions, its principles, its laws, and the fundamental decency of the governed and those who govern. When that disappears, the nation is put in peril. The build-up to the Civil War and then its actual fighting demonstrates what is possible when consensus is lost. The same was true when a president and members of his party violated the oath they took to "preserve, protect and defend the Constitution of the United States"[55] in favor of the politics of grievance.

Connections Across Time

The results were eerily similar, but this is what comes of ignoring the inherent contradictions that were present from the beginning of the Republic. If one thinks about it, a version of the politics of grievance drove the South to secede in 1861. Ironically, though, both during the Civil War and during the failed Trump putsch and its aftermath, those who felt themselves most aggrieved were those who wanted to keep those who were *truly* aggrieved—people of color, women, and the poor—"in their place."

Following the Civil War, and well into the twenty-first century, white males who believed themselves marginalized came to identify with white males of privilege who were not, around the two things that they had in common—their race and their gender. By blinding lower-class individuals—regardless of race, color, ethnicity, or gender—to what they had in common, the wedge that had given elites their advantage since before there was a Republic continued very much in place.

On the eve of the Civil War, though exact numbers are debated, most poor whites did not own slaves and had little stake in preserving the institution. One study suggests that even with conscription laws and inducements for poor whites to fight for the Confederacy, of the approximately 3.9 million free whites in the South, slave owners fought in disproportionally higher numbers than did non–slave owners because they had a more direct economic interest in the outcome of the conflict.[56] Taken in conjunction with the election results of 1860, one is struck by how easy it is for a determined minority to imperil the Republic.

In the case of 2020–2021, the statistics are equally revealing. If the consensus required for a republic to function lies in the middle, between 2004 and 2020, Americans were fairly evenly divided between Democrats, Republicans, and Independents. Citizens who called themselves Democrats ranged from a high of 38 percent to a low of 26 percent, with that number being 31 percent in December 2020. For Republicans, the range was between 38 percent and 20 percent, with 25 percent identifying as Republicans in December 2020.

Independents, meanwhile, ranged from 47 percent to 27 percent and, in December 2020, were 41 percent of the population. The numbers averaged out to a roughly one-third, one-third, one-third split, with the number of Independents being on the high end of that average, Republicans on the low end, and Democrats in the middle, with minor variations up and down depending on when the poll was taken.

The point, be it in the twenty-first century or the nineteenth, is that extremism does not resonate with most Americans. When asked whether they lean more to the Democratic or the Republican side, with few exceptions, Independents usually split about evenly during the period covered by the survey. One telling exception was in December 2020, when Independents supported the Democrats 50 percent to 39 percent.

Viewed another way, 51.5 percent of the population in December 2020, when Democrats and Democrat-leaning Independents were combined, did not support the Republican agenda, which was largely focused on stealing the election. When combined with the 36.5 percent of Independents who continued to identify simply as Independent, that meant that 88 percent of citizens rejected the Republican coup attempt and continued to operate in the middle.[57]

Those numbers were reminiscent of the reality after the 1860 election. Just as significantly, as in 1860, when a vote for Breckenridge was not necessarily a vote for secession, not all those who voted Republican in 2020 supported Trump's extremist agenda. One need only consider the split-ticket voting that returned fifty Republicans to the Senate, boosted their numbers in the House, and allowed them to retain control of many state governments.

Granted that the Republican base became more hard-core in its Trumpism,[58] but the central point is that such extremism was no more indicative of the nation as a whole than had been the secessionists in 1860. Of course, as with the secessionists and the Nazis in Germany, the legacy of the Trump base left its mark, and it would do so well into the future. That is the nature of movements that spring from unresolved issues. To that point, it bears repeating that the roots of Trumpism were firmly entrenched in the events that fomented the Civil War and were brought forward in time by the backlash against first Reconstruction and then, in the twentieth century, the civil rights movement.

There are several important takeaways here. A consensus in favor of the Republic has long been the hallmark of the nation. When taken in conjunction with the checks at the federal and state levels against the abuse of power, it is why the nation has been able to weather the inevitable "stormy times" born of liberty.

Still, the fringe that fueled secession in 1861, that has manifested in America's paranoid style of politics, and that fed the delusions of a president in 2020 and 2021 cannot be avoided. In fact, it constitutes a clear and present danger, even in the best of times. For its effects to be blunted and even thwarted, the citizenry must remember not only the wisdom of the Founders but also the lessons of what can happen when that wisdom is forgotten.

CHAPTER FOUR
THE INTANGIBLES

The Civil War and the failed coup attempt of 2020–2021 are instructive in many ways, but perhaps the most important aspect involves consensus. It is clear that finding common ground is essential if a republic is to survive. Compromise is a big part of that. Unfortunately, it does not necessarily serve the cause of social justice. For a nation premised on a belief in liberty and equality for all, that is a problem. Especially when the divisions can be exploited to fragment and undermine the unity needed for the Republic to function.

The solution, though glaringly obvious, has been difficult to implement. That is because, as Martin Luther King Jr. observed, the American "who is more devoted to 'order' than to justice . . . prefers a negative peace which is the absence of tension to a positive peace which is the presence of justice." Such an attitude leads those with power and privilege to "paternalistically believe . . . [they] can set the timetable for another man's freedom."[1]

This situation adds yet another layer of complexity to the negotiation of an acceptable middle ground, and it illustrates the truth of Tocqueville's observation that liberty is "born in stormy times."[2] To understand the nature of the challenge, one need only consider how the United States has dealt with inequity. Since its founding, the country has lived with, and has periodically sought to address, the fundamental inconsistency of a republic founded on glaring injustice. The mixed results speak both to human frailty and to the power of principle and hope.

The Specter of Race

In the original draft of the Declaration of Independence, Thomas Jefferson listed among the many reasons for the break from His Majesty's government that the king had

> waged cruel war against human nature itself, violating it's [sic] most sacred rights of life & liberty in the persons of a distant people who never offended him, captivating & carrying them into slavery in another hemisphere, or to incur miserable death in their transportation thither. . . . [T]he CHRISTIAN king of Great Britain determined to keep open a market where MEN should be bought & sold . . . [and] is now exciting those very people to rise in arms among us, and to purchase that liberty of which he has deprived them, & murdering the people upon whom he also obtruded them; thus paying off former crimes committed against the liberties of one people, with crimes which he urges them to commit against the lives of another.[3]

The charge was deleted in discussion before the Continental Congress because of the objections of Southern planters, and so it did not appear in the final draft of the Declaration.

Several things are worth noting here. First, that Jefferson, a slave owner, would mention the issue at all speaks to what a lawyer might call "consciousness of guilt." That is, "that a person is aware of the fact that they are guilty of committing a crime."[4] In this, he was not alone. Many of the Founders were conscious of and uncomfortable with the hypocrisy of fighting a war for liberty while allowing slavery to exist undisturbed.

Second, Jefferson's indictment of King George makes a point of the monarch's disingenuousness in cynically enlisting those he had enslaved and foisted on America to now murder those who were seeking their freedom, thus paying off a crime "against the liberties of one people" with crimes "against the lives of another." It was an interesting rationale, but it ignored the fact that Americans had accepted the benefits of slavery for generations before King George.

Finally, and more to the point, faced with their own complicity, white Americans chose to do nothing. The matter of race, being so intimately tied to economics, was simply too dicey to deal with, especially if creation of a nation was the goal. So the precedent was set: union or justice, and when in doubt, choose union.

Thus in Philadelphia eleven years later, when the matter came up again, it was finally resolved in a compromise over taxation and representation that counted African American slaves as three-fifths of a person and permitted "the Migration or Importation of such Persons as any of the States now existing shall think proper to admit"[5]—in other words, the slave trade by which, in Jefferson's telling, a heartless king callously uprooted "a distant people who never offended him . . . to incur miserable death in their transportation thither."

As the issue of race became institutionalized, it mixed with other political considerations, again involving compromise so that the Union might be established and preserved. The Tenth Amendment reserved all power not delegated to the federal government to the states. Article I, Section 9 of the Constitution left the issue of the slave trade to "the States now existing" to determine how many slaves they "shall think proper to admit."[6] Such language reflected the subtle compromises and dynamic tension involved in balancing a diverse republic with different socioeconomic realities and agendas. It also kicked the issue of slavery and racism down the road for some future generation to deal with.

Along the way, states' rights became a rallying cry for slave owners who felt themselves increasingly embattled, first by Northern economic interests, then over the issue of the expansion of slavery West, and, finally, over the very institution of slavery itself. As long as the matter remained one of economics and politics, compromise could and was reached and the Union preserved. Indeed, starting with the Missouri Compromise of 1820 and ending with the Kansas-Nebraska Act of 1854, that was the pattern that allowed the nation to survive.[7]

It did so at a cost, however, ignoring the obvious inconsistency that everyone had always known was there. It turned a blind eye to what Jefferson had categorized as the "cruel war against human nature itself" that was being waged against the "most sacred rights of life & liberty in the persons of a . . . people who [had] never offended" by those who held them captive. But make no mistake. The scars went deep, and they would be carried by everyone, defying real healing because they were never fully acknowledged or dealt with.

The reason is grounded in basic biology. Trauma is internalized across generations, genetically coded, and handed down across time. Ancestors who were brutalized pass on their trauma to the next generation as the evolutionary processes that drive the adaptations that make human survival possible kick in. In this way, the past matters in ways of which most people are completely unaware. We literally carry it around in our bodies. It lives within our DNA. One of the leading authorities on the subject, Resmaa Menakem, explains it this way:

> During the Middle Ages in Europe, torture, mutilation, and other forms of savagery . . . were seen as normal aspects of life. Public executions were literally a spectator sport.
>
> As a result, when European "settlers" first came to this country centuries ago, they brought a millennium of inter-generational and historical trauma with them, possibly stored in the cells of their bodies. Today, much of this trauma continues to live on in the bodies of most Americans.[8]

Joy Dugruy observes simply and profoundly, "Although slavery has long been a part of human history, American chattel slavery represents a case of human trauma incomparable in scope, duration and consequence to any other incidence of human enslavement."[9]

The costs, as these researchers on trauma attest, exist below our consciousness, but, as with all things, they must first be acknowledged at that level before real healing can begin. Jefferson's charge against King George was an abortive step in that direction. It was met with denial, but others took up the cause, challenging America to take a look at itself, at the jarring inconsistency between what it professed to be and what it was.

Whenever people are confronted with such cognitive dissonance, they have essentially two choices: accept the truth and learn from the experience, or deny and rationalize away reality.[10] In the antebellum period, that dichotomy manifested itself in the abolitionists, who called on America to face what some have since called its original sin, and Southern defenders of slavery, who manufactured a mythos around what they euphemistically called the "peculiar institution."

As the situation deteriorated and the nation tore itself apart in war, President Abraham Lincoln sought a compromise. Like his forebears, he searched for the balance between union and the ideals of the Republic and, like his predecessors, found it difficult to achieve, much less hold. Indeed, circumstances drove the evolution of his and, by extension, the nation's principles.

Writing to newspaperman Horace Greeley in August 1862, Lincoln explained his war aims this way:

> My paramount object in this struggle is to save the Union, and is not either to save or to destroy slavery. If I could save the Union without freeing any slave I would do it, and if I could save it by freeing all the slaves I would do it; and if I could save it by freeing some and leaving others alone I would also do that. What I do about slavery, and the colored race, I do because I believe it helps to save the Union; and what I forbear, I forbear because I do not believe it would help to save the Union.[11]

Lincoln was a man of his word. On January 1, 1863, he issued the Emancipation Proclamation. First, he declared which states were in rebellion, noting exceptions in parts of Louisiana and Virginia, which were, "for the present, left precisely as if this proclamation were not issued." He then declared "all persons held as slaves within said designated States" were "free," a condition that was to be recognized by all Union forces.

He subsequently encouraged those he had just emancipated "to abstain from all violence, unless in necessary self-defense" and to "labor faithfully for reasonable wages." Finally, any former slave "of suitable condition" would be "received into the armed service of the United States to garrison forts, positions, stations, and other places, and to man vessels of all sorts in said service."[12]

The Proclamation did to the Confederacy what King George had sought to do to the American colonies. It also sought to shame and dissuade any foreign power thinking about supporting the South by making the war about slavery. In truth, though, the Emancipation Proclamation did nothing about slavery in the short term. Only slaves where the Union had no jurisdiction were freed, and in areas of the South that remained loyal to the Union, an exemption was granted "for the present." As he had told Horace Greeley, the president was simply doing "about slavery, and the colored race" what would help "to save the Union."

Then came the aftermath of the battle of Gettysburg. For three days at the beginning of July 1863, Union and Confederate forces engaged in some of the bloodiest fighting of the war. On November 19, 1863, Lincoln traveled to the battlefield to dedicate a cemetery for the fallen. His rhetoric moved the Civil War to a whole new level of moral imperative. In some of the most powerful and eloquent words ever spoken, the president called on Americans to reaffirm their commitment to the ideals on which their country had been founded.

"Four score and seven years ago," he began, "our fathers brought forth on this continent, a new nation, conceived in Liberty, and dedicated to the proposition that all men are created equal. Now we are engaged in a great civil war, testing whether that nation, or any nation so conceived and so dedicated, can long endure." For Lincoln, the cause that Union soldiers had fought and died for was sacred, and it necessitated a commitment by their countrymen to dedicate themselves "to the unfinished work which they who fought here have thus far so nobly advanced." That meant nothing short of pledging themselves to ensure "that this nation, under God, shall have a new birth of freedom—and that government of the people, by the people, for the people, shall not perish from the earth."[13]

It was stirring rhetoric and in the best traditions of the aspirational values of the Republic. But, as has been the challenge since its founding, creating a Union that lived up to those ideals was hamstrung when there were those who benefited from the exploitation of others, trafficked in prejudice, and were free, because of the logic of liberty, to do so. Compromise of ideals was then inevitable and, with it, the resulting implications for social justice.

When the war ended and the time came for Reconstruction, the so-called Radical Republicans pushed hard to make Lincoln's challenge at Gettysburg real. However, even had he lived, Lincoln would not have been one of them. His scheme for Reconstruction involved something called the Ten Percent Plan. For a Southern state to be readmitted to the Union, only 10 percent of its voters would have to swear their allegiance to the United States. After that, all voters in the state—even a potentially unrepentant 90 percent—could elect delegates to draft a revised state constitution. Additionally, all Southerners except high-ranking Confederate officials would be granted a full pardon and all their property (except for slaves) would be protected. Andrew Johnson, who inherited the presidency after Lincoln was assassinated, was even less sympathetic to African American rights.

In fairness, there was progress, most notably the Thirteenth, Fourteenth, and Fifteenth Amendments. However, the nation could not have hoped to have a "new birth of freedom" in twelve short years, which is how long Reconstruction lasted. And even during that period, an emphasis on union ultimately allowed the South to return to many of its old ways, institutionalizing racism with the Black Codes even before the Compromise of 1877 and the subsequent rise of Jim Crow laws.

Finding a true middle ground, where ideals and union coexist in harmony, was the challenge set forth by Lincoln at Gettysburg. It was what Frederick Douglass meant when he said that the Civil War was a fight for "unity of idea, unity of sentiment, unity of object, unity of institutions, in which there shall be no North, no South, no East, no West, no black, no white, but a solidarity of the nation, making every . . . [one] free, and every . . . [one] a voter."[14]

Unfortunately, such a simple objective proved elusive because the underlying issues that divided the nation, at a level deeper than region or ideology, persisted. After the Civil War, denial returned, as it did when the Founders opted to let King George (and themselves) off the hook for slavery in the first place.

The Dance of Liberty

The Glorious Lost Cause was concocted by Southern apologists to rationalize a war that had been fought to defend slavery. They resurrected the Confederate battle flag and idolized Southern generals as an act of defiance that sought to portray the South as the victim of Northern aggression. The tactic was a political one, driven by those of privilege, to justify preservation of segregation and racism and to stir up a base of support among average citizens, much in the same way that the fire-eaters did before them. From the post-Reconstruction era forward, the themes remained the same.

Still, that was only part of the story. In many cases, one could look at the 1950s and 1960s as a second Reconstruction period, focused on addressing the unfinished business of the post–Civil War period. As with the first, there were significant steps forward but also much left undone. Legislation was passed to protect civil and voting rights, and to begin addressing the causes of systemic poverty, but other issues, like the inequities created by centuries of racism, were more difficult.

It was a point that was not lost on so-called militants like Black Panther Eldridge Cleaver, who clearly explained the problems confronting the nation in the 1960s. With a few modifications, what he wrote could have been penned at any time in American history:

> Police brutality is only one facet of the crystal of terror and oppression. Behind police brutality there is social brutality, economic brutality, and political brutality. From the perspective of the ghetto, that is not easy to discern: the TV newscaster and the radio announcer and the editorialists of the newspapers are wizards of the smoke screen and the snow job.[15]

With that, Cleaver hit on the legacy of denial and the resulting backlash against reform by those who failed to see a problem or who feared that change could undermine their privilege. The issue was encapsulated in Dwight Eisenhower's hedge on the issue of civil rights. At his first press conference after announcing he was a candidate for the presidency of the United States in 1952, Eisenhower asserted that his support for "fairness and equality among all types of citizens" was "unalterable." However, it was a mistake to try to legislate such ideas, he added, because not "all the evils in men's hearts [can be] cured by law."[16]

True enough, but laws can facilitate change. Without them, the problems remain, abetted by denial born of cognitive dissonance and/or self-interest and, with them, the justifications and rationalizations that inform "the smoke screen and the snow job."

Which returns us once again to the wisdom of Tocqueville's assessment about liberty and the importance of, in Jefferson's words, "a little rebellion now and then,"[17] or, as John Lewis put it, getting into "good trouble, necessary trouble."[18] A republic will always demand that each new generation commit itself to a "new birth of freedom." It is the only way that the "Blessings of Liberty" can be secured "to ourselves and our Posterity."[19]

This was a point not lost on Reverend William Barber. In the face of the assault against civil rights during the first decades of the twenty-first century, he spoke of the need for a third Reconstruction to advance the unfinished work of the first two. As with any movement for change, certain things were necessary, he explained:

> You have to know your history, practice the moves of those who have gone before you, and make their music your own. But you haven't mastered the art until you've learned to improvise—to take the wisdom passed down to you and write the next verse of humanity's collective song. The art of improvisation is about negotiating the unexpected.[20]

Truer words have seldom been penned. What Barber pointed out lies at the heart of what makes a republic possible. Liberty unleashes people to be all they are. That necessitates accepting both the good and the bad, even as one strives to maximize the best and minimize the worst. The result is a synergy impossible under any other system of government except a republic. But the dance is complex, ever evolving, free flowing, with no prescribed steps. It is in that, however, in its improvisation, that lies its beauty, its power, its strength, and, ultimately, its humanity. And in its humanity lies its blessing, even with all its imperfections and messiness.

Moralism versus Morality

Since this is true, a functioning republic also requires citizens who have a moral compass. John Adams explained that if virtue "cannot be inspired into our People . . . they may change their Rulers, and the forms of Government, but they will not obtain a lasting Liberty—They will only exchange Tyrants and Tyrannies."[21] But what is virtue, and how does one inspire it? It is a question that has plagued philosophers and theologians for centuries. Although coming up with an answer can be difficult, it does not excuse us from dealing with the issue, at least not without risking, as Adams pointed out, condemning ourselves to an endless cycle of "Tyrants and Tyrannies."

There are two trends in American history that seem instructive to any discussion of the virtues necessary for a functioning republic—specifically, the tension between moralism and morality. The first speaks to an all-too-human tendency toward self-justification and rationalization. The second to a set of values and principles that inform action and a sense of right and wrong, justice and decency. Both can exist in the same individual and be manifested in any given movement or group. But while the first can polarize, the second can inspire and bring about deep and meaningful change.

Although there are historical examples aplenty of both moralism and morality, two will suffice, since they speak to many of the other themes raised in this chapter. Consider that the same Bible, the same profession of Christian faith, gave birth to Jerry Falwell Sr. and Martin Luther King Jr.

Falwell, the pastor of Thomas Road Baptist Church in Lynchburg, Virginia, began his media career in 1956 at the tender young age of twenty-two, when he founded his church and began broadcasting *The Old Time Gospel Hour*. Featuring gospel music, preaching, and Bible teaching, the program usually concluded with Falwell's testimony on salvation and developing a personal relationship with Jesus Christ.

Ostensibly eschewing politics in the Baptist tradition of keeping matters of church and state separate, Falwell nonetheless was not averse to having rabid segregationists like Governors Lester Maddox of Georgia and George Wallace of Alabama appear on *The Old Time Gospel Hour*. He also used the show to criticize Martin Luther King Jr. and the civil rights movement.[22]

Falwell's theology and politics were part of a seamless whole that blended racism and a commitment to religious fundamentalism. Updated for the 1950s and 1960s, it was a recycling of the arguments made by Confederate apologists after the Civil War. For

Falwell, like the White Citizens Councilers of the same period, the first line of defense was segregation.

In 1967, he opened Lynchburg Christian Academy, a whites-only private school under the umbrella of Thomas Road Baptist Church. The fact that the academy integrated two years later did not change Falwell's take on integration. Like other conservative Southerners, he realized he was fighting a rear-guard action and had to be flexible. After all, federal law and public policy were clearly shifting against segregation, and Washington, DC, had the power of the purse.

Though the issue was defense of segregation, it was easily blurred with what became a cover to keep it in place. Evangelicals had long argued that since their schools did not accept federal funds, the government had no right to dictate policy to them. It was, they contended, a matter of religious freedom, of the separation of church and state, not of race, even as the de facto result constituted resistance to integration.

Leaders like Jerry Falwell had significant followings around which a powerful base of support could be developed, not just against desegregation but also against a host of other hot-button items like abortion, women's rights, and homosexuality. The Lynchburg preacher even tested the waters during the 1976 presidential election, when he organized a series of "I Love America" rallies, ostensibly to tout a return to traditional values.

In June 1979, he and Paul Weyrich, along with fellow evangelical preachers Pat Robertson and Tim LaHaye, got together and founded the Moral Majority. Its goal: to mobilize the Christian conservative right and elect a Republican president in 1980 who would begin reclaiming the America they felt that they were losing.

Contrast that story with that of Martin Luther King. Much could be written about his life and his theology and, in fact, has.[23] Suffice it here, as a point of comparison with Falwell's brand of Christian moralism, to reflect on the morality that informed King's work for civil rights.

In an article published in *The Christian Century* in 1957, he clearly laid out the logic that drove everything he would do to deconstruct the segregationist system Falwell sought to perpetuate. For King, the movement he led had to be based on love. To engage in protest against an unjust system in any other way was to court "not only external physical violence, but also internal violence of spirit." Taking a page from Jesus, King observed that "In struggling for human dignity the oppressed people of the world must not allow themselves to become bitter or indulge in hate." Doing that only intensifies "the hate of the world." The cycle of violence and oppression would end only when someone had "sense enough and morality enough to cut off the chain of hate."

That required agape love, which was much more than some sentimental notion for King. It had real power, as well as practicality. It involved a leap of faith that put God in charge. Agape love was about "understanding . . . [the] redeeming good will for all men" that overflowed and sought nothing in return because it was "the love of God working in the lives of men."[24]

Armed with such a commitment, King and his followers withstood imprisonment, invective, fire hoses, beatings, and police dogs, secure in the knowledge of what all African Americans knew since the days of slavery. They were "somebody." Their religion told them "that God loves all his children and that the important thing is . . . the quality of . . . [their] soul." With such "self-esteem and sense of dignity," they could undermine "the South's negative peace," even as "the white man refused to accept the change."[25]

Respect for Tradition and the Law

If the power of morality breeds self-respect and dignity and can motivate change, it can also engender respect for the nation's positive traditions, values, institutions, laws, and norms. Indeed, the first is essential to the second. That is why America's *real* leaders have always had a strong sense of duty, grounded in a fundamental understanding that there were things more important than feelings or egos.

A few examples will suffice. In 1800, the first real test of the notion of a peaceful transfer of power occurred. John Adams had narrowly beaten out Thomas Jefferson for the presidency in 1796, and the two men served as president and vice president, respectively, over the next four years. Their political agendas were hardly conducive to cooperation. Adams was a Federalist. Jefferson was what came to be known as a Democratic-Republican, the logical evolution of the Anti-Federalists who had contested the Constitution.

In 1800, factionalism had become institutionalized. The Democratic-Republicans nominated a ticket consisting of Jefferson and Aaron Burr. The Federalists put forth Adams and Charles C. Pinckney. Under the rules then in play, each elector cast two ballots. The plan was for each party to have their electors either split their vote or abstain on their second ballot. That would theoretically allow their preferred candidate, in a worst-case scenario, to squeak out a victory by one vote.

After a contentious fight that involved bickering among the Federalists and mudslinging in all directions, the election ended in a tie. Although the Federalists had executed the vote-splitting strategy successfully, it had been for naught. Adams received sixty-five electoral votes, and Pinckney six-four. Meanwhile, Jefferson and Burr tied for first, with seventy-three votes each. The Democratic-Republican electors had messed up. This situation threw the election into the House of Representatives, with the choice between Jefferson and Burr. It took thirty-six ballots for Jefferson to win.[26]

Jefferson knew that the tone he set at his inaugural would define the course of the future. The nation was still fragile, and the bitterness of factional politics had been clearly on display during the 1800 campaign. So, he chose his words carefully and deliberately for his inaugural address. Acknowledging the rancor of the previous year, he reminded his countrymen that since the election had been decided by the voice of the nation, announced according to the rules of the Constitution, all will, of course, arrange themselves under the will of the law, and unite in common efforts for the common good. All, too, will bear in mind this sacred principle, that though the will of the majority is in all cases to prevail, that will to be rightful must be reasonable; that the minority possess their equal rights, which equal law must protect, and to violate would be oppression. Let us, then, fellow-citizens, unite with one heart and one mind. Let us restore to social intercourse that harmony and affection without which liberty and even life itself are but dreary things. . . . [E]very difference of opinion is not a difference of principle. We have called by different names brethren of the same principle. We are all Republicans, we are all Federalists.[27]

At an even more perilous time, there was the inauguration of 1861. John Breckinridge, the Southern Democrat who had swept the South in the 1860 Electoral College, was still the vice president. He had also, despite running for president, won election to the Senate.

What followed was a testament to country over party. As one of his final acts as vice president of the outgoing Buchanan administration, Breckinridge was to announce the vote of the Electoral College to a joint session of Congress on February 13, 1861. Rumors swirled around Washington that he would tamper with the vote in an effort to deny Lincoln's victory.

Knowing that some legislators planned to attend the session armed, Breckinridge had guards posted in and around the congressional chambers. One legislator raised a point of order, requesting that the guards be removed. Breckinridge refused. Things were tense and looked ominous.

The electoral vote proceeded, and Breckinridge dutifully announced Lincoln's election as president. More significant, after Lincoln arrived in DC, Breckinridge visited the president-elect at the Willard Hotel. Then, in the final act of the peaceful transition of power, on March 4, after making a valedictory address, he swore in Hannibal Hamlin as his successor as vice president. Hamlin then swore in Breckinridge and the other incoming senators.[28]

Herein lies the through line and the mark of true leadership, regardless of political agenda. Indeed, even those who have had no reason to respect the laws and traditions that excluded and oppressed them understood their importance. Once again, Martin Luther King's insights are instructive on this point. He wrote to clergymen in Birmingham who questioned his tactics, "In no sense do I advocate evading or defying the law, as would the rabid segregationist. That would lead to anarchy. One who breaks an unjust law must do so openly, lovingly, and with a willingness to accept the penalty."[29]

Doing so requires decency, integrity, and a deep sense of morality, to say nothing of a commitment to the bedrock values on which the United States was founded. The nation has been fortunate to have had leaders with such qualities emerge, often during its darkest hours, both to push for change and to heal the wounds of excessive partisanship.

They reminded Americans, as did Abraham Lincoln, and Jefferson, and Washington before him, that "Though passion may have strained it must not break our bonds of affection. The mystic chords of memory, stretching from every battlefield and patriot grave to every living heart and hearthstone all over this broad land, will yet swell the chorus of the Union, when again touched, as surely they will be, by the better angels of our nature."[30]

In the aftermath of the 2020 election, as the incumbent president did everything he could to burn the house down, President-elect Joe Biden reached back to that fundamental decency and the principles that had always informed the Republic and allowed it to weather every previous storm. Speaking on multiple occasions of the importance of bipartisan cooperation to solve both the country's deep divisions and the multiplicity of challenges, he struck a chord in his victory speech that was reminiscent of Thomas Jefferson after America's first peaceful transition of power.

I pledge to be a president who seeks not to divide but unify. Who doesn't see red states and blue states, only sees the United States. And work with all my heart with the confidence of the whole people, to win the confidence of all of you. And for that is what America I believe is about. . . .

Let this grim era of demonization in America begin to end here and now. The refusal of Democrats and Republicans to cooperate with one another, it's not some mysterious force beyond our control.

It's a decision. A choice we make. And if we can decide not to cooperate, then we can decide to cooperate.[31]

With all that might undermine a functioning republic, and all the things that allow it to function which cannot be quantified or codified, the truly amazing thing about the United States is that it has survived and thrived despite the odds. Keeping a republic is no small undertaking, and some might even call it a miracle. But what all miracles require, in truth, is faith and a willingness to work hard—two things Americans have had in great abundance throughout their history.

CHAPTER FIVE
POWER AND PRINCIPLE

W hen he accepted the Democratic nomination for president in 1960, John F. Kennedy told delegates at the party convention in Los Angeles that "the old era is ending." Complacency was impossible given the challenges both at home and abroad. In the area of foreign policy, the world found itself divided into three camps—one free, one "the victim of a cruel repression," and the third "rocked by poverty and hunger and disease." Meanwhile, Communism was making inroads in Asia and the Middle East and "now festers some ninety miles off the coast of Florida." Friends had become neutral, and neutrals had become enemies. What was needed was bold new leadership by a generation of "men who are not bound by the traditions of the past, men who are not blinded by the old fears and hates and rivalries—young men who can cast off the old slogans and the old delusions."

Whether it liked it or not, America was facing a "New Frontier," and, as it had in the past, it needed to meet the challenge posed by such a reality head-on. In the nineteenth century, the pioneers had forgone "their safety, their comfort and sometimes their lives" all with a determination "to make the new world strong and free—an example to the world, to overcome its hazards and its hardships, to conquer the enemies that threatened from within and without."

Now, Kennedy observed, the United States needed to deal with a world of "unknown opportunities and perils . . . of unfilled hopes and unfilled threats." Citizens needed to rise to the challenge of proving "all over again . . . [that] this nation, conceived as it is with its freedom of choice, its breadth of opportunity, its range of alternatives, can compete with the single-minded advance of the Communist system."[1]

JFK's reading (or, perhaps more accurate, his misreading) of history was a familiar one. The past had proven time and again the rightness of America and, by extension, of democracy and freedom. It was this fundamental faith in these virtues that set the United States apart, which had allowed it to achieve so much over the course of its history. It was in that sense, if not in his choice of examples, that Kennedy's message spoke to a fundamental truth about the United States in the world. Her ideals demanded that every generation rise to the challenge of making them real and relevant.

The roots of America's sense of its own exceptionalism run deep. As early as 1630, John Winthrop had admonished his fellow Puritans, "we must consider that we shall be as a city upon a hill . . . [because] [t]he eyes of all people are upon us."[2] Grounded in a unique religious vision, Winthrop's words have resonated across time because they spoke to an enduring sense that the United States should be a model to the rest of the world.

Of course, Americans are human, and their actions inevitably fall short of the principles they espouse, both at home and abroad. As it expanded west, for example, bringing it into conflict with Native Americans and Mexicans in the nineteenth century, the United States reassured itself that its expansionism was in keeping with the values of democracy. John L. O'Sullivan gave voice to that opinion when he argued:

> [W]e are the nation of progress, of individual freedom, of universal enfranchisement. Equality of rights is the cynosure of our union of States, the grand exemplar of the correlative equality of individuals. . . . We must [move] onward to the fulfilment [sic] of

our mission. . . . This is our high destiny, and in nature's eternal, inevitable decree of cause and effect we must accomplish it. All this will be our future history, to establish on earth the moral dignity and salvation of man.[3]

Taking that reasoning a step further, he would later assert that it was America's "manifest destiny to overspread and to possess the whole of the continent which Providence has given us for the development of the great experiment of liberty and federated self-government entrusted to us."[4] Rhetoric aside, the fact was that the West was ripe for the taking. Land hunger and a growing economic juggernaut unleashed by the building of roads, canals, and eventually railroads drove the growth of the nation. These factors, far more than any sense of national mission, shaped the decisions of politicians and of average citizens moving west.

Although Kennedy's words about pioneers who gave their all by "conquer[ing] the enemies that threatened from within and without" made sense to Americans, Native Americans and Mexicans would likely have had a different interpretation of the historical process that allowed the United States "to make the new world strong and free." Indeed, they very well might have questioned the applicability of those words to what the pioneers did.

Not that ethnocentrism was unique to the United States or something unfamiliar to Americans. However, its use in Kennedy's acceptance speech hardly bespoke "men who are not bound by the traditions of the past, men who are not blinded by the old fears and hates and rivalries—young men who can cast off the old slogans and the old delusions." The simple truth was that even had he been predisposed to do so (and there is no evidence that he was), Kennedy was bounded by the demands of the familiar script dictated by America's historical sense of self.

This is not meant as a condemnation of President Kennedy, but rather to point out some of the historical assumptions that have helped to shape and define the United States' role in the world, both for good and for bad. Kennedy was typical of many modern (read: post-1900) policy makers. His view of his country and of the world was framed by a narrative with which most Americans could easily identify, even as it did not always comport with historical truth.

Still, like everything else about the American story, foreign policy was shaped by the effort to operationalize the ideals on which the Republic was founded within the context of the practical realities that limited their applicability, despite the universalist language in which they were expressed. "We hold these truths to be self-evident that all men are created equal" seems unambiguously clear: *ALL* men (understood as humankind) meant that all individuals were equal and thus entitled to certain "unalienable rights."[5] That was hardly the case when one remembers the status of women. Even when read in terms of all *men*, realities fell short. But the ideals remained a beacon, a goal toward which to aspire, so, despite the gaps, the ideals framed the course of the nation's evolution, tumultuous and uneven as it was.

The same can be said about US foreign policy. The principles defined the nation's understanding of itself, but what that meant in terms of how the country operated in the world was informed by practicalities, to say nothing of competing agendas at home and abroad. Because they saw their country as a unique experiment in federated self-government—a conscious effort to put into practice the ideas of Enlightenment thinkers like John Locke and Adam Smith—Americans believed that they were given a special mission in the world. The logic predated the founding and was expressed in the religiosity of John Winthrop.

But, as with the domestic challenges posed by taking ideals and applying them to the real world, there were questions to be asked, compromises that had to be made. Perhaps the most fundamental issue was how was the cause of democracy to be advanced, and for and by whom? These questions were answered differently depending on the realities and time period, at home and, likewise, with the United States' encounters with the world. And therein lies the animating force in the American story—a nation evolving its under-standing of itself in terms of the principles that called it to a higher standard.

What Does Commitment to Democracy Entail?

On July 4, 1821, the United States celebrated its forty-fifth anni-versary. President James Monroe's secretary of state, John Quincy Adams, was asked to deliver a speech to Congress about the Dec-laration of Independence. Standing on the floor of the House of Representatives, wearing an academic robe, he told his listeners that wherever freedom and liberty were advocated, there the nation's

> heart, her benedictions and her prayers [would] be. But she goes not abroad, in search of monsters to destroy. She is the well-wisher to the freedom and independence of all. She is the cham-pion and vindicator only of her own. . . . She well knows that by once enlisting under other banners than her own, were they even the banners of foreign independence, she would involve herself, beyond the power of extrication, in all the wars of interest and intrigue, of individual avarice, envy, and ambition, which assume the colors and usurp the standard of freedom. . . . She might become the dictatress of the world: she would be no longer the ruler of her own spirit.[6]

This statement distilled the challenges involved in balancing ide-als and practicalities. Like any nation, the United States needed to understand not only where its national interest lay but also the state of the world and thus its ability to advance its agenda. That agenda, as made clear in the Preamble of the Constitution, was to secure "the blessings of liberty to ourselves and our posterity."[7] *Ourselves* and *our* posterity says it all. The blessings of liberty were first and foremost for *Americans*. Adams's statement was hardly earth-shattering in that context and, indeed, has remained a constant despite overt changes in the level of US involvement in the world.

In the first one hundred-plus years of the Republic, when America was relatively weak, protecting the rights of Americans was a tall enough order. George Washington had advised the country in 1796, "It is our true policy to steer clear of permanent alliances with any portion of the foreign world, so far, I mean, as we are now at liberty to do it. . . . Taking care always to keep ourselves by suitable establishments on a respectable defensive posture, we may safely trust to temporary alliances for extraordinary emergencies."[8]

That did not, however, mean isolationism. After all, to survive, the United States needed to trade with Europe. Unfortunately, in the aftermath of its independence, it no longer had the protection of the British navy. Unable to withdraw from the world, it had to engage with it carefully and with a healthy dose of realism. Still, that carried its own dangers, not the least for the ideals of the Republic itself.

The history surrounding the creation of the US Navy is instructive in terms of the search for a balance between the need to "provide for the common defense" and to "secure the blessings of liberty."[9] Pressed by crushing debt, in August 1785, the United States sold its last remaining warship, the *Alliance*, effectively leaving the country without a navy. Unfortunately, the challenges of surviving in a hostile world remained. Algerian pirates menaced American merchant vessels. Then, to complicate matters, the French Revolution soon brought England and France into conflict. As a neutral power, the United States could technically trade with both sides. Without a navy, however, it was powerless to enforce its prerogative, and American vessels were routinely stopped by both the British and the French navies.

At home, fear of what building a navy would mean for the fledging Republic fueled opposition despite the economic losses and the affront to American sovereignty on the high seas. The logic was that a Navy Department would create a bureaucracy and ever-increasing demands to expend public funds in the building of vessels. Despite continued assaults by Algerians and the British, a reluctant House of Representatives barely passed the Naval Act of 1794. Even so, it would be three years before the first three frigates of a proposed six were built, and another three years until the last slid down the ways.[10]

That did not stop the world from threatening. Between 1798 and 1800, the United States fought what became known as the Quasi-War with France. American and French ships battled wherever they encountered each other. The conflict had been a long time coming. The French objected to the terms of the so-called Jay Treaty in 1794, which settled long-standing disputes between Great Britain and the United States dating back to the end of the American Revolution. Seeing the agreement as a violation of the 1778 treaties between France and the United States, the French began seizing American vessels that traded with the English.

America struck back by suspending payment on loans France had provided during the Revolution. Efforts at peace broke down during the infamous XYZ Affair, when French officials tried to extort bribes in exchange for agreeing to negotiate. With that, the shooting started, and with it the worst nightmares of the Anti-Federalists, who had long questioned the efficacy of imbuing the president with the power of commander in chief.[11]

Arguing that the Quasi-War posed a threat to national security, Federalists pushed through four new laws that became known as the Alien and Sedition Acts. In sum, they made it harder for immigrants to become naturalized; empowered the president to jail and deport non-citizens who were considered a threat to the United States, or who were from a hostile country; and made it illegal to criticize the federal government.

The response was quick and not surprising. Thomas Jefferson and James Madison led opposition to the acts by secretly authoring the Virginia and Kentucky Resolutions, which were passed by those states' respective legislatures. Arguing that the laws were unconstitutional, the resolutions contended that states retained the right to nullify any act by the federal government that they deemed to be in violation of the Constitution. It was a bold assertion, and one that others would use in the build-up to the Civil War.[12]

If American politics were naturally complicated because of the character of liberty and democracy, its effort to negotiate the treacherous waters of foreign policy while maintaining the ideals of freedom and self-governance made them even more so. At the heart of the issue was the requirements imposed by being able to defend the country. As James Madison explained:

> Of all the enemies to public liberty, war is, perhaps, the most to be dreaded because it comprises and develops the germ of every other. War is the parent of armies; from these proceed debts and taxes. And armies, and debts, and taxes are the known instruments for bringing the many under the domination of the few. In war, too, the discretionary power of the Executive is extended. Its influence in dealing out offices, honors, and emoluments is multiplied; and all the means of seducing the minds, are added to those of subduing the force of the people. The same malignant aspect in republicanism may be traced in the inequality of fortunes, and the opportunities of fraud, growing out of a state of war, and in the degeneracy of manners and morals, engendered by both. No nation could preserve its freedom in the midst of continual warfare.[13]

There were lessons here that would resonate across time, from the paranoia that drove the Cold War to the fear that led to the passage of the Patriot Act, which restricted rights in the name of national security after the 9/11 terrorist attacks in 2001.[14] Before the late nineteenth century, however, John Quincy Adams's logic had an even more existential component: the United States was in no position to engage itself in "other banners than her own."

The safest course for the United States as it came of age was to heed George Washington's advice "to steer clear of permanent alliances" and pursue a foreign policy focused primarily on what can best be characterized as a continental foreign policy. Here, calculations of power and domestic politics also played a role.

Americans might not have been able to play hardball with the Europeans, but they had a military advantage over weaker Indian nations and Mexico; even then, however, struggles were hard fought.[15] Framed within the context of Manifest Destiny, the aim of the United States' western expansion was to dislodge those who occupied the land, not to convert them to democracy. The clear beneficiaries of such policy were the citizens of the United States who were moving west, theoretically advancing the noble experiment in democracy, and certainly growing the power and prestige of their country.

As with the nation's more outwardly focused foreign policy, the impact of Manifest Destiny shaped the debate over the future of the Republic, as advocates for slavery and Free Soilers argued over the fate of the Western lands and, by extension, the future of the country itself. When the arguments devolved to the point where compromise collapsed, the logic of nullification and out and out secession inevitably led to the Civil War.[16]

Principle in Service to Power

As with most things in history, the thirty-five years between the end of the Civil War and the beginning of the twentieth century were a product of timing. Circumstances came together in just the right way to bring about major changes in the nation and, with them, not only American attitudes about themselves and their government but also their role in the world.

The transcontinental railroad linked east and west when trains from the Central Pacific and Union Pacific Railroads met at Promontory Point, Utah, on May 10, 1869. The growth of cities and railroads fueled additional growth, creating jobs and encouraging immigration. Building railroads and urban infrastructure required steel. Producing steel required coal, coke, and iron ore. Getting these raw materials to places like Pittsburgh required more railroads, which in turn required more steel. Demand for more steel created more jobs. More jobs meant more mobile people, which meant more railroads and streetcars, which fueled the demand for steel. And on and on it went. The economy became a perpetual motion machine fueled by its own energy and momentum.[17]

Before the Civil War, most Americans lived in small communities and rural areas. It was not until 1820 that New York had one hundred thousand residents. It would remain the only American city that big until 1840. Ten years later, there would be five more cities of that size: Boston, Philadelphia, Baltimore, Cincinnati, and New Orleans. By 1890, there were twenty-three such metropolises strung across the country. In 1800, no American had lived in a city that large. Ninety years later, more than 40 percent of urban dwellers resided in such communities.

Just as significant, the number of municipalities with populations between five thousand and ninety-nine thousand mushroomed. In 1800, only 4 percent of Americans lived in a city as defined by that statistical standard. By 1890, 35 percent of Americans were by that measure urbanites.[18] In 1890, Robert Porter, the director of the US Census Bureau, declared that the frontier was closed. According to that year's census, the so-called frontier line—defined as a point beyond which the population density was less than two persons per square mile—no longer existed.[19]

The United States was now a two-ocean nation, with interests in the Atlantic and the Pacific. Its industrialization had turned it into a first world power and gave it not only the wherewithal to acquire an empire but also the economic imperative to do so. But empire ran counter to the nation's sense of itself. As Adams had observed in 1821, "The fundamental maxims of her policy would insensibly change from liberty to force. . . . [T]he ineffable splendor of freedom and independence . . . would soon be substituted [with] an imperial diadem, flashing in false and tarnished lustre [sic] the murky radiance of dominion and power."[20]

But the end of the nineteenth century was a different time, and the United States was a different country. The urbanization and industrialization of the nation had challenged the fundamental assumptions of many Americans about the nature of their government and society. Progressive reformers, appalled by what they read in the press about their cities, politicians, and industrialists, and driven by the logic of Social Gospel, which challenged them to put their Christian faith into action, pushed for reforms to return the country to its founding principles.[21]

Of course, there were those who pushed back. Applying the logic of Charles Darwin's theory to human affairs, men like Charles Spencer in England and William Graham Sumner in the United States explained that, as in nature, so, too, in society—the fittest rose to the top, the unfit naturally sank to the bottom. Their ideas received widespread traction on both sides of the Atlantic.[22]

The connections between domestic realities and foreign policy objectives are never very far apart, and that was certainly the case at the end of the nineteenth century. In 1890, Alfred Thayer Mahan published *The Influence of Sea Power upon History, 1660–1783*, which explored the role of the navy in the rise of the British Empire. Mahan, and politicians like Theodore Roosevelt, believed that the English model was instructive, especially as America sought to expand its markets overseas.[23]

Mahan's argument was boosted by the work of historian Frederick Jackson Turner. Writing in 1893, Turner argued that closing the frontier would have serious social and economic implications, necessitating a new approach to foreign policy that would require the United States to step beyond the continent to meet its demand for continued economic growth.[24] Such a new foreign policy would build on the efforts of Secretary of State William Seward after the Civil War to expand America's commercial reach into the Pacific with the purchase of Alaska and with her meddling in Hawaii following the Reciprocity Treaty of 1875 that gave the United States free access to Hawaiian produce.[25]

As Americans sought to perfect their democracy at home, ninety miles off the coast of Florida in Cuba those ideals were being thwarted by Spanish oppression. If ever the logic of Monroe Doctrine applied—that Europe should stay out of affairs in the Western

Hemisphere—this was it. Cuban freedom fighters had been struggling for their independence since 1895. The Spanish had brutally relocated thousands of refugees into reconcentration camps. The American press had a field day exposing the atrocities, just as they did with the social and political corruption at home.

When the USS *Maine* exploded in Havana Harbor on February 15, 1898, the demand for action grew increasingly more strident. By the end of April, America and Spain were at war. It took sixteen weeks for the United States to squelch the Spanish both in the Caribbean and in the Pacific. With victory, it acquired the Philippines, Guam, and Puerto Rico, and it made Cuba a protectorate.[26]

Over the course of the next decade and a half, the United States involved itself in China, Latin America, and the Philippines, ostensibly in the name of democracy but more often than not in the interest of empire and economic and national self-interest.[27] As Senator Albert J. Beveridge put it when justifying America's war with the Philippines:

> The Philippines are ours forever. . . . And just beyond the Philippines are China's illimitable markets. We will not retreat from either. We will not repudiate our duty in the archipelago. We will not abandon our opportunity in the Orient. We will not renounce our part in the mission of our race, trustee, under God, of the civilization of the world. . . . He has marked us as His chosen people, henceforth to lead in the regeneration of the world. . . . It is God's great purpose made manifest in the instincts of our race, whose present phase is our personal profit, but whose far-off end is redemption of the world and the Christianization of mankind.[28]

Beveridge's reasoning managed to combine the religious rationalization of Winthrop, the logic of O'Sullivan's Manifest Destiny, and the rhetoric of Rudyard Kipling's poem "White Man's Burden," which called on Americans to search their "manhood," sending forth their best and brightest to serve their "new-caught, sullen peoples, / Half-devil and half-child."[29]

In Kipling's logic, Americans found an interesting composite of Social Gospel and Social Darwinism that allowed them to forge facile connections between their understanding of changing dynamics at home and the new role of their nation abroad. It did not hurt that America's duty to better the world was compatible with her national self-interest.

The idea that America's commitment to democracy extended only to Americans had thus been reframed, but the ultimate rationale—that the nation's prime concern was the advancement of American interests—had not. Still, the moralistic logic undergirding the self-serving rationalizations for acquiring empire could easily morph into less Machiavellian excuses for moralistic crusading, and when that occurred, the warning that Adams had sounded—the United States "might become the dictatress of the world: she would be no longer the ruler of her own spirit"—became all too real.

Power in Service to Principle

That tendency began with the presidency of Woodrow Wilson and would continue thereafter. At the beginning of his first term, Wilson announced his administration's desire to "cultivate the friendship and deserve the confidence of our sister republics of Central and South America." The caveat was that

> Cooperation is possible only when supported at every turn by the orderly processes of just government based upon law, not upon arbitrary or irregular force. We hold, as I am sure all thoughtful leaders of republican government everywhere hold, that just government rests always upon the consent of the governed, and that there can be no freedom without order based upon law and upon the public conscience and approval. We shall look to make these principles the basis of mutual intercourse, respect, and helpfulness between our sister republics and ourselves. We shall lend our influence of every kind to the realization of these principles in fact and practice, knowing that disorder, personal intrigue,

and defiance of constitutional right weaken and discredit government and injure none so much as the people who are unfortunate enough to have their common life and their common affairs so tainted and disturbed.[30]

Disorder was bad not only for the processes of republicanism but also for capitalism, and influence could take many forms. As the president wrote to British diplomat William Tyrrell about eight and a half months later regarding Mexico, "the United States Government intends not merely to force [General Victoriano] Huerta [Mexico's autocratic ruler] from power, but also to exert every influence it can exert to secure Mexico a better government under which all contracts and business concessions will be safer than they have been."[31]

Two interventions in Mexico later, to say nothing of incursions elsewhere in Latin America, made Wilsonian moralism appear little different from William Howard Taft's dollar diplomacy, the policy for which the president had criticized his predecessor. Taft had sought to exert US influence through its economic power. If anything, moralism added an even stronger layer of self-righteousness to the assumptions guiding American foreign policy, eschewing ulterior economic motives while assuming that free trade and democracy were flip sides of the same coin.

While the United States dealt with issues in the Western Hemisphere, World War I had broken out in 1914. Seeking to avoid engagement with the Europeans, the United States asserted its neutrality. That did not stop it from trading with the combatants. In practical terms, though, that meant England and the Triple Entente, because of Great Britain's blockade of the Central Powers. To stanch the flow of American arms, which gave the Allies an advantage on the battlefield, Germany deployed submarines, sinking vessels like the *Lusitania*, endangering civilian lives, and enraging US public opinion.

When the French ferry *Sussex* was attacked without warning in the English Channel, the president announced that if Germany did not cease and desist its attacks on passenger vessels, he would break off diplomatic relations with Berlin. Wanting to avoid US entry into the war, the Germans announced on May 4, 1916, that they would not attack passenger ships, that merchant craft would be stopped and searched for weapons before they were sunk, and that if it were deemed necessary to sink such a vessel, the passengers and crew would be off-loaded first.

Wilson ran for re-election that year in part on the slogan "He kept us out of the war." It was not to last. As the new year dawned, the Germans had plans to resume submarine warfare. They also sought to hedge their bets by approaching the Mexican government, which was frustrated with American intervention. Berlin posited a radical proposition: a Mexican-German alliance whereby if the United States went to war with Germany, Mexico would reconquer the territory it had lost during the Mexican-American War of 1846–1848. The contents of the proposal were in a telegram sent by Foreign Secretary Arthur Zimmermann of Germany.

The British intercepted and decoded the message. Sharing it with American officials, this news added fuel to growing anti-German sentiment in the US government. Washington had severed diplomatic relations in February 1917 when Germany had resumed unrestricted submarine warfare. On March 1, Wilson authorized release of the telegram. Two days later, Zimmermann acknowledged the communique was authentic. The die was cast. Wilson called on America to enter the conflict on April 2, 1917:

> Neutrality is no longer feasible or desirable where the peace of the world is involved and the freedom of its peoples, and the menace to that peace and freedom lies in the existence of autocratic governments backed by organized force which is controlled wholly by their will, not by the will of their people. . . . We are at the beginning of an age in which it will be insisted that the same standards of conduct and of responsibility for wrong done shall be observed among nations and their governments that are observed among the individual citizens of civilized states.[32]

Nine months later, the president outlined the means by which this new age would be realized. Known as the Fourteen Points, Wilson's worldview called for "Open covenants of peace, openly arrived at"; "Absolute freedom of navigation upon the seas, outside territorial waters"; "The removal, so far as possible, of all economic barriers and the establishment of an equality of trade conditions among all the nations"; "Adequate guarantees given and taken that national armaments will be reduced to the lowest point consistent with domestic safety"; "A free, open-minded, and absolutely impartial adjustment of all colonial claims"; and specific assurances and proposals for dealing with the peoples of Russia, Belgium, Austria-Hungary, Rumania, Serbia, Montenegro, the Ottoman Empire, and Poland that would ultimately guarantee their "place among the nations we wish to see safeguarded and [that would ensure] . . . the freest opportunity to autonomous development."

For Wilson, the key to achieving most of these goals lay in creation of "a general association of nations . . . formed under specific covenants for the purpose of affording mutual guarantees of political independence and territorial integrity to great and small states alike."[33] This point would become the basis for the League of Nations.

As things turned out, neither Europeans nor Americans were much in the mood to create a new age. The victors at the Versailles Peace Conference in 1919 were more concerned with punishing the Central Powers. As Prime Minister David Lloyd George of Britain put it, the negotiations at Versailles had more to do with "squeezing the orange until the pips squeak" than implementing the Fourteen Points, making the world safe for democracy, or creating a victorless peace.

Members of the United States Senate were equally unsympathetic. Though objections to the Treaty of Versailles were myriad, the strongest opposition centered on the League of Nations. Opponents believed that the League threatened American sovereignty and the nation's long-standing policy of avoiding European entanglements. There was also suspicion of the provisions calling for joint economic and military action against aggression under the proposed covenant, even though these remained at the discretion of the member states.[34]

With the outbreak of World War II about twenty years after the signing of the Treaty of Versailles, there were those who wondered whether the world had missed an opportunity by ignoring Wilson's vision. Certainly, the spirit of Wilson informed the terms of the Atlantic Charter signed by President Franklin Delano Roosevelt of the United States and Prime Minister Winston Churchill of England in August 1941. About three and a half months before America entered the war, the two leaders met to plan for "a better future for the world . . . after the final destruction of the Nazi tyranny."

They agreed that the war would result in no nation seeking "aggrandizement, territorial or other"; that no territorial changes would occur that did "not accord with the freely expressed wishes of the peoples concerned"; that "the right of all peoples to choose the form of government under which they will live" would be guaranteed; that "all States, great or small, victor or vanquished" would have "access, on equal terms, to the trade and to the raw materials of the world which are needed for their economic prosperity"; that "fullest collaboration between all nations in the economic field with the object of securing, for all, improved labor standards, economic advancement and social security" should occur; and that a peace be established that would "afford to all nations the means of dwelling in safety within their own boundaries, and . . . afford assurance that all the men in all the lands may live out their lives in freedom from fear and want." Such a peace would allow everyone to "traverse the high seas and oceans without hindrance." It would also necessitate abandoning the "use of force" and moving toward disarmament "pending the establishment of a wider and permanent system of general security."[35]

In the post-1945 world, Wilsonian idealism persisted as the stated agenda of the United States, but it was tempered by the realization that the world was a dangerous place. That meant charting a course between idealism and realism and seeking to create rationality where it often did not exist. Thus, the United States wrapped its foreign policy in the rhetoric of democracy, freedom, and international cooperation while thwarting popular movements that smacked of Communism. All while trying to deal with the insanity of Mutual Assured Destruction (MAD) created by the nuclear arms race. Later, the same would be true in the nation's war on terrorism, which played out against the backdrop of nuclear proliferation.

Certainly, one can draw an almost straight line from Wilson's ideals to the principles of the Atlantic Charter to the logic of Truman Doctrine (which said it was America's duty to "assist free peoples to work out their own destinies in their own way"[36]) to President Dwight Eisenhower's Doctrine on the Middle East that promised to help nations in that region defend democracy because it was America's purpose to "support free and independent governments."[37]

These ideas found new expression under John Fitzgerald Kennedy, who asserted that leadership had passed to "a new generation of Americans—born in this century, tempered by war, disciplined by a hard and bitter peace, proud of our ancient heritage," who were willing to "pay any price, bear any burden, meet any hardship, support any friend, oppose any foe to assure the survival and the success of liberty."[38]

Kennedy's words mirrored the rhetorical logic that informed US foreign policy between 1945 and 2017. Certainly, it was evident when Lyndon Johnson asked Congress for a resolution authorizing that he take action against North Vietnam following the Tonkin Gulf incident in 1964.[39]

Even as the Cold War wound down, Ronald Reagan characterized the threat from the Soviet Union in 1983 in much the same language that all his predecessors had used since President Harry Truman. Speaking to the Annual Convention of the National Association of Evangelicals in Orlando, Florida, Reagan said it was a mistake to "ignore the facts of history and the aggressive impulses of an evil empire, to simply call the arms race a giant misunderstanding and thereby remove yourself from the struggle between right and wrong and good and evil."[40]

There can be little doubt that, like the successful conclusion of World War II, the end of the Cold War marked a watershed event that validated such rhetoric. It certainly provided future leaders with a place for lessons, even if those lessons did not quite apply. Indeed, President George W. Bush turned to the Reagan model for clues on how to deal with terrorism after the attacks of September 11, 2001.

It seems hardly coincidental that Reagan's rhetoric about the Soviet "evil empire" was modified to define an "Axis of Evil" by Bush. Citing Iraq, Iran, and North Korea, the president remarked in his State of the Union address on January 29, 2002:

> States like these, and their terrorist allies, constitute an axis of evil, arming to threaten the peace of the world. By seeking weapons of mass destruction, these regimes pose a grave and growing danger. They could provide these arms to terrorists, giving them the means to match their hatred. They could attack our allies or attempt to blackmail the United States. In any of these cases, the price of indifference would be catastrophic.

He went on to observe, "History has called America and our allies to action, and it is both our responsibility and our privilege to fight freedom's fight."[41]

Bush's successor, Barack Obama, criticized such reasoning during his campaign for the presidency in 2008, arguing that it reflected a "failure of imagination" that was most obvious in the US invasion of Iraq. According to Obama:

> Instead of adjusting to the stateless threats of the twenty-first century we invaded and occupied a state that had no collaborative relationship with al Qaida. Instead of taking aggressive steps to secure the world's most dangerous weapons and technology we've spent almost a trillion dollars to occupy a country in the

heart of the Middle East that no longer has any weapons of mass destruction.[42]

Even with the truth of such assertions, the new president was unable to escape the limits imposed by history. In his inaugural address, Obama told the world:

> As for our common defense, we reject as false the choice between our safety and our ideals. Our Founding Fathers, faced with perils we can scarcely imagine, drafted a charter to assure the rule of law and the rights of man, a charter expanded by the blood of generations. Those ideals still light the world, and we will not give them up for expedience's sake.[43]

Like every other president before him, Obama had been shaped by the logic of the American experience.

It is tempting to look at this history and hear the voice of John Quincy Adams in Donald Trump's advocacy of "America First" as a cure for what he called the United States' "endless wars." It is doubtful, however, that he knew about Adams, and even if he had, the world that Trump sought to avoid was not the world of 1821.

The United States has to be involved with the world in a myriad of ways. If the imperative driving foreign policy has always been the defense of American interests, in a globalized world order that task requires being aware of the real threats that exist to democracy, to health, and to the environment, to name but a few. It means working with allies and dealing with "bad actors," wherever they may imperil the security of the nation.

Realistic Idealism

It is no small task, nor is it easily accomplished. After all, there are so many moving parts. The impact of "endless wars" has had serious implications for the stability of democracy itself, as James Madison wrote in 1795, and as President Eisenhower pointed out in his 1961 farewell address, when he warned of the dangers of the "military-industrial complex."[44] The role of the nation in the world is never static, nor is the world itself. Then there is the issue of history and its impact on a nation's self-perception.

Put simply, the United States could not have easily changed its approach to foreign policy without changing its political character and national culture, to say nothing of human nature. Because culture is a human construct, the same truth applies to every nation with which the United States has ever had to deal. Each is or was bound by their own expectations, interests, perspectives, agendas, and values, each seeking to balance competing and conflicting goals in a changing and uncertain world.

The optimism that informed the American perspective that sought a better world following World War I grew naturally from the United States' values and the past that created them. At the very least, the notion of the American self that the interpretation of history and culture created fed a very natural human impulse for order and rationality, for answers in a world of seeming chaos. The problem was that the answers were uniquely American and did not always comport with those arrived at in other countries operating from different and diverse political, cultural, and historical experiences.

It should come as no surprise that dissent over policy, both foreign and domestic, has been inevitable. That, in turn, has limited the options open to policy makers. The problem lies in the very nature of freedom, both at home and abroad. As James Madison put it in "Federalist No. 10":

> There are . . . two methods of removing the causes of faction: the one, by destroying the liberty which is essential to its existence; the other, by giving to every citizen the same opinions, the same passions, and the same interests.
>
> It could never be more truly said than of the first remedy, that it was worse than the disease. Liberty is to faction what air is to fire, an aliment without which it instantly expires. But it could not

111

be less folly to abolish liberty, which is essential to political life, because it nourishes faction, than it would be to wish the annihilation of air, which is essential to animal life, because it imparts to fire its destructive agency.

The second expedient is as impracticable as the first would be unwise.[45]

There is much truth here about the nature of politics, generally, and international relations, in particular. Whenever there is freedom, there will be conflict. After all, it is a simple fact that liberty encourages diversity of opinion. Human reason is flawed because of the impossibility of perfect information, the corrupting influences of self-love and passion, and the tendency to rationalize. Conflict and factionalism over self-interest and truth are inevitable, especially given the various factors that shape how people develop logical narratives to explain their realities and justify their actions. To examine the history of US foreign policy is to be reminded again and again of these truths—and of their natural connectedness in a system governed by liberty.

Herein lies the challenge. Certainly, few Americans would deny the value of liberty, and most would wish its blessings for others. However, liberty is a slippery slope, as Madison indicated, especially when combined with the foibles of human nature and life in an unpredictable universe. When fueled by factionalism, especially in the area of foreign policy, the consequences produce everything from confusion to catastrophe. Moreover, seeking to promote democracy abroad in a world that is already factionalized creates a conundrum of enormous proportions. If Madison was correct, the only way for such a world to come about was either to repress freedom or for people to be made to have the same opinions, passions, and interests.

The first option runs counter to what the United States has long articulated as its agenda, even though at times it has not been averse to employing it. The second is not likely to occur, a fact that should be abundantly clear from an examination of American society or from the broader sweep of human history.

That said, a consensus about the power of freedom to improve the quality of life wherever it is institutionalized has often been enough to create a façade of unity among Americans and to foster what amounts to efforts to give everyone around the world "the same opinions, the same passions, and the same interests" (specifically, America's).

When taken to its logical extreme, the resulting policies have often sounded eerily similar to the imperialist posturing of Rudyard Kipling or Albert Beveridge. It has also sometimes led to ignoring or dismissing legitimate opposition to US actions because they did not fit into the nation's preconceived notions of right and wrong, good and evil. Since the end of World War II, that has been the case in responding to anti-American sentiment, especially from the so-called developing world.

Even when countries have moved in the direction of democracy, they have not always chosen leaders of whom the United States approved or who followed the United States' lead, especially when compared to the authoritarian regimes they sometimes replaced. Additionally, liberty has encouraged just as much factionalism in other countries as it has in the United States. Thus, even traditionally democratic allies have not always agreed on what path to follow. Finally, sovereignty, like freedom, breeds factionalism among nations, making global agreement on any issue exceedingly difficult to achieve.

These facts, however, are easy to forget because the ideals on which the Republic was founded are so deeply engrained in the American consciousness and so easily tapped to frame US action in the world. The assumptions undergirding US ideals defined the approach of liberals and conservatives alike until the Trump administration. They even inspired advocates of human rights and freedom around the world. When ideals and reality overlapped, the results were usually positive. When they did not, the outcomes were negative or at best ambiguous.

Viewed in this way, it is easy to understand the US record in foreign policy. American values set the bar high. They have the power to inspire, just as they do at home. They also have the power to act as a smokescreen for more insidious agendas, just as they do at home. Good and bad, however, the stated ideals have been based on the expectation that somehow something better was possible.

On this foundation rests the hope of the nation, both domestically and internationally. When the United States has been able to balance its commitment to principle with the practical considerations and constraints imposed by reality, it has blazed new paths and served as a beacon of hope to downtrodden immigrants seeking a new life, to oppressed groups demanding that the country live up to its creed, and to the world as it faced down the challenges not only to its own freedom but also to that of citizens around the world. It has not been a smooth ride, nor will it ever be, because liberty allows people to be what they are—and that means, as historian Walter McDougall once noted, being good, bad, and ugly, often at the same time.[46]

CITIZENS AND SOLDIERS

There are bumper stickers, coffee mugs, T-shirts, plaques, and greeting cards emblazoned with the bold declaration "Well-behaved women seldom make history." (Sometimes the slogan appears as "rarely make history.") Variously attributed to Eleanor Roosevelt, Marilyn Monroe, and Anne Boleyn, the statement was first articulated in its current form by historian Laurel Thatcher Ulrich in 1976, in, of all places, an article on Puritan women in the late seventeenth and early eighteenth centuries.[1] As with many things taken out of context and popularized, the statement does not mean what it at first seems to imply.

In an offhand remark in the first paragraph of her article, Ulrich noted, "Well-behaved women seldom make history; against Antinomians and witches, these pious women have had little chance at all."[2] The qualifier makes all the difference. It speaks to a deeper truth that Ulrich sought to point out.

As she noted in a book titled *Well-Behaved Women Seldom Make History*, published thirty-one years after her article, "Nobody has proposed printing T-shirts with any of the other one-liners in my article on funeral sermons. It is hard to imagine . . . women . . . voluntarily wearing buttons that read, 'The real drama is in the humdrum.'"[3] That's because there is little "sex appeal" (often quite literally) in celebrating the so-called humdrum.

Ulrich's unintended pop culture phenomenon has become the rationale for many things, including refrigerator magnets featuring leopard print stiletto heels and a cigarette, which, as she pointed out, reflected the meaning the slogan has taken on for many: "Bad girls have more fun." Even without such sexual overtones, the message seems to give license for breaking the rules, which Ulrich found out when she contacted sellers of a T-shirt bearing the sentence and her picture, used without her permission. The response: "I guess we are not very well-behaved girls."[4]

This story speaks to the fact that meaning is all too often in the eyes of the beholder, especially when divorced from the broader narrative of which it is a part. As Ulrich observed:

> So what do people see when they read that well-behaved women rarely make history? Do they imagine good-time girls in stiletto heels or do-good girls carrying clipboards and passing petitions? Do they envision an out-of-control hobbyist or a single mom taking down a drunk in a bar? I suspect it depends on where they stand themselves.[5]

Ulrich's academic article would have received little public attention had it not been for half a sentence in a twenty-page essay. Indeed, the piece remains largely unknown except in academic circles, and even then it is probably of interest only to those concerned with late seventeenth- and early eighteenth-century New England Puritans. More is the pity, because Ulrich's insights into that culture (and, by extension, the average Americans of that day) is instructive about how the nation has developed and who have been the real heroes and heroines shaping the course of its history.

Which gets us back to Ulrich's quotation about the real drama being in the humdrum. Ordinary people make history every day, and how they make it is a function of who they are and how they understand themselves. Most do not even see themselves in these terms or consider that they are the product of their individual and collective pasts. Yet both of these things are the case. As such, it is important to consider their role in shaping culture. Although this is true for an understanding of any society, it is especially so for America, which professes the value and equality of each individual.

Consider that the roots of the Republic go back to the seventeenth century, to those Puritans who so fascinated Professor Ulrich. Rather than dismiss these individuals out of hand as a bunch of misogynistic, uptight religious bigots, we would do well to look more closely at their ideals and their lived experiences, as Ulrich did. Among other things, she found that despite their second-class status in society—nothing unique to the Puritans of that time, or for most of history, for that matter—women were viewed as equals, at least when it came to issues of piety. Because all people were equal before God, the same qualities were expected for both genders.

Given that belief, ministers sought to encourage the same values in both men and women: prayerfulness, hard work, charity, modesty, study, and devout writing. All of this spoke to a certain humbleness of demeanor that should inform the conduct of any God-fearing individual. The often-explicit assertion of the equality of the sexes—at least theologically—posed a conundrum for the Puritans, though. Women may have been equal before God, but not in everyday life or politics.

Ministers like famed Boston cleric Cotton Mather addressed the problem in three potentially contradictory ways. In some of his writings and sermons, he encouraged women to expand their activities in ways that would win them acclaim. In others, he challenged his fellow Puritans to rethink their assumptions about women, encouraging them to celebrate the many things they accomplished, usually without fanfare or recognition. His third approach straddled the fence, falling back on the humility that all Puritans should practice. Status seeking was irrelevant in a society whose members should be focused on the spiritual.[6]

Mather's wrestling with the issue of women spoke to what Ulrich characterized as a real tension between "private worth and public position." Although no one would make the case that Puritan women were liberated, it was hard, after examining the literature from the period, to ignore the fact that the "confining notions of 'femininity' might grow out of a genuine concern with equality." Such an insight, Ulrich argued, required that "more intricate questions about the interplay of values and practice over time" be asked.[7]

In this statement, she has put her finger on the pulse of a theme that is central to understanding the very nature of American life. Whether for women, or people of color, or average white males, the ideals of the nation, even before there was a nation, centered on the gap between the promise of equality and the social realities that prevented it. Puritan John Winthrop had argued that if they were to create a "city upon a hill," his co-religionists needed to be "knit together . . . as one man." They should "rejoice together, mourn together, labor and suffer together" to ensure the accomplishment of their great undertaking.[8]

One cannot help but hear echoes of Martin Luther King's speech on the steps of the Lincoln Memorial 333 years later, when he said, "With this faith we will be able to work together, to pray together, to struggle together, to go to jail together, to stand up for freedom together."[9] Or perhaps Benjamin Franklin's alleged comment after the signing of the Declaration of Independence springs to mind: "We must all hang together, or most assuredly we shall all hang separately." The point is that bold experiments like creating a "city on a hill," launching a new nation grounded in the principles of equality and unalienable rights, or sustaining movements that demand that those rights be universally accessible requires people to recognize their common purpose and their shared humanity.

It also creates cognitive dissonance when ideals do not align with the social, political, and economic realities, be it in seventeenth- and eighteenth-century New England, late eighteenth-century Philadelphia, the American South in the 1950s and 1960s, or anytime in between or since. Leaders struggle to reconcile the incongruities, just as did Cotton Mather, or Thomas Jefferson, who abortively tried to get America to confront the evils of slavery in an early draft of the Declaration of Independence. Other leaders, often outside the power structure, push the country ahead by demanding that it live up to the promise of its creed. In fact, therein lies the clear connection among all reformers.

Against this background, which captures headlines and makes it into the history books, there are average citizens from all backgrounds and experiences. Their lives, seemingly "humdrum," are where the real work of moving the nation forward occurs. After all, they are the ones who make up the majority of the country, and it is they who, navigating the space between what should be and what is, forge the national character.

Such a view might be questioned by those who grew up thinking that history was made by great men and women. Those folks who headed movements, who accumulated great fortunes, who built and invented things, or who led the nation through times of crisis and war—these are the movers and shakers to be admired and emulated. The notion is not a new one, and certainly there is truth in such an assertion. As philosopher and essayist Thomas Carlyle observed:

> Universal History, the history of what man has accomplished in this world, is at bottom the History of the Great Men who have worked here. They were the leaders of men, these great ones; the modellers [sic], patterns, and in a wide sense creators, of whatsoever the general mass of men contrived to do or to attain; all things that we see standing accomplished in the world are properly the outer material result, the practical realization and embodiment, of Thoughts that dwelt in the Great Men sent into the world: the soul of the whole world's history, it may justly be considered, were the history of these.[10]

Such an interpretation begs the question: What makes for greatness? Is it the time in which the person lived, as an individual rises to

119

the challenges of his era? According to Carlyle, no. "Alas," he wrote, "we have known times *call* loudly enough for their great man; but not found him when they called!"

Imagine, he posited, that any era is analogous to "dry dead fuel, waiting for the lightening out of Heaven that shall kindle it." It is into this space that the great man enters, "with his free force direct out of God's hand. . . . His word is the wise healing word which all can believe in." He becomes the "indispensable saviour of his epoch." Logically, then, asserted Carlyle, "the history of the world . . . [is] the Biography of Great Men."[11]

For that to be true, the personality of the individual was important. "[N]o man adequate of doing anything, but is first of all in right earnest about it." That means being possessed of a sincerity that "he cannot speak of, is not conscious of." The trait is ingrained, a matter of his very character, according to Carlyle.[12] Of course, it was possible that "a little man" may possess such an attribute, but "a Great Man cannot be without it."[13]

Aside from ignoring women, such a view of the past ignores the fact that more than a few "little" people made history because they had character and acted on it wherever they found themselves, even if not on the grand stage trod by the great. These were the unsung of every era, whether it was graced by a "Great Man" or not. Admittedly, academic historians and others concerned with such matters have long since dismissed the assumptions undergirding Carlyle's thesis, but the fact that the notion remains alive and well in popular culture is reason enough to elucidate the obvious truth that the humdrum is where history is made and where a nation's character is defined.

To Build and Sustain a Nation

In the United States, the most egregious manifestation of the "Great Man Theory" is the tendency to conflate greatness with money. After all, in a country that is the bastion of both democracy and free market capitalism, the equation seems logical enough.

Consider the popular History Channel mini-series from 2012, *The Men Who Built America*. Focusing on the lives of Cornelius Vanderbilt, John D. Rockefeller, Andrew Carnegie, J. P. Morgan, and Henry Ford, the programs traced the impact that these individuals had on the creation of modern American life. It did an excellent job of documenting their rivalries, their tactics, and society's response to what they had wrought.

Their seamier sides, their foibles, and their strengths were explored through a combination of reenactments, use of archival material, and interviews with historians and the supposed modern-day exemplars of their entrepreneurial spirit, including Donald Trump, Mark Cuban, Steve Case, Charles Schwab, and Ronald Perelman.[14] According to the Internet Movie Database, the series

> shines a spotlight on the influential builders, dreamers and believ-
> ers whose feats transformed the United States, a nation decaying
> from the inside after the Civil War, into the greatest economic
> and technological superpower the world had ever seen. *The Men
> Who Built America* is the story of a nation at the crossroads and of
> the people who catapulted it to prosperity.[15]

Think about the underlying premise here: Five white male property owners were almost completely responsible for transforming the nation, bringing it out of a state of decay to prosperity, measured by its economic and technological prowess. But at what cost to workers, immigrants, and the environment? At what sacrifice to the founding principles of the Republic?

There can be no denying that Vanderbilt, Rockefeller, Carnegie, Morgan, and Ford left their marks, but they did not "build America"—certainly not without a lot of help from those who went about their lives anonymously. Or without those who reacted to the world they were creating and sought to offer a counternarrative to what America was all about.

That has always been the case. For every "Great Man" endowed with "the lightening out of Heaven" to kindle change and define an age, there are others with their own lightning who stand in opposition to what the so-called great would create.

Such a person was Mary G. Harris Jones.[16] Born in 1837 to Roman Catholic tenant farmers in Cork, Mary and her family fled Ireland to avoid the devastation of the potato famine of the mid-1840s and early 1850s. Arriving in Canada, the family experienced the fate of many Irish Catholic immigrants—discrimination and prejudice. This was, after all, the time when employers freely posted signs reading, "No Irish Need Apply." At the age of twenty-three, the young woman moved to Michigan, where she took a teaching job at a convent.

The position failed to stimulate her, and she moved to Chicago and then to Memphis. There she met and married George E. Jones, a member and organizer for the National Union of Iron Moulders. Mary settled into the life of a housewife, raising four children. Two years after the end of the Civil War, yellow fever spread through Memphis, taking her family. Devastated, the young widow returned to Chicago determined to support herself as a dressmaker. More bad luck seemed to follow. In 1871, Mary lost her house, shop, and everything she owned in the Great Chicago Fire.

As she worked with other Chicagoans to rebuild the city, Jones was drawn to the union movement, joining the Knights of Labor and helping to organize its members. The Knights fell into disrepute after the Haymarket Riot of 1886. A peaceful rally in support of workers demanding an eight-hour workday ended in violence. Someone threw dynamite at police trying to break up the crowd. The cops fired at the protesters. By the end of the melee, seven police officers and at least four civilians lay dead while dozens of others were wounded. Anarchist involvement complicated the situation. Jones would later reflect on the tragedy:

> The city went insane and the newspapers did everything to keep it like a madhouse. The workers' cry for justice was drowned in the shriek for revenge. Bombs were "found" every five minutes.

Men went armed and gun stores kept open nights. Hundreds were arrested. Only those who agitated for an eight-hour day, however, were brought to trial, and a few months later hanged.[17]

Haymarket had been the culmination of a hard winter in which "long unemployment resulted in terrible suffering. Bread lines increased. Soup kitchens could not handle the applicants. Thousands knew actual misery." Seeking to arouse awareness, anarchists organized a march to the affluent section of Chicago on Christmas Day. As "hundreds of poverty stricken people in rags and tatters, in thin clothes, in wretched shoes paraded," the only thing they managed to do was "increase the employers' fear . . . make the police more savage, and the public less sympathetic to the real distress of the workers."[18]

This stark disparity between what justice meant for workers and what it was for the affluent was something Jones learned firsthand in Chicago, and it would inform her work for the rest of her life. She became involved with the United Mine Workers and traveled to coal towns in Virginia, West Virginia, and Pennsylvania. One of her favorite tactics was engaging the wives and children of striking workers in protests against employers.

Her disarming Irish brogue and diminutive stature hid the fact that she was a force with which to be reckoned. A powerful orator, she had a magnetism and approachability that drew followers. By the turn of the twentieth century, she had become "Mother Jones" to those whom she called "her boys."

Like any good mother, Jones had high expectations for her children. During an organizing drive in West Virginia, she arrived to find the miners in the local church where they had paid to use the sanctuary. She reached over and took the money from the priest and said, "This is a praying institution. You should not commercialize it. Get up, every one of you and go out in the open fields." They did as they were told. Noticing a schoolhouse across the way as she spoke, she pointed to it and declared:

Your ancestors fought for you to have a share of that institution over there. It's yours. See the schoolboard, and every Friday night hold your meetings there. Have your wives clean it up Saturday morning for the children to enter Monday. Your organization is not a praying institution. It's a fighting institution. It's an educational institution along industrial lines. Pray for the dead and fight like hell for the living![19]

A woman of her word, Mother Jones did just that. In 1903, in one of her most famous organizing efforts, she led children who worked in mills and mines in a march from Philadelphia to the home of President Theodore Roosevelt in Oyster Bay, New York, a distance of about 135 miles. Their demand: to go to school and not have to work in the mines and factories.

Revisiting Ulrich's analysis of well-behaved women, Mother Jones was a quintessential archetype. She was unassuming. There was nothing in her background or early life to suggest anything but the humdrum. Yet she also proved the more popular interpretation of Ulrich's statement about well-behaved women and history. Jones inspired a movement, went to jail on multiple occasions for the cause, and helped found the International Workers of the World. At one of her trials, she was characterized by the prosecuting attorney as "the most dangerous woman in the country today."[20] It turned out that this little woman had all the characteristics—the sincerity and lightning—of any of Carlyle's great men and, certainly, of the movers and shakers of her age.

Nor was Mother Jones alone. Her work and that of others down through the years spoke to the plight of workers who toiled under the conditions that "the men who built America" helped to create and that needed to be addressed to make the dream of America more universally accessible.

Of all the challenges that workers have confronted, perhaps their invisibility as they contribute to "catapulting" the nation "to prosperity" (and keeping it there) has been one of the biggest, if seemingly least obvious. It is what lay behind the indifference that Mother Jones described in the lead-up to the Haymarket incident and that she witnessed in the mining communities in which she later toiled.

Awareness of the unseen millions who go about the daily business of life might be a bit easier if somewhere the advice of steelworker Mike LeFevre of Cicero, Illinois, were taken seriously. As he told Studs Terkel in the early 1970s:

> Somebody built the pyramids. Somebody's going to build something. Pyramids. Empire State Building—these things just don't happen. There's hard work behind it. I would like to see a building, say the Empire State, I would like to see on one side of it a foot-wide strip from top to bottom with the name of every bricklayer, the name of every electrician, with all the names. So when a guy walked by, he could take his son and say, "See, that's me over there on the forty-fifth floor. I put the steel beam in." Picasso can point to a painting. What can I point to? A writer can point to a book. Everyone should have something to point to.[21]

Of course, no one is likely to do what LeFevre proposed, but his statement bespeaks an important truth about who has always kept the nation going. The people who have no archives preserving and documenting their contributions, who will never be the subject of a movie or a mini-series, are, at the very least, equal partners with those accorded such recognition.

These individuals include those who wear hard hats and blue collars and those who work the soil so that the nation might eat. They are those who serve meals and operate late-night drive-thrus so that we can indulge our cravings for a Big Mac. They are also the first responders and the healthcare workers who put their lives on the line for little thanks and often less pay. These are the folks who have made and sustained the country without fanfare and without whom there would be no nation.

Answering the Call of Duty

There are, of course, times when we do celebrate the instances of ordinary people changing the course of history. It was, after all (at least according to Henry Wadsworth Longfellow), Paul Revere, a silversmith, who alerted the minutemen to fall out to meet the British army as it marched out of Boston looking for weapons caches in Lexington and Concord on the evening of April 18, 1775. It was simple farmers who grabbed their muskets and stood against the world's most powerful military. The sacrifices of the Continentals at Valley Forge are widely acclaimed.[22] Indeed, citizen soldiers have long played a central role in the narrative of America's fight for and defense of freedom.[23]

However, who exactly these citizens were and what their lives were like has not always been fully appreciated. Take, for example, the story of sixteen-year-old Sybil Ludington. On April 26, 1777, two years and eight days after Paul Revere's celebrated ride, Sybil's father, Colonel Henry Ludington, received word that British forces were attacking Danbury, Connecticut. His regiment was on leave so that they could plant their crops. The messenger who brought the news was exhausted. The colonel was preoccupied with battle plans. That left Sybil. She mounted a horse and took off across the countryside.

Riding through the woods on a dark and rainy night, she rallied troops from the neighboring farms. By the time she returned the next morning, hundreds of soldiers were massing to meet the English threat. Arriving too late to turn the tide of battle, the men Sybil had raised managed to harass the Redcoats as they withdrew from the city. Not exactly the same scenario as the more famous events surrounding Lexington and Concord, but similar enough to merit more than passing comparison.

Then there was Esther de Berdt Reed, at first glance the epitome of an eighteenth-century well-behaved woman. Born in London in 1746, at the age of twenty-three she married American Joseph Reed, who was studying law in England. Shortly thereafter, she moved to

Philadelphia with her widowed mother and husband. Settling into her duties as the wife of a prominent attorney and political leader, Esther played hostess to colonial America's elite. With the outbreak of the Revolution, she would entertain many members of the Continental Congress, including George Washington and John Adams.

Not satisfied with such a narrow role, Esther took it on herself to organize women in support of the Patriot cause. In May 1780, shortly after news reached Philadelphia that the British had taken Charleston, South Carolina, Esther, only thirty-three years old, published a broadside titled "The Sentiments of an American Woman." She bluntly stated that women were committed to assisting the cause of the Continentals in meaningful ways. Citing historical precedent in which women from the past had advanced patriotic causes, Reed drew a direct connection between those foremothers, herself, and her fellow American sisters.

It was time for them to donate the money they would spend on vanity to the troops who were fighting for freedom. Three days after the publication of "The Sentiments of an American Woman," thirty-six Philadelphia women met to decide how to carry out Esther's recommendations. Dividing the city into ten equal districts, they assigned between two and five women to canvass each area. It was an unprecedented undertaking, not the least because women of high social rank were soliciting assistance from friends and neighbors, as well as from strangers.

Thus was formed the Ladies Association of Philadelphia. At the suggestion of George Washington, the group used the money it raised to buy linen and sew clothing to make more than 2,200 shirts for soldiers. Each volunteer seamstress sewed her name into the clothing she made. Unfortunately, Reed died before the initiative she began was completed.

The work then fell to Sarah Bache. The daughter of Benjamin Franklin, Sally (as she was called) was born in 1743 and was the only surviving child from the marriage of her famous father and Deborah Reed. As she grew up, Ben, like so many other men of his time, was busy pursuing his career and held his daughter at arm's length. Franklin wanted Sally to get the sort of "useful" education that would prepare her for marriage. She learned reading, writing, and arithmetic and was taught French. She also became proficient in spinning, knitting, and embroidery, and she attended dance school.

At the age of twenty-four, she was ready to enter her "career"— she married merchant Richard Bache. The couple had eight children. This seemingly unassuming American woman proved to be a formidable force. When her father returned from his diplomatic mission to France in 1775, Sally dutifully acted as his hostess at many an important political gathering, her mother having died the year before. With the creation of the Ladies Association, she found an even more effective way to serve, bringing to fruition the dream of her fellow socialite, Esther de Berdt Reed.

Ludington, Reed, Bache, and all the seamstresses whose names were known only to the men who received the shirts they had made were but some of the many women who played a role in the American Revolution. Like Laurel Thatcher Ulrich's "well-behaved" Puritan ladies, they never intended to be heroines, nor would they likely have viewed themselves as such if they had been asked. Yet their contributions to the war effort were just as real and significant as that of any of their male contemporaries.[24]

And if women played a vital role in founding the Republic, even as they were excluded from the promise of liberty outlined by Thomas Jefferson in the Declaration of Independence, so, too, did African Americans. Estimates suggest that some 29,000 African Americans participated in the Revolution. Of these, nine thousand fought for the United States. The remaining twenty thousand joined the British in search of the same ideals that the fledging nation espoused but selectively limited to white, property-owning men.

Governor John Murray of Virginia, Fourth Earl of Dunmore, understood the lure of freedom, which is why he issued what became known as Dunmore's Proclamation on November 7, 1775. A cynical move to blunt the Patriot cause, the edict declared martial law and promised freedom to any slave who left an owner who stood against the Crown. For African Americans in bondage, Dunmore offered them something that they, like their owners, understood was fundamental to their humanity and their dignity: liberty.

The same motivation informed those African Americans who sided with the Revolution. Indeed, if one can judge by their length of service to the cause, African Americans who enlisted with the Continentals were even more patriotic than their white counterparts. On average, blacks fought for four and a half years, and some for the entire eight-year duration of the war. By comparison, white soldiers served for about six months. Equally significant, African Americans made up approximately 4 percent of available manpower, but they represented about 25 percent of the Patriots' strength in terms of labor contributed to the cause, which included serving in both fighting and support roles.

Put simply, African Americans were a fixture in the nation's fight for its independence from beginning to end. One man's story serves to illustrate the point. About thirty-four years old in 1775, Prince Estabrook lived in Lexington, Massachusetts, with his owner's family. Benjamin Estabrook, Prince's master, spent his days working the fields with Prince, who also assisted with daily household chores. As with many master-slave relations in the North, Benjamin and Prince were reportedly friends.

When word of the approaching British mobilized the minutemen in Lexington on April 19, Prince was among them, even though according to law he was technically prohibited from training with the militia. Once the Redcoats showed up, it did not take long for tensions to boil over. In the ensuing melee, Prince Estabrook became one of the first causalities of the American Revolution, taking a musket ball to his left shoulder.

Within a couple of months, he had recovered. Prince then enlisted with the Continental Army. Alongside his fellows from the Lexington Company, he served as a sentry during the Battle of Bunker Hill. In July 1776, he found himself marching on Fort

Ticonderoga in New York. Estabrook regularly re-enlisted, doing everything from guarding British prisoners to building forts. On September 3, 1783, the Treaty of Paris was signed, ending the American Revolution.

Two months later, Prince and fellow members of the Third Massachusetts Regiment were discharged and returned home to life as free Americans. Estabrook was either emancipated by Benjamin or released because of the Quock Walker case. Walker, a slave, had sued and won his freedom by successfully arguing that the Massachusetts Constitution implicitly outlawed slavery. Whatever the reason, Prince's long fight for liberty had finally come to an end.[25]

Such stories serve as a testament not only to the character of ordinary and often forgotten individuals but also to the very nature of the country itself. From the beginning, one of America's distinguishing characteristics has been its diversity. That Americans from all walks of life answered the call to serve during the Revolution should hardly be surprising. Neither, though, should the fact that some enlisted on the British side in the hopes of realizing what the nation was ostensibly fighting for. The common link is nothing less than the transcendent power of America's founding principles, even when the country has failed to live up to them.

This has been true for nearly every conflict fought by the United States. Thus, during the Civil War, the rhetoric of democracy (most dramatically articulated in Abraham Lincoln's "Gettysburg Address") made the cause of preserving the Union sacred in a way that Lincoln's explanation of his war aims to Horace Greeley never could. Although it is easy to dismiss Lincoln's words as so much rhetoric used to give meaning to the otherwise senseless slaughter of some estimated 620,000 Americans, the more important takeaway lies in the belief that a "new birth of freedom" was possible and that the United States could nurture it into being.

Thus Woodrow Wilson rallied support for American involvement in World War I by reminding his fellow citizens that democracy was a sacred responsibility. Faced with the provocation of

German submarine warfare and the Zimmermann Telegram, US entry into the Great War had to be propelled by higher ideals than national self-interest. "We must put excited feeling away," Wilson observed. "Our motive will not be revenge or the victorious assertion of the physical might of the nation, but only the vindication of right, of human right, of which we are only a single champion."[26] And so American doughboys marched off to war in a crusade to advance the ideals of human rights, as so many soldiers had done before them and have done since.

Indeed, some twenty-seven years later, American soldiers, sailors, and aviators and their allied compatriots prepared to embark on the greatest amphibious invasion in history. The Supreme Allied Commander of the European Theater, General Dwight David Eisenhower, reminded them in the Order of the Day for June 6, 1944, what they were fighting for:

Soldiers, Sailors, and Airmen of the Allied Expeditionary Force!
You are about to embark upon the Great Crusade, toward which we have striven these many months. The eyes of the world are upon you. The hope and prayers of liberty-loving people everywhere march with you. In company with our brave Allies and brothers-in-arms on other Fronts, you will bring about the destruction of the German war machine, the elimination of Nazi tyranny over the oppressed peoples of Europe, and security for ourselves in a free world.
The free men of the world are marching together to Victory![27]

To return to the words of Lincoln at Gettysburg, American service personnel have always been willing to give their last full measure of devotion so that the ideal of the United States, if not always its reality, might live: that "a new birth of freedom" is always possible, both at home and abroad. The rhetoric has sometimes been abused to justify engagement in questionable conflicts, but that fact has not diminished the nation's belief in its efficacy or the zeal with which its citizens have fought for it.

To state the obvious, the words of those who lead armies or who call for the wars that the nation fights are what passes into history and are remembered. By contrast, those of the men and women who answer the call are largely unknown except, perhaps, to the members of their families. What monuments exist to them tend to speak in aggregates about their collective stories.

That is, except for the Vietnam Memorial, which takes a page from Mike LeFevre's suggestion about how American workers should be honored. Adjacent to the National Mall in Washington, DC, it consists of two black granite walls with the names of the 58,318 Americans who died as a result of the Vietnam War. As with every conflict before and since Vietnam, it was average citizens who served, individuals with hopes, dreams, aspirations, and families.

To drive that point home, imagine a professor (like the author of this book), who asks his students to visit the wall website.[28] He tells them to search for someone they know or to put in their own name (or that of a family member). They are asked to do a similar search for those from their hometown, and then for those with the same birthday. They are told to be sure to click on the "Info Page" and the "Personal Comments or Pictures" page. The results are always sobering.

Consider, for example, the case of Michael Santos. A twenty-two-year-old sergeant with the Ninth Infantry Division, he was single and hailed from Monterey Park, California. He had been in country a little more than six months when he received multiple fragment wounds during ground action in Quảng Tri Province. He left behind people who still mourn his passing. A nephew said this:

I WAS ONLY A YEAR AND A HALF OLD WHEN YOU DIED UNCLE SO I CAN'T SAY I KNEW YOU. BUT I DO LOVE YOU[.] I REMEMBER YOUR FUNERAL STILL. STRANG[E] HOW I REMEMBER THAT DAY. I LOVE YOU SO MUCH UNCLE AND FEEL YOU WITH ME ALWAYS[.][29]

Michael's name appears on panel 53E, line 22, of the Vietnam Wall. Had this writer been born earlier, there might have been two Michael Santoses listed on that polished black granite. Only this one would have come from the small town of Acushnet, Massachusetts.

A town of some eight thousand in the 1960s, two of its native sons lost their lives in Vietnam. Both were only nineteen years old and both were Marines. Lance Corporal James Ferro died on May 26, 1966, in Quảng Nam Province. A childhood buddy remembered:

> Jimmy and I were school mates in our hometown and lived really close to each other. Lots of memories of fun times and just learning how to grow up. Jimmy quit High School to join the Corps, I guess he was going to make a career of it, that would have been nice. Jimmy's death was a shock to all of us who had grown up with him, it was the first impact of the cost of war to me, to know him and then to lose him at such a young age and be without his friendship really hurt. It's been a long time but the memories never leave, I can still see his face and hear his voice and watch him walk, now he walks with the Lord.[30]

Leonard Picanso died in Quảng Tri about a year after Jimmy Ferro. Like Ferro, Lenny was well known and liked in Acushnet. As one of his friends recalled:

> This young man I will always remember, lots of fun to know and just be with. We were all too young and just getting to live life. The memory of Lenny I will always carry and the loss of him had and still carries a sobering impact of what war is all about and the cost it can be to those who serve our country. I know if [he] had been allowed to grow old with us he would have been a fine man and an example to all who would have known him, thank you Lenny![31]

One hundred sixty-eight Americans who were born on December 3, this writer's birthday, never came home.[32] Many more obviously did, but few were left unscathed by the experience. This exercise is one any American should undertake, if for no other reason than to remember not only those who fell in Vietnam but also all those who have ever served.

The People Who Make America

Clearly, presidents, generals, and business leaders have done much to shape the development of the United States. Some for the good and some for the bad. So, too, though, the often-invisible Americans who go about their daily lives making a living or who answer the call to defend the country when duty demands.

The nation has accomplished amazing things in its relatively short history. Much of it can be credited to the no-nonsense attitude of its citizens who have, often against long odds and in the face of great personal sacrifice, made it so. Since at least 1775, the American people have believed, along with the US Army Corps of Engineers, Navy Seebees, and others who claimed variations on the motto during World War II, that "the difficult we do immediately, the impossible just takes a little longer." It was a mantra that could only have been made real because of the liberty on which the Republic was founded.

CHAPTER SEVEN
KEEPERS OF THE FLAME

I n his classic study of America, published in 1888, Irish observer James Bryce opined that there is "in the American people . . . a reserve of force and patriotism more than sufficient to sweep away all the evils which are now tolerated, and to make the politics of the country worthy of its material grandeur and of the private virtues of its inhabitants."[1] He went on to note that American patriotism was such that it was "so proud of the real greatness of the Union as frankly to acknowledge its defects."[2] Further, "There is in the United States abundance of patriotism, that is to say, of a passion for the greatness and happiness of the Republic, and a willingness to make sacrifices for it."[3] The truth of Bryce's analysis speaks to the power of America's founding principles to inspire individuals to stand up for them and so push the nation closer to its true greatness.

Bucking the System

Ordinary people and transformational leaders who have challenged the status quo and demanded justice have intuitively known this fact, and it has been this intuition that has moved them to action. The civil rights movement had Dr. Martin Luther King, whose words and organizing prowess mobilized Americans of all kinds to demand an end to discrimination. It also had Rosa Parks, the woman whose act of defiance in refusing to give up her seat to a white person on a Montgomery, Alabama, bus on December 1, 1955, triggered a 361-day boycott of the city's mass transit system. What followed propelled King into the national spotlight and ended with a Supreme Court ruling that outlawed segregation in public transportation. Parks's action was the culmination of a lifetime of living with (and understanding the injustice of) racism.

Indeed, what she fought for was so fundamental, so self-evident, that even as a youngster Parks understood the issue. As she observed, "For half of my life there were laws and customs in the South that kept African Americans segregated from Caucasians and allowed white people to treat black people without any respect. I never thought this was fair, and from the time I was a child, I tried to protest against disrespectful treatment."[4] Her insights about the fundamental equality of all people harkened back to one of her first recollections growing up. As Parks recalled:

> Moses Hudson, the owner of the plantation next to our land in Pine Level, Alabama came out from the city of Montgomery to visit and stopped at the house . . . [with] his son-in-law . . . a soldier from the north . . . [who] patted me on the head and said I was such a cute little girl. . . . In those days in the South white people didn't treat little black children the same way as little white children. And old Mose [sic] Hudson was [so] uncomfortable. . . . [His] face turned red as a coal of fire.[5]

The contrast between the old planter and what Parks called the "Yankee soldier" left an indelible impression on her. She became active in the local chapter of the National Association for the Advancement of Colored People (NAACP) in 1943 and served as its secretary. She and her husband also became members of the League of Women Voters. When all was said and done, her struggle for basic human dignity could be traced back to her earliest experiences. Reflecting on that fateful day in December 1955, when she started the boycott that would make history, Parks noted, "I had no idea when I refused to give up my seat on that Montgomery bus that my small action would help put an end to segregation laws in the South. I only knew that I was tired of being pushed around. I was a regular person, just as good as anyone else."[6]

No complicated political agendas. No grandiose visions. Just a simple recognition of right and wrong and an instinctive understanding that humans are born with unalienable rights. Parks, and countless others in the civil rights movement, had the sort of patriotism that frankly acknowledged the nation's defects and inspired the passion to demand and even sacrifice so that it would live into its greatness.

The Indigenous Spirit of Freedom

Of course, such individuals have not just been advocates for the rights of African Americans. Consider the experience of the first Americans, who understood the principles of freedom long before Christopher Columbus sailed west. While Europe was in the throes of chaos and ruled by secular and ecclesiastical oligarchies, for example, the Iroquois had created a republic.[7]

Organized under the Great Law of Peace, the Iroquois Confederacy guaranteed freedom and rights to every individual, clan, and nation under its jurisdiction. Resources were shared and all religious beliefs tolerated. Migration among nations of the Confederacy was encouraged as long as individuals accepted the Great Law.[8]

Some have argued that the Iroquois helped to inspire the United States Constitution. Although that claim has been the subject of debate among historians,[9] what is not is the joint congressional resolution passed in 1988, which recognized that the "original framers of the Constitution . . . are known to have greatly admired the concepts of the . . . Iroquois Confederacy." Additionally, because the confederation of the original Thirteen Colonies into one republic was influenced by the political system developed by the Iroquois Confederacy as were many of the democratic principles which were incorporated into the Constitution . . . Congress, on the two hundredth anniversary of the signing of the United States Constitution, acknowledges the contribution made by the Iroquois Confederacy and other Indian Nations to the formation and development of the United States.[10]

Perhaps the most important phrase in the resolution was the last: "the contribution made by the Iroquois Confederacy and other Indian Nations to the formation and development of the United States." All American Indian nations had a part to play in the way in which America turned out, even when that was not always acknowledged by the federal government.

Such was clearly the case with Tecumseh. A Shawnee warrior, he had fought against American expansionism from an early age, witnessing the loss of his people's ancestral territory after their defeat at the Battle of Fallen Timbers in 1794 and the signing of the Treaty of Greenville the following year. These early experiences made it abundantly clear to Tecumseh and many other Native Americans what was at stake if events continued to unfold as they were.

Meanwhile, his younger brother, Tenskwatawa, would provide a focus for the growing angst. Born in 1775, he was once an incorrigible alcoholic. All that changed when he became a prophet at the age of thirty. Emerging from a drunken stupor, he was enlightened by a vision. As he told it, the Master of Breath visited him and revealed a land of great abundance for those who lived virtuously and according to the old ways. That meant renouncing the influences of white settlers, whom he called spawn of the Evil Spirit. The solution demanded nothing short of purification and unity among all Native Americans.

It was a message that resonated with many Indians, not the least of whom was Tecumseh. Together, the brothers established Prophetstown in 1808 and began making their shared vision a reality. Prophetstown soon grew into a heterogeneous mix of Native peoples. Still, the threat of white encroachment persisted. In 1809, William Henry Harrison, governor of the Indiana territory, was able to persuade several Indian leaders to sign the Treaty of Fort Wayne, which sold over three million acres of land to the United States. The deal outraged many Native Americans, including Tecumseh and Tenskwatawa.

The stage was set for confrontation. The following year, Tecumseh met with Harrison and insisted that he abrogate the treaty. If that did not happen, Indian opposition to white settlement was guaranteed. A federation was being created to prevent further concessions. Harrison was having none of it, asserting that the land had been bought fair and square and that Tecumseh's claim that it was held in common by all Native Americans was specious.

Tecumseh left the meeting intent on building his confederacy, enlisting allies among the Potawatomis, Winnebagos, Sauks, Foxes, Kickapoos, and Missouri Shawnees. He also tried to solicit British assistance in the event of a war with the United States. In 1811, work on the confederacy continued with a trip to Ohio to recruit the Shawnees, Wyandots, and Senecas to the cause. A delegation was also sent to the Iroquois in New York.

In July, Tecumseh met with Harrison again, informing him of the growing confederacy and announcing his intention to continue to organize to the south. True to his word, Tecumseh traveled some three thousand miles in six months. Forewarned of his efforts, and knowing his nemesis was away on his diplomatic mission, Harrison initiated a preemptive strike on Prophetstown on November 7, 1811. Tenskwatawa and his forces were caught completely off guard and eventually were forced to flee. The Americans burned the village and then left.

More violence ensued. As the situation on the frontier deteriorated, the United States went to war with England in what would become known as the War of 1812. It was a fortuitous break for Tecumseh and his confederacy. Great Britain constituted a powerful ally with whom he shared a common cause: stop the American juggernaut. Unfortunately, it was not to last. After the Americans won the Battle of Lake Erie on September 10, 1813, Tecumseh's British friends withdrew from the area.

With the English proving to be unreliable allies, many of Tecumseh's Indian army gave up in despair. The end came on October 5, 1813. Outnumbered three-to-one at the Battle of the Thames, the outcome was a foregone conclusion for the British and Indian forces. Tecumseh fell in battle, and what remained of his Indian supporters scattered. The victorious American soldiers stripped and then scalped the Shawnee chief, some even taking pieces of his skin as souvenirs.[11]

It was a symbolic enough commentary on the relationship between the United States government and the Indigenous peoples of America, and it would be replayed, in some form or another, with various people and their leaders, for years to come. While Tecumseh was dead, his vision remained alive in the soul of any Indian who understood, as he had, what the loss of their way of life meant.

So in his stead, in different places and at different times, stepped individuals like Red Cloud, Sitting Bull, Crazy Horse, Geronimo, and Chief Joseph, to name but a few.[12] Each fought just as hard as Tecumseh did against the assaults by an expanding nation that believed it had a manifest destiny to seize a continent in the name of liberty and a self-proclaimed great and noble experiment in federated self-government.

It meant little to those in Washington, DC, that creation of a continental nation destroyed the very principles that expansion was ostensibly supposed to bring to the western lands, whose people already knew freedom and self-government.[13] However, it was the power of those ideals, when possessed and lived, that informed the pushback of American Indians, just as surely as it had the motivations and actions of white settlers during the Revolution.

The closing of the frontier in 1890 did not end the Indians' struggles for recognition of their basic human rights. In a testament to their resilience in the face of genocide, acculturation, and a host of other indignities, Native peoples fought on. The road was hard and progress slow, but it won them the right to vote in 1924 and led to creation of the American Indian Movement (AIM) in 1968.

AIM was a response to a long list of standing grievances that had been left to fester as the twentieth century rolled on. By the mid-1950s, Native Americans faced federal policies designed to force them to leave their reservations and traditional lands. With states given more control over residents of reservations as part of a scheme to assimilate Indians into mainstream American culture, by the late 1960s, Native peoples found themselves displaced and more marginalized than ever before. Approximately 70 percent of them had moved to cities where they confronted high unemployment, lack of educational opportunities, poor housing, and discrimination. Frustrated, the American Indian Movement fought back.

AIM began as a local grassroots organization in Minneapolis, Minnesota, organizing AIM Patrol to help victims of police brutality, a Legal Rights Center, and the Indian Health Board, which employed Indigenous medical practices in the service of its clients. In 1972, Heart of the Earth Survival School was established to educate Indigenous children in their own communities free from the racism they regularly encountered in Minneapolis's public schools.

That same year, AIM took its mission to the national level, joining other Native rights organizations in a march from the West Coast to Washington, DC, called the Trail of Broken Treaties. In the nation's capital to demand that the federal government honor its treaty commitments, AIM members opted for direct confrontation. They occupied the Bureau of Indian Affairs Building.

After almost a week, the Nixon administration agreed to consider their demands and paid for their trip home. The continuing disconnect between Native American concerns and federal policy evidenced since the days of Tecumseh was obvious when the issues were ignored and AIM became the target of the FBI's Counter Intelligence Program, which routinely engaged in illegal and covert operations against domestic political organizations deemed subversive.

In 1973, AIM again ran afoul of Washington. Gladys Bissonette of the Oglala Sioux Civil Rights Organization informed the group that the traditional Lakota people on the Pine Ridge Reservation were being terrorized by white vigilantes and supporters of tribal president Dick Wilson. In response, AIM joined the traditional Lakotas in occupying the village of Wounded Knee, South Dakota.

They were surrounded by hundreds of federal authorities armed with military-grade hardware. The Indians skirmished with the feds for seventy-one days. When it was over, two Native Americans were dead and nothing had been done to meet their demands for hearings on their treaty and for a full investigation of the circumstances that they faced. It was a scene eerily reminiscent of events some eighty-three years earlier on the same site. Three hundred Lakota had been killed by the US Seventh Calvary during a raid to disarm the Indians' camp in 1890.

Federal persecution of AIM members and leaders persisted through most of the 1970s, but the group fought on. In 1978, for example, it organized the Longest Walk, demanding the release of AIM activist Leonard Peltier and defeat of eleven federal bills that threatened treaty rights. The anti-Native bills were defeated. More significant, President Jimmy Carter signed the American Indian Religious Freedom Act, ending a ban on Native American spiritual practices that had been in place since 1884. It was a step forward, as had been the granting of suffrage in 1924, but it spoke volumes that, once again, the first Americans were the last to be guaranteed so fundamental a right.

Like so many Native American resistance efforts, the American Indian Movement was about more than politics. AIM members saw themselves as part of a spiritual revival, regularly engaging in Sun Dances, sweat lodges, and other spiritual ceremonies that had long been driven into hiding. That such efforts mirrored the work of Tenskwatawa, Tecumseh, and so many others down through the years speaks both to the legacy of these ancestors and to the persistent threat posed to Indigenous culture by white society.[14]

Sadly, the problem was not just an American one. In 2007, the United Nations (UN) passed the Declaration of the Rights of Indigenous Peoples, which affirmed "that indigenous peoples are equal to all other peoples . . . [and] contribute to the diversity and richness of civilizations and cultures"; that racism is "scientifically false, legally invalid, morally condemnable and socially unjust"; and that Native peoples "have suffered from historic injustices as a result of . . . colonization and dispossession of their lands, territories and resources, thus preventing them from exercising, in particular, their right to development in accordance with their own needs and interests."

As a result, the UN asserted that Native people had the right to "the full enjoyment, as a collective or as individuals, of all human rights and fundamental freedoms as recognized in the Charter of the United Nations, the Universal Declaration of Human Rights and international human rights law." That meant the right to "self-determination" and to "maintain and strengthen their distinct political, legal, economic, social and cultural institutions, while retaining their right to participate fully, if they so choose, in the political, economic, social and cultural life of the State." Perhaps most important, indigenous populations had the right to "not to be subjected to forced assimilation or destruction of their culture."

Also of significance in light of the long history of dislocation that they had suffered, people of the First Nations had "the right to the lands, territories and resources which they have traditionally owned, occupied or otherwise used or acquired." That meant they could "own, use, develop and control" these lands, and countries and governments would grant "legal recognition and protection" of the "territories and resources" of the Indigenous population and do so with respect to their "laws, traditions, customs and land tenure systems."[15]

Interestingly, only four countries voted against the resolution when it was first introduced: Australia, Canada, New Zealand,

and the United States, all with a history of mistreating their Native populations.[16] Although it is true that they later reversed their votes, such actions reflect (at least in the case of America) not only a clear tone-deafness to Indian concerns but also the power of Indigenous people who have refused to capitulate.

That much remained to be done if the ideals of the UN resolution were to have any meaning was evidenced when the Standing Rock Sioux and the Cheyenne River Sioux began their protests against the Dakota Access Pipeline. In December 2014, Texas oil firm Energy Transfer Partners asked the federal government for permission to build the 1,200-mile, $3.8 billion Dakota Access Pipeline. When completed, it would be able to carry half a million barrels of North Dakota oil per day through the Dakotas and Iowa to Illinois.

Although it would bypass their land, the pipeline would cross under Lake Oahe, the source of drinking water for the Cheyenne River and Standing Rock Sioux. In April 2016, the Army Corps of Engineers published the results of a survey of the Energy Transfer Partners' proposal. Its senior field archaeologist noted that there were five documented cultural sites within the area that would be affected by building the pipeline, and more than thirty more believed to be within a one-mile radius. In a bit of specious logic, the Corps concluded that because the construction would run the pipeline under Lake Oahe, no serious threat to Native American heritage locations existed. Even if theoretically true, the obvious danger to the health of the Sioux who got their water from the lake remained.

In response, Indian and non-Indian opponents of the project organized the Oceti Sakowin Camp. Protests and lawsuits followed each other in quick succession. Not surprisingly, given the history of relations between Native Americans and government forces, confrontations sometimes turned violent. Meanwhile, construction on the pipeline got underway. By November 2016, the situation boiled over into a scene reminiscent of events at Wounded Knee in 1973.

November 21 was a cold night, the temperature hovering at about twenty-three degrees Fahrenheit. Suddenly, heavily armed law enforcement officials attacked those encamped at Oceti Sakowin, firing rubber bullets and tear gas and drenching people with water cannons in the subfreezing weather. One hundred sixty-seven people were injured, and seven were hospitalized. In what can only be called the height of hypocrisy, Governor Jack Dalrymple of North Dakota asked people to leave the encampment and then signed an evacuation order for Oceti Sakowin, explaining the move was taken because of the harsh weather.

The outgoing Obama administration sided with the Cheyenne River and Standing Rock Sioux, but its actions to block the building of the pipeline were reversed on January 24, 2017, when incoming President Donald Trump signed an executive memorandum ordering the Corps of Engineers to instruct the army to fast-track approval of the unbuilt section of the pipeline. By the end of February, those who remained at Oceti Sakowin were forcibly removed and the National Guard and police occupied the camp.[17]

The matter then went to the courts. Even following the election of a new, more sympathetic president, Joe Biden, who took office some four years later, no clear-cut victor emerged.[18] All of which may suggest that little has changed since William Shakespeare penned *Hamlet* in 1603 and probably long before that. In the play, the troubled Danish prince asks plaintively, "For who would bear the whips and scorns of time, / The oppressor's wrong, the proud man's contumely?"[19]

Native Americans have wrestled with that question for a long time and know firsthand the despair that is possible as a result. Indeed, the Dakota Access Pipeline was just another example of the challenges that American Indians have had to face since the arrival of white settlers.

Still, their resistance speaks to something deeper and perhaps more hopeful. Unlike Hamlet, who thought the solution might well lie in suicide, from Tecumseh to AIM to the Standing Rock and

Cheyenne River Sioux, America's Indigenous people have refused to be silenced, to "go gentle," as Dylan Thomas put it, "into that good night."[20]

Social Constructs and Human Reality

The same is true of everyone who has ever had a sense of (and respect for) his or her own humanity. Indeed, such an awareness is the cornerstone on which a functioning republic rests and from which it draws its national conscience. Native Americans and African Americans speak to what all people of color know, and what all people regardless of color should know—that race in no way diminishes their humanity and, as such, their right to be treated with the respect to which all people are entitled. Toni Morrison put it succinctly when she observed:

> There is no such thing as race. Racism is a construct; a social construct. And it has benefits. Money can be made off of it. People who don't like themselves can feel better because of it. It can describe certain kinds of behavior that are wrong or misleading. So [racism] has a social function. But race can only be defined as a human being.[21]

The same can be said about sexism, homophobia, and ableism. Certainly, women have understood their worth and sought to maximize its impact, even as they sometimes did so in the guise, as Laurel Thatcher Ulrich put it, of being "well behaved." Of course, the unintended popular interpretation of Ulrich's statement also applies—women who "misbehaved" by challenging societal expectations did their part to "make history."

Both kinds of women have been part of the feminist struggle, from the Puritan women Ulrich wrote about to the efforts of Sybil Ludington, Esther de Berdt Reed, Sarah Bache, Susan B. Anthony, Elizabeth Cady Stanton, Mother Jones, Rosa Parks, Betty Friedan, and Gloria Steinem. So, too, the leadership and rank and file of the

National Organization for Women and the work of Tarana Burke, the founder of the Me Too movement that seeks to put an end to sexual harassment and abuse.[22] More important, their stories have been an important part of the American narrative.

The same applies to members of the LGBTQ+ community. People have been lesbian, gay, bisexual, cross-dressers, transgendered, or queer for as long as there have been people. Hidden in plain sight by the denial forced on them by a culture unable to deal with its own sexuality, they had to reside in the proverbial closet because of who they were. That did not change the fact that they were persons and, as such, entitled to the rights that attach to that status. Nor did it diminish their many contributions to the arts, entertainment, literature, and science—indeed, to every walk of life. Certainly, measured by that yardstick, the history of the LGBTQ+ community in America is far richer and more central to the nation's story than traditional history textbooks are wont to admit.

Equally significant, though, are those who dared to step out of the closet and assert their equality and demand their rights. Such was the case with Henry Gerber, who knew from personal experience the challenges of being gay in America. Migrating from Germany to Chicago in 1913 at the age of twenty-one, he was committed to a mental institution for being a homosexual four years later.

Shortly thereafter, with Germany and the United States at war, he was given the choice of being incarcerated as an enemy alien or joining the US Army. He opted for the latter and was stationed with the Allied Army of Occupation in Coblenz, Germany. There, Gerber learned about the work of German physician Magnus Hirschfeld and the Scientific-Humanitarian Committee to decriminalize sex between men. He also routinely visited Berlin, with its active gay subculture.

Returning to the States, Gerber decided to replicate the Scientific-Humanitarian Committee, founding the Society for Human Rights (SHR) in 1924, the first LGBTQ+ rights advocacy group in the United States. The group published the newsletter

Friendship and Freedom, dedicated to issues of concern to gay men. Unfortunately, it lasted for only two issues. Under the Comstock Act, sending material deemed pornographic through the mail was illegal, and, until 1958, that included anything dealing with homosexuality.

The Society for Human Rights soon went the way of its newsletter. Its vice president, Al Weininger, was a bisexual who was married with two children. His wife filed a complaint against SHR, charging that the organization was a haven for "degenerates." A police investigation followed, which led to the arrest of Gerber and several other SHR leaders. Though the charges against him were eventually dismissed, Gerber ended up penniless. He also lost his post office job for "conduct unbecoming a postal worker." With the Society for Human Rights in shambles, Gerber eventually re-enlisted in the military.

He continued to dabble in LGBTQ+ issues, becoming one of the first members of the Washington, DC, branch of the Mattachine Society. Founded in 1950, the society was, after the SHR, the second oldest national gay rights organization in the United States. By the 1960s, Gerber, now an old man, carried on a regular correspondence with members of a new generation of LGBTQ+ community advocates.

These individuals were part of the liberation movements that were transforming the American landscape in that decade. Gay and lesbian Americans came to view their struggle as part of a broader initiative to root out the effects of racism, sexism, Western imperialism, and Victorian mores about drugs and sexuality. The movement coalesced, in earnest, in the aftermath of the Stonewall Riots in 1969.

In the early morning hours of June 28, 1969, police raided a gay/transgender bar known as the Stonewall Inn in Greenwich Village, New York. A common enough occurrence, this time some of the patrons vehemently fought back. Anger over the incident boiled over, spurring many heretofore apolitical members of the LGBTQ+ community to action. Three days of rioting were characterized by increasing militancy against police harassment and brutality, demands that organized crime's hold over gay bars come to an end, and insistence that anti-vice laws targeting LGBTQ+ individuals be repealed.

The Stonewall incident led to the founding of the Gay Liberation Front (GLF) and the Gay Activists Alliance. Reflective of the times, these groups used street theater to draw attention to issues and spoke of the need for liberation. The GLF published "A Gay Manifesto," which was subtitled "Out of the Closet and into the Streets!" Like so many other such documents of the period, the manifesto pulled no punches. It explained that gay people were

> children of a straight society. We still think straight. That is part of our oppression. One of the worst straight concepts is inequality. Straight (also white, English, male, capitalist) views things in terms of order and comparison. . . . There is no room for equality. This gets extended to male/female, on top/on bottom, spouse/not spouse, heterosexual/homosexual, boss/worker, white/black, and rich/poor. Our social institutions cause and reflect this verbal hierarchy. This is Amerika [sic].

> We've lived in these institutions all our lives. Naturally, we mimic the roles. For too long, we mimicked these roles to protect ourselves—a survival mechanism. Now we are becoming free enough to shed the roles we've picked up from the institutions which have imprisoned us.[23]

Given these realities, LGBTQ+ citizens were every bit as oppressed as others, even when there were those in related movements who argued that "homosexuals [are] not being oppressed as much as blacks or Vietnamese or workers, or women." To such thinking, the reply was "Bull! When people feel oppressed, they act on that feeling. We feel oppressed."[24] Those words pretty much summarize the story of America going back to the Revolution.

The movement took many forms after that. In 1973, the National Gay and Lesbian Task Force was organized to mobilize change at the local and state level. Three years later, Steve Endean established the Gay Rights National Lobby (GRNL). In 1978, he founded the Human Rights Campaign Fund, which eventually merged with the GRNL to form the Human Rights Campaign, the largest LGBTQ+ advocacy and lobbying organization in the United States. On October 24, 1979, some one hundred thousand people traveled to the nation's capital for the first national gay rights march in American history.

The road forward was bumpy, punctuated by persistent anti-gay violence and the supposed compromise that dealt with the question of LGBTQ+ military members by implementing the self-explanatory "Don't Ask, Don't Tell" policy in 1993. Still, there were also victories. "Don't Ask, Don't Tell" was repealed in 2010. The Supreme Court ruled on June 26, 2015, that under the Fourteenth Amendment, all states were required to allow same-sex marriages and recognize such marriages performed in other states. Although a landmark decision, it was passed by a five-to-four majority, which spoke to the continued prejudices faced by the LGBTQ+ community.[25]

Then there is the case of America's largest minority: disabled people, who, like LGBTQ+ individuals, were subject to imprisonment for simply being who they were. That was the essential message of the so-called ugly laws, passed by many cities and states across the nation between 1867 and 1913. Prohibiting individuals characterized as "unsightly beggars" from soliciting alms, the laws were usually quite explicit, singling out any person with "physical and mental deformities" or whose body was "deformed, mutilated, imperfect or has been reduced by amputations, or who is idiotic or [an] imbecile."[26] This was an interesting set of criteria, seeing as the first laws came into being just two years after the end of the Civil War, which left some sixty thousand Americans "mutilated, imperfect . . . [and] reduced by amputation."[27]

The ugly laws would soon become part of a more insidious campaign driven by the eugenics movement that targeted individuals with disabilities, gays, lesbians, people of color, certain immigrants, and the poor. Focusing on eradicating so-called undesirables, eugenicists argued that there was a need to improve the quality of the nation's gene pool.[28]

What that meant for people with disabilities and others was sterilization laws. In 1907, Indiana passed legislation legalizing the forced sterilization of institutionalized individuals with the goal of keeping career criminals and "idiots and imbeciles" from having children. Over the coming decades, thirty-three states would pass similar or even more draconian laws. The goal was always the same: to weed out the "feebleminded," criteria for which often included hearing or vision impairment.

In the 1927 case of *Buck v. Bell*, the Supreme Court ruled eight-to-one that forced sterilization was constitutional. The story began some ten years earlier in Virginia. Between 1916 and 1917, Albert Priddy, superintendent of the Virginia State Colony for Epileptics and Feeble Minded in Lynchburg, Virginia, performed some seventy to eighty forced sterilizations. Unsuccessfully sued by one of his victims, and wanting to make sure that his actions would be protected by law in the future, Priddy asked state senator Aubrey Strode to draft a sterilization law.

On March 20, 1924, the Virginia Eugenical Sterilization Act was signed. Priddy sprang into action. Prowling the halls of the State Colony, he selected eighteen candidates for sterilization whom he presented to the institution's board of directors. His plan was to have a lawsuit filed on behalf of whoever was the first to be operated on under the new law. This would prove once and for all the constitutionality of eugenics. The board selected unmarried seventeen-year-old Carrie Buck, whose foster mother had had her institutionalized for being pregnant.

A little over a week after passage of Virginia's sterilization law, Carrie's daughter, Vivian, was born. With Carrie at the Colony, Vivian was labeled feebleminded and sent to a poorhouse. She was later adopted by Carrie's foster parents on the condition that if she continued to show signs of mental deficiency, she would be incarcerated at the Colony. For the moment, two generations of Buck women were inmates: Carrie and her mother, Emma Adeline Harlowe Buck, who had been admitted in 1920 suffering from a list of ailments ranging from rheumatism to syphilis. Both were labeled feebleminded.

As per his plan, Priddy had an attorney appointed for Carrie, and the issue shifted to the courts. Over the next several years, the case meandered through the system and, in 1927, reached the US Supreme Court. Buck's lawyer argued that sterilization violated the Fourteenth Amendment, which guarantees all citizens due process under the law. The Court disagreed, and with that, eugenics continued to rob those the government labeled "defective" of their reproductive rights. More ominously, America's laws would serve as inspiration for Hitler's campaign to create a "master race."[29]

Despite such an onslaught against them, people with disabilities were never simply victims to be scorned, pitied, or eradicated, as society might have it. Consider that during the height of the eugenics craze, the nation elected Franklin Delano Roosevelt, a man who had suffered the effects of polio, four times. Granted, polio was not the sort of "heredity disease" that eugenicists worried would contaminate future generations, but the president's leadership during twelve years in office spoke eloquently to the fallacy that people with disabilities were doomed to meaningless, unfulfilled lives, characterized only by suffering and pain.

Franklin was a distant cousin of President Theodore Roosevelt, the Republican Progressive who had helped to redefine the office of the president at the beginning of the twentieth century. A Democrat, FDR entered politics at twenty-eight years of age, winning election to the New York State Senate in 1910. A rising political star, he served as assistant secretary of the navy in the Wilson administration and was the Democratic Party's vice presidential nominee in 1920. Though he and his running mate, James M. Cox, lost to the Republican ticket of Warren G. Harding and Calvin Coolidge, his career seemed bright.

Then, the following summer, without warning, everything changed. Enjoying a day of sailing on the Bay of Fundy, Roosevelt fell overboard. The next day, his legs became weak, and soon thereafter they would not support his weight. It took doctors a while to figure out what had happened: FDR had contracted infantile paralysis, or, as it is more commonly known, polio. Retreating from public life, he concentrated on rehabilitation. By the end of the year, he had regained strength in his arms, his nervous system was back to normal, and his stomach and lower back seemed much improved. With the dawn of the new year, Roosevelt was fitted with braces, and by the spring he was able to stand with help.

It did not take long for FDR to return to politics, despite some trepidation about how he would be received by the voting public at a time when people with disabilities were usually shunned. In 1922, he wrote an open letter endorsing Al Smith for governor of New York. Two years later, he acted as Smith's floor manager at the Democratic National Convention and formally placed Smith's name in nomination to be the party's candidate. It was not to be. After 101 ballots, the party nominated John W. Davis, who went down to defeat in the November election.

Roosevelt, however, was back. Smith named him to the Taconic State Park Commission, where he became chair. In 1928, he reprised his role as Smith's floor manager at the Democratic National Convention, this time successfully getting Smith chosen as the party's standard-bearer. Although Smith lost to Herbert Hoover, Roosevelt swept into the governor's mansion in Albany. As the nation plunged deeper and deeper into depression after the 1929 stock market crash, Roosevelt was well positioned to make a run for the presidency in 1932. The rest, as the old cliché goes, is history.

Except that beyond the familiar narratives about a president who led the nation through the Great Depression, and then on to victory in World War II, there is the story of a man who never viewed his impairments as handicaps. At home in the White House, FDR used a wheelchair he designed himself that was both discreet and easily maneuverable in an age when wheelchair accessibility did not exist.

In public, the president insisted that he not appear helpless. He therefore honed a technique that simulated walking by which he leaned on a cane with one arm and on either his son or an advisor with the other, shifting his hips and swinging his legs. Stairs he tackled on his own, supporting his entire weight with his arms as he held onto the banisters. Roosevelt also asked the media not to show him in any way that would make him seem weak or disabled. It was a request that most members of the press respected, and when they did not, the Secret Service was dispatched to prevent any such images from being taken.

Though it is easy to characterize these efforts as attempts to hide his impairment, FDR's relationship to his disability was more complicated than that. Roosevelt had begun traveling to Warm Springs, Georgia, in the mid-1920s because of the reputed therapeutic effects of the water there. With the facility facing economic hard times in 1926, he bought it for $200,000 and built a rehabilitation center for polio patients.

In 1934, a Birthday Ball was held to honor the president. He urged people to donate to the Warm Springs Foundation. In the years that followed, Birthday Balls continued in order to support both Warm Springs and the National Foundation for Infantile Paralysis (NFIP), which Roosevelt established in 1938 to encourage research and education on polio. NFIP would soon become more popularly known as the March of Dimes, a phrase coined by actor Eddie Cantor, who believed that asking for only 10¢ per person was a way to encourage children and those hard hit by the Depression to participate in the president's fight against polio without any real economic hardship.[30]

By the 1950s, the work had paid off with vaccines that turned the tide of the disease. The National Foundation went on to develop initiatives designed to improve healthcare for mothers and babies through medical research, education, community efforts, government advocacy, and programs aimed at supporting pregnant women and mothers.[31] As important as Roosevelt was in redefining government's role in social and economic policies and in defending democracy in the face of Nazi tyranny, his experiences as a person with a disability helped to inform a legacy that was far more personal for countless children in future generations than anything that came from the New Deal or the Atlantic, Casablanca, Teheran, or Yalta Conferences.

Then there was the work of Roosevelt contemporary Helen Keller. Born in Alabama in 1880, at nineteen months old she contracted an unknown disease that left her unable to see or hear. It did not stop her. Like many hearing-impaired children, she communicated by home signs, a self-created system of gestures unique to each individual and household. At age seven, Keller met Anne Sullivan, her first teacher and the woman who would be her lifelong friend. Sullivan taught her young charge to read, write, and speak and to understand what others said.

So armed, Keller went on to leave an indelible mark on the world. She attended Radcliffe College, graduating as a member of Phi Beta Kappa at the age of twenty-four, the first so-called deaf-blind person to receive a bachelor of arts degree. Her intelligence and her values informed everything she did thereafter. As an advocate for the rights of people with disabilities, she traveled the globe on behalf of members of the deaf community and worked for the American Foundation for the Blind for forty-four years, until her death in 1968.

A pacifist, she labored tirelessly for world peace. A supporter of workers' rights, in the early part of the twentieth century she joined the Socialist Party of America and the International Workers of the World. She was also a vocal proponent of women's suffrage and took a stand against racism. A member of the NAACP, Keller was quick to point out the un-Christian treatment of African Americans by white Southerners. In 1920, she helped found the American Civil Liberties Union. A dynamo of energy, she wrote books and essays and delivered hundreds of speeches, remaining active until her late seventies, when declining health took its toll.[32]

As Roosevelt's and Keller's stories attest, Americans with disabilities have had many role models to inspire them in their struggle for rights, respect, and dignity. Certainly, it is within the context of pioneers like FDR, Helen Keller, and so many others that the disability rights movement must be understood. After all, nothing occurs in a vacuum. Like other disenfranchised groups, individuals with disabilities had their early advocates who laid the groundwork for change. They also had those who, caught up in the post–World War II quest for greater inclusivity, pushed forward the agenda of reform.

With the end of the Second World War in 1945, disabled veterans demanded that the government provide them with rehabilitation and vocational training, something a grateful nation was more than willing to do. Still, serious obstacles remained. Access to public facilities, including transportation, telephones, and bathrooms, was restricted. Stores, offices, and worksites posed physical barriers that essentially said that no person with disabilities need apply, even before some employers said it explicitly.

Quite simply, the same sort of discrimination that relegated African Americans to segregated schools and water fountains and demanded that they ride in the back of the bus confronted disabled people—only many of them could not even get on the bus. The parallels were not lost on disability advocates, who, inspired by the civil rights movement, began partnering with other groups demanding equity.

Starting at the grassroots level in the 1960s, demands for change grew more insistent. By the 1970s, pressure was being brought to bear on Congress to institute meaningful change. In October 1972, and again in March 1973, President Nixon vetoed the Rehabilitation Act, which would have granted people with disabilities greater rights. His reasoning—it would have negative financial implications. Frustrated, disability rights advocates responded. The group

Disabled in Action staged a sit-in in New York City after the first veto. Meanwhile, in Washington, DC, it joined the Paralyzed Veterans of America, the National Paraplegia Foundation, and other organizations in demonstrations demanding passage of the act.

Nixon reversed himself, but only because the measure had been significantly amended. Even watered down, the law contained Section 504, which guaranteed equal employment opportunities with any federal agency or federally funded programs, outlawed discrimination on the basis of physical or mental impairment, and created the Architectural and Transportation Barriers Compliance Board, which was charged with establishing accessibility standards for all public facilities.

Legislation is one thing; enforcement is something else again. For Section 504 to be meaningful, a legal definition of what constituted a disability had to be established, as did a clear articulation of actions that could be considered discrimination based on a person's disability, how protection would be carried out, and on what timetable. The task for defining these issues fell to the Department of Health, Education, and Welfare (HEW). Between passage of the bill and 1977, it did nothing.

Mobilized, people with disabilities would not be ignored. A lawsuit was filed in federal court that resulted in a judge's order requiring that the regulations be issued. Unfortunately, no deadline was established, and the matter remained gridlocked in bureaucratic and congressional politics. In response, the American Coalition of Citizens with Disabilities was organized to push the issue forward. They set April 4, 1977, as the deadline for regulations to be announced.

When that day came and went, sit-ins were held at eight HEW regional offices and in Washington. At the capital, some three hundred individuals met with HEW Secretary Joseph Califano but received no satisfaction. They remained inside HEW headquarters overnight before dispersing. Meanwhile, in San Francisco, the sit-in lasted twenty-five days. Protests played out with greater or lesser intensity across the country.

Although officials sought to wait them out, it proved to be an ineffective strategy. Disability advocacy groups had done a good job of cultivating political allies and establishing a network of support from a wide variety of groups, including the Black Panthers, the Gay Men's Butterfly Brigade, labor unions, and churches, including the Salvation Army. On April 28, 1977, the regulations necessary to give Section 504 teeth were signed into law.

It was an important step, but more work remained to be done. So the push for change continued, culminating with passage of the Americans with Disabilities Act (ADA) in 1990, which consolidated the gains that had been made piecemeal since the 1960s. As with other legislation aimed at equity, there was a gap between the ideals set forth by the ADA and their realization. That meant continued advocacy, but also progress, even when sporadic and inconsistent.[33]

And herein lies the common thread in all these stories. Whether an African American, female, Native American, lesbian, gay, bisexual, cross-dresser, transgendered, queer, or a person with disabilities, each individual whom society has sought to marginalize has had to come to terms with the labels that branded them and then decide a very fundamental question, the same question that African Americans struggled with in the 1960s. Writing in *Ebony* in 1968, Lerone Bennett Jr. put the matter clearly: "On one level or another, every 'Negro' and/or 'black' and/or 'Afro-American' is going to have to choose a name in the process of choosing his being. Who are you? What is your name?"[34]

The profound insight of Bennett's observation lies in the fact that in coming to understand oneself, one inevitably has to come face to face with Shakespeare's truth that "a rose by any other name would smell as sweet."[35] Or, more bluntly put, that a human by any other name is still a human. Once a person recognizes that they are not ugly, deviant, or less than, they cannot help but take the next step: to dismiss the labels that have been imposed on them, declare their equality, and claim, as the Declaration of Independence and the Declaration of Sentiments at the Seneca Falls Convention of

1848 put it, the rights "to which the Laws of Nature and of Nature's God entitle them."[36] After that, the nitty-gritty and hard work of operationalizing this fundamental truth is the space within which history occurs.

There are, of course, a lot more stories about those who bucked the system than a quick survey like this one allows. To not include them is not to diminish their importance. And acknowledging that we have but scratched the surface is proof enough of the central point being developed here. Those the country might wish to shun or ignore are often closer to its true heart than those who would silence or ignore them. When the marginalized realize that and demand their just desserts as human beings, change is inevitable, and the nation, often despite itself, draws closer to its roots and so to its underlying strength.

Daring to Dream

The struggles and triumphs outlined above point to a sort of national schizophrenia that keeps America in dynamic tension between what it espouses and how some of its citizens conduct themselves. The bottom line is that although few would disagree with the value of freedom and unalienable rights in theory, there are those who would deny them to certain "others" in reality.

This has been true whether one focuses on the nation's track record on gender, race, class, ethnicity, sexual orientation, and disability issues, or immigration. A central theme of the American narrative is that the United States is a nation of immigrants. She has drawn people from around the world who took the promise on the plaque located on the pedestal of the Statue of Liberty seriously. Here was a country that opened its doors wide, calling on the world to "Give me your tired, your poor, / Your huddled masses yearning to breathe free."[37]

Unfortunately, this was also the nation that made life miserable for many of those who arrived. Or that turned old immigrants into nativists within a generation or two when they followed the quickest way to acceptance—adopting the prejudices of the dominant culture.[38] Clearly not true for all citizens, naturalized or born in the United States, the persistence of prejudice (like the selective application of liberty to which it is related) has been an ongoing challenge.

Despite the odds, or against them, just as with those who bucked the system, immigrants have made their mark. And perhaps for the same reason: they believed in the promise of America. Certainly, it takes a special breed of person to risk all in pursuit of a dream. And it has never been an easy path. No universal one-size-fits-all narrative can tell of the diversity of experiences of those who have come to the United States from every continent, save Antarctica. Yet each generation has contributed to the American Dream, defining it in new ways and on their own terms.

It is easy to indulge in glowing generalizations about the melting pot or to focus on the harsh realities that faced the first generations of those fresh off the boat or the airplane. On the one hand, Lady Liberty raises her torch by the Golden Door. Opportunities unheard of in the old country keep people flocking to the supposed land of opportunity. On the other hand, workers are exploited and viewed as threats to some vague concept of the American way. These are both common threads that connect every immigrant saga and that reflect the love-hate relationship that the United States has with all newcomers.

So, we know of Irish who fled the potato famine in the mid-nineteenth century and found hard work and low wages to be a staple of life—that is, when they were not confronted by signs that read, "No Irish Need Apply." Southern and Eastern Europeans coming to the United States in the late nineteenth and early twentieth centuries provided the labor for a burgeoning post–Civil War industrial economy that needed their strong backs but felt they were a threat to the very fiber of the nation. Likewise the Chinese who helped to build America's transcontinental rail system, among many other things.

Even as they contributed to the growth of the nation's economy, the sheer number of newcomers often frightened those already here. Thus so-called progressives like sociologist Eugene Ross and President Theodore Roosevelt warned of "race suicide" if white Anglo-Saxon Protestants—the supposed backbone of American culture—continued to have small families, while the teeming hordes of Catholics and Jews procreated unassimilated in the nation's urban ghettoes. The same logic took on even more blatantly racist overtones when applied to migrants from East Asia, who were variously characterized as the Yellow Peril, the Yellow Specter, and Yellow Terror.[39]

Certainly, such logic was behind every form of restrictive immigration policy that has ever been implemented. The list is a long one and includes the Chinese Exclusion Act of 1882; the Immigration Acts of 1921 and 1924, which sought to limit immigration from Southern and Eastern Europe; and Executive Order 9066, which uprooted some 120,000 Japanese immigrants and Japanese Americans and moved them to internment camps for the duration of World War II. Then there is the Trump administration's "zero tolerance policy" that necessitated the arrest of anyone illegally crossing America's southern border. The result separated children from their families and led to thousands of Latinos and Latinas being housed in camps whose conditions were little different from what Japanese and Japanese Americans endured during the 1940s. Such discriminatory initiatives occurred alongside what came to be known as the Muslim ban. Justified as an effort to strengthen national security against potential terrorists, it targeted immigration from mostly Islamic countries and suspended Syrian refugee relocation.

Still, there has been recognition that to dream is to be American and that the nation needs to encourage the influx of new blood from around the world to keep itself vibrant and, ultimately, to make itself stronger. Thus, among other things, the Naturalization Act of 1870 expanded the right of citizenship to those of African ancestry. The Refugee Relief Act of 1953 provided visas for refugees from Europe and Asia. The Cuban Adjustment Act of 1966 granted permanent resident status and aid to Cubans fleeing Fidel Castro's regime. The similar 1975 Indochina Migration and Refugee Assistance Act helped those fleeing Southeast Asia after the fall of Saigon. Finally, the Dreamers Policy, established by President Barack Obama's executive order in 2012, guaranteed protection from deportation for those who had come to the United States as minors and had lived in the country since June 15, 2007.[40]

America's "self-evident truths" have always had the power to inspire. And it is these that have brought people to its shores since the founding of Jamestown in 1607. The nation's conflicted relationship with those who have risked so much to realize their dreams, if not for themselves, then for their children and children's children, cannot diminish the reason that they have kept coming. Indeed, it speaks to something fundamental about the country at its best. Immigrants serve to remind the nation that its dream and promise are real, even when there are those who would forget.

The Measure of a Nation's Character

Heroes, heroines, and role models come from all walks of life. Certainly, the litany of the famous has inspired schoolchildren and average Americans for generations. However, there are others who have been forgotten because they have been marginalized. Still, that has not prevented them from shaping the character of America, because their fundamental humanity permitted nothing less.

Mayor David Dinkins of New York liked to call his city a "gorgeous mosaic."[41] The same characterization could be applied to America. The individuals who constitute the mosaic and who have embraced the values that founded the nation have kept its flame of hope alive. This is especially true of those who have repeatedly been denied their freedom but refused to take no for an answer. Knowing the truth about themselves as people, they have challenged the nation, time and again, to do the same.

The bottom line is that diversity is the sinew of the Republic, as is the collective recognition that the self-evident truths Jefferson described really are self-evident and thus apply to everyone. Appreciating that fact, even when the nation's ideals have not been fully actualized, has been the basis on which each generation has built, as it met the unique challenges of its time. US history is, after all, the story of individuals who have sustained the nation and moved it forward, sometimes despite itself. Any reflection on America must take special note of that reality.

CHAPTER EIGHT
WILL THE REAL AMERICA
PLEASE STAND UP?

*T*o *Tell the Truth* has been a popular TV gameshow staple off and on since 1956. The rules and premise are pretty straightforward: One challenger with a unique job or an intriguing story is partnered with two imposters in an effort to stump a celebrity panel of four. The show begins with the three challengers standing side by side. The announcer asks, "What is your name, please?" Each in turn claims to be the real individual in question. The emcee then reads a description of the person, and the celebrities are given the opportunity to question each challenger. The imposters may lie, but the real challenger must tell the truth.

At the end of the questioning, the celebrities vote for who they think the individual really is. With the votes cast, the host asks, "Will the real [person's name] please stand up?" One or the other challenger usually feigns rising before the real challenger gets to his or her feet. The impostors say who they really are, and prize money is allocated to the team of challengers based on the number of incorrect votes the impersonators received.[1]

Imagine if one were able to play the same game with America. Only in this case, each imposter would have to truthfully tell part of the story of the nation. The real America would likewise have to be honest in her answers. The panel charged with determining who the real America is would be made up of average citizens from all walks of life.

In a real sense, that is exactly the storyline of the United States. There are several contenders for the title of America. Which one most accurately describes the country has a lot to do with who the panelists are, who is asking the questions, and what details are being discussed. Having reviewed the history of America from a variety of perspectives, it is now time to ask, "Will the real America please stand up?" So without further ado, here are the challengers.

Challenger Number I

For all its struggles, the history of America can be summed up in one word: "democracy." No matter how one looks at it, the history of the United States has been a never-ending effort to make the ideals and promises of freedom accessible to as many people as possible. Whether it was fighting a revolution against the British, structuring a new Constitution, moving toward industrialization, expanding westward, fighting a civil war, or rebuilding from its aftermath, the course of the nation was determined by an abiding commitment to the ideals of the Enlightenment. That all people are created equal. That they are endowed with certain unalienable rights.

How else does one explain the abiding concern of both Federalists and Anti-Federalists with ensuring the preservation of liberty? Or the demand for universal manhood suffrage that eliminated property requirements as a criterion for voting in the North by the 1830s? Or the commitment to those ideals that drove the work of mid-nineteenth-century reformers who pushed for everything from free public education, to abolition, to women's rights? The struggle for control of the West was framed within debates about slavery and free soil. The Civil War, meanwhile, became a referendum on freedom, not only because of the words of Abraham Lincoln at Gettysburg but also because of the Radical Republicans' reform agenda during Reconstruction.

After the Civil War, much work remained to be done. New challenges posed by immigration, urbanization, and industrialization challenged the very core of what it meant to be an American. Still, the country responded to the challenges. Progressive reformers at the end of the nineteenth century and into the early twentieth century pushed for a new role for government that would provide, in the parlance of Theodore Roosevelt, a "Square Deal" or, in the words of Woodrow Wilson, a "New Freedom." At the same time, internationally, the United States came to realize that with its growing power came new responsibility to promote and defend democracy beyond the water's edge.

As the twentieth century unfolded, that would lead to America's defense of democracy in the face of Nazism and Fascism, Communism, and later terrorism. Granted, the path was not smooth. There were abuses, including imperialism and ill-advised proxy wars. But at the end of the day, there was the truth that the world was better off, despite the lapses, when the United States took on a leadership role. Indeed, it was America's commitment to freedom that established liberal internationalism and informed the peace, even when uneasy, after World War II.

Domestically, slowly and often painfully, marginalized individuals, from people of color to women to members of the LGBTQ+ community to disabled Americans, have moved ever closer to the ideals of equity and fairness promised by the Declaration of Independence and guaranteed under the Constitution and Bill of Rights. Indeed, the power of the American idea, of the American Dream, for *all* citizens is what has inspired all reformers to, in one way or another, echo the words of Martin Luther King Jr. when he said, "I have a dream that one day this nation will rise up and live out the true meaning of its creed: 'We hold these truths to be self-evident: that all men are created equal.'"[2]

There is no assumption that the promise of freedom is unattainable in these words or in the actions of those who have challenged the system. Rather, in the demands for change lies an affirmation that America is the land of eternal possibilities because of the power of its founding principles: liberty and democracy for all. It is a belief in those bedrock beliefs that have attracted millions of immigrants to its shores, braving hardships and challenges so that future generations might live a better life than would have been possible in the old country, wherever that might be.

America is not perfect, but her story is unique in world history. Ever aspirational, the United States has dared to do the impossible from its birth. That it has failed occasionally is not the surprise of the miracle. Rather, that it has succeeded as often and as spectacularly as it has for as long as it has is the true miracle. This is the real America.

Challenger Number 2

The story of the United States has been about the constant exploitation of the poor by the rich. Americans might like to wrap their revolution up in Jeffersonian ideals, but the truth was that colonial economic interests were tired of having their profits interfered with by British taxes, period. Liberty had nothing to do with it—unless, of course, measured in terms of the freedom to acquire land, wealth, and power. If it had meant more than that, slavery would have been abolished there and then. Likewise, elites promoted the limitations on freedom that were institutionalized in the Constitution and that led to development of industrialization and western expansion. Even the Civil War and Reconstruction were economic affairs, played out between rival economic interests that ignored the plight of African Americans both during and after slavery.

Consider that power in America between 1800 and 1860 was concentrated in the hands of the few, a small cadre who used their positions to advance their economic agenda. Driven by greed, mill owners exploited workers and immigrants. Land speculators encouraged western expansion and displaced Native Americans and Mexicans who lacked the economic and military power to resist them. In the South, planters sat atop a hegemony that kept African Americans and poor whites subjugated.

The resulting continental foreign policy fixated on creation of empire justified by the logic of Manifest Destiny but ultimately driven only by self-interest and economic gain. Even debates over freedom had economic interest at their root. As Congress wrestled over whether a territory would be admitted as a free or slave state, the bottom line was not the immorality of bondage but the balance of economic power between Northern and Southern interests.

Movements to change the system and make it more "democratic" were either scams or proof of the power of a wealthy, white male-dominated system. Horace Mann may have advocated for free public education, but those who attended government schools received an inferior education because property owners failed to allocate adequate funds for the purpose, preferring to put their economic interests ahead of the common good. Women protested for more rights, but the truth remained that they were largely ignored as cranks. Once established, the elite had all the tools at their disposal to maintain their power and to deflect any challenges to it.

Certainly, the Civil War only became about freedom and the abolition of slavery as a political ploy by Abraham Lincoln to make it difficult for Great Britain and France to side with a Confederacy dedicated to the preservation of slavery. After the war, a twelve-year "Reconstruction" was ended by the infamous Compromise of 1877 and was a sad joke well before that, at least when it came to advancing the rights of newly freed African Americans.

There is a reason that one hundred years later, the United States would have to revisit the unfinished business left in the aftermath of the Civil War and Reconstruction. It is the same reason that two decades into the twenty-first century, the same issues haunted African Americans that their forebears dealt with in the 1860s and 1960s (and during every decade in between). Systemic racism, grounded in the economic advantage afforded to white males since the establishment of the nation, is really the foundational corner-stone of the so-called American Republic.

And what is true of African Americans has been true with only minor modifications for all people of color, for women, for gays, for lesbians, for trans people, for peoples with disabilities, and for immigrants. The prejudices that lock these individuals in chains are systemic in large part because they afford one group economic privilege and political control over others.

The power structure has not changed dramatically since the late eighteenth century and, if anything, has become starker in the divisions that it perpetuates. Industrialization earned robber barons millions, allowing them every luxury, including the ability to spend leisurely summers at palatial summer cottages in places like Newport, Rhode Island. Meanwhile, men, women, and children labored on the fringes of poverty, subject to unsafe working conditions, overcrowded and substandard housing, disease, and early death.

Economic growth might have expanded the size of the middle class after World War II, but the suburbs were segregated. The affluent society that came to characterize postwar America still tolerates poverty. Urban and rural poor experience shrinking economic opportunities and face the dismal reality of what have been euphemistically called food deserts. What can be said about a nation where some of its citizens cannot access healthy or affordable nourishment because of how little money they have and where they live?

The same dynamics shaping the domestic narrative have informed America's foreign policy. When the frontier closed in 1890, the aggressive quest for wealth and power that had swept Native Americans and Mexicans away in its wake now targeted people in Latin America and Asia. The story of early twentieth-century US imperialism has little to distinguish it from its oft-condemned European equivalent. Even when she entered into conflicts ostensibly in the name of democracy, there was always a subtext driven by economics and power considerations.

How else does one explain the fact that Woodrow Wilson, who ran for re-election on a campaign slogan that he kept American boys out of war, was willing to enter that war only five months later? Rhetorical flourishes about making the world safe for democracy aside, the impact of German submarine warfare and its effect on the bottom line for US munitions manufacturers—to say nothing of the Zimmermann Telegram, which posed a direct threat to American dominance of the Western Hemisphere—were the real issues.

Nor was concern for defense of democracy and freedom any more evident during World War II. Had it been, it would not have required a direct assault on US interests at Pearl Harbor to bring America into the war. And even before that, whatever aid the United States provided to the Allies was motivated by enlightened self-interest at best. As Franklin Roosevelt once explained in justifying the need for the Lend-Lease program, if your neighbor's house is on fire, it just makes sense to lend him a hose to put it out before your house is also consumed by flames. And let us not even get into the internment of Japanese and Japanese Americans during a war that was ostensibly being fought in the name of liberty.

After World War II ended, the struggle between the United States and her allies, and the Soviet Union and hers, had less to do with the advancement of ideological principles than with global domination, overlaid with the awful specter of Mutual Assured Destruction. Nations that had once been colonies found themselves victims of a game of cat and mouse between the superpowers that left their needs largely unmet or that hopelessly enmeshed them in the weird logic of proxy war and neo-imperialism. With the end of the Cold War, the underlying challenges confronting these countries persisted because, as with their domestic counterparts in the United States, the problems were systemic, rooted in long-standing economic agendas overlaid with equally old racist assumptions.

America is far from the ideal she would have her citizens believe or the world accept. Her track record speaks to an ongoing struggle in human history between wealth and poverty, between the powerful and the powerless. What makes her story all the sadder is that, unlike other cultures, her citizens all too often believe the hypocritical rhetoric. Certainly, there are few who would dare challenge the accepted narrative of US exceptionalism. And those who do inevitably find themselves marginalized, demonized, or ostracized. This is the real America.

Challenger Number 3

America, at both her best and her worst, is a function of what her citizens choose to make of her. This comes naturally from her founding values, which, in enshrining liberty, allow humans to be fully human. That means that people are free to be the best version of themselves, the worst version of themselves, and, perhaps most of the time, an amalgam of the two.

The Founders understood both the power and the danger accompanying freedom, which is one reason they sought to build so many safeguards into the Constitution, including the Bill of Rights. Even so, they understood the complexity of human nature and, in particular, how division based on self-interest was inevitable in a free society and so engendered conflict and disagreement.

This is clearly a challenge to building a nation, which by definition requires union and consensus to function. To be foolhardy enough to make freedom the building block for union was to create a perpetual and dynamic tension that could never be fully resolved without sacrificing either liberty or unity. No wonder, then, that American history is littered with so much division and strife.

Thus, despite a common background and a shared viewpoint on the rights of man, Americans and the British came to blows in the American Revolution, to say nothing of the struggle between Patriots and Tories that was also so much a part of that conflict. Federalists and Anti-Federalists argued over the nature of the national government. Disputes between Hamilton and Jefferson informed the debate about whether the nation should industrialize or remain rural. Likewise, the Civil War was quite literally, as Lincoln put it, a test of whether a nation founded on the idea of government of, by, and for the people could long endure.

Reconstruction failed and industrialization took its toll. For every Progressive reformer, there was a corrupt political boss or a captain of industry who sought to derail meaningful change. There has never been consensus about the role of government, even in the face of the Great Depression or the upheavals of the 1960s. Internationally, two world wars, a Cold War, and a war on terror brought the same debate and disagreement as had America's policy of western expansion in the nineteenth century.

All of the conflict, though, stands as a magnificent testimonial to America's founding principles. It is the result of the paradox that lies at the very heart of the Republic: a free and united nation is a tall order when freedom is inherently corrosive to union, but necessary if one believes that all human beings are born free, equal, and with rights. The story of United States has required, and will always require, a continuing reinvention of the meaning and purpose of the Republic, all within the parameters first framed in Philadelphia in 1787.

After all, the Founders defined the purpose of the Constitution as creating a "*more* perfect Union."[3] That modifier reflects the complexity of life in a democracy, then and since. Perfection, despite the idealism of reformers over the years, was never (and will never be) possible. Only slow progress.

And therein lies the rub. The definition of progress is in the eyes of the beholder. For the poor, for African Americans, for women—indeed, for anyone who has been marginalized by the system—it has been slow. Given the enormity of the injustices they have confronted, those who have experienced the lingering legacies of prejudice and discrimination have often not perceived progress. Nor, ironically, have those who controlled the economic system or otherwise have felt threatened by changes that promote equity.

All this is why Winston Churchill's assertion rings so true: "Many forms of Government have been tried, and will be tried in this world of sin and woe. No one pretends that democracy is perfect or all-wise. Indeed it has been said that democracy is the worst form of Government except for all those other forms that have been tried from time to time."[4] That is because of all forms of government, democracy is the most adaptive to the nature of humanity.

People are complex, contradictory, and imperfect creatures. That means democracy is as well. Dealing with that truth, however, causes problems given the sense that most Americans have about their national identity and the mythology surrounding it. After all, the United States has often framed itself as exceptional, mostly because of its enduring commitment to liberty. It is this quality which informs the country's collective national conscience, and which ultimately keeps it on track.

Of course, freedom allows for interpretation—which perhaps gets to a fundamental truth about democracy. A consensus is difficult to come by and even harder to sustain because not only do times, challenges, and opportunities change but so, too, do personal perspectives and values, to name but a few of the variables at play at any given moment. That makes constant reinterpretation and debate about what it means to be an American inevitable. And if something so fundamental is up for grabs, "progress," by whatever yardstick it is measured, will inevitably be fitful, sporadic, and uneven.

The takeaway in all this is that there will always be a gap between what America aspires to be and what it will be able to accomplish in a world that is by its very nature complex and diverse. That the United States defies easy characterization is a function of its true character. A free society pays the price for its commitment to liberty by suffering perpetual conflicts. Each, though, has the power to make the nation stronger and inch it ever closer to its true promise. This is the real America.

The Real America and the Power of Choice

Depending on the reader, the "real America" could be any of the challengers. Certainly, there is truth to be found in each of the narratives above. However, after the feinting is done, a fair reading of US history would end with challenger number 3 rising to her feet, for all the reasons outlined in her testimony.

The nation is complicated, like the people who make it up. The characteristics and optimism implicit in the story of challenger number 1 cannot be erased by the truths attested to by challenger number 2, any more than the critique of her failings outlined by challenger number 2 can be erased by the positive read of history spun by challenger number 1.

Both challengers 1 and 2 are America, at her respective best and worst. That leaves the truth of challenger number 3. Still, it is not enough to stop there. Liberty demands choice and civic responsibility. In a republic, people, even when they do not always know it, have real power to shape what their country stands for, what it is, and what is can become.

Too much complacency about the real problems that confront the nation, usually informed by a blind faith in the power of the founding principles to somehow magically sustain the Republic, can lead not only to the worst described by challenger number 2 but also to the very erosion of the system. Certainly, there is more than a little reason for concern when one considers how the United States has scored on the Democracy Index in the twenty-first century.

The supposed exemplar of liberty, the United States ranked between seventeenth and eighteenth between 2007 and 2010, hovered between nineteenth and twenty-first between 2012 and 2016, and plummeted to twenty-fifth in 2018, where it remained in 2020. Once among the ranks of "Full Democracies," America since the Trump era has found itself classified as a "Flawed Democracy."[5] Left unchecked, the slide can and will continue unless the majority of citizens choose a different course.

That means not only voting against insanity and acting to check those who would seek to foist it on the nation but also calling to account those within the power structure who would aid and abet the dismantling of the Republic. It also requires honestly confronting the nation's past sins, not seeking to hide them because discussion might make certain people who have been traditionally privileged feel uncomfortable.[6]

That said, fixation on the nation's weaknesses can easily lead to cynicism and despair, especially when one realizes how much has been left unchanged since 1776 and thus how much still remains to be done. Yet, at the risk of being cliché, the tendency to view the glass as half empty can lead one to give up on the possibility that it can ever be filled. That is as dangerous an alternative as complacency or denial, for without hope there is no basis on which a republic can function. People must believe, and with good reason, that they can affect meaningful change, for themselves, for their children, and for their children's children, in perpetuity.

America, like her citizens, is fully human. As such, her humanity has the power to transform her in positive and negative ways, sometimes unknowingly as people go about their day-to-day existence. There is something oddly comforting in that fact.

A nation that grants its citizens the power of choice must also be peopled with individuals who have the courage to face themselves and the challenges confronting their country, warts and all. When that happens, humanity's innate resiliency is unleashed. If that fact is accepted and acted on, current and future generations of Americans become worthy heirs to what the Founders bequeathed to them— nothing more nor less than the blessings of liberty, in all their glory and messiness.

NOTES

Chapter One

1. Thomas Jefferson to Henry Lee, May 8, 1825, Founders Online, National Archives, accessed November 5, 2020, https://founders.archives.gov/documents/Jefferson/98-01-02-5212.

2. John Locke, *Second Treatises of Government*, ed. C. B. Macpherson (Indianapolis, IN: Hackett, 1980).

3. David Armitage, *The Declaration of Independence: A Global History* (Cambridge, MA: Harvard University Press, 2007).

4. Declaration of Independence: A Transcription, America's Founding Documents, National Archives, accessed November 5, 2020, https://www.archives.gov/founding-docs/declaration-transcript.

5. John Koblin, Michael M. Grynbaum, and Tiffany Hsu, "Tension, Then Some Tears, as TV News Narrates a Moment for History," *New York Times*, November 7, 2020, accessed November 8, 2020, https://www.nytimes.com/2020/11/07/business/media/presidential-election-tv-networks-call.html; Oliver Darcy, "Analysis: Fox News, Last to Call Election, Offers Subdued Coverage of Biden's Victory," CNN, November 7, 2020, accessed November 8, 2020, https://www.cnn.com/2020/11/07/media/fox-news-joe-biden-elected/index.html; Brian Slodysko, "Explaining Race Calls: How AP Called the Race for Biden," AP, November 7, 2020, accessed November 8, 2020, https://apnews.com/article/ap-explains-race-calls-0b1988605f9101f4b799fc63b01e0090.

6. "Americans Celebrate Joe Biden's Victory," Deutsche Welle (DW), November 7, 2020, accessed November 8, 2020, https://www.dw.com/en/us-celebrates-biden-harris-win/a-55532961.

7. Julie Bosman, Sabrina Tavernise, and Lucy Tompkins, "'A New Day in America': Biden Victory Prompts Spontaneous Celebrations," *New York Times*, November 7, 2020, accessed November 8, 2020, https://www.nytimes.com/2020/11/07/us/election-biden-reaction.html; Joshua Bote and Jay Cannon, "Popping Champagne and Dancing, People Take to the Streets Across the US to Celebrate Biden, Harris Win," *USA Today*, November 7, 2020, accessed November 8, 2020, https://www.usatoday.com/story/news/politics/elections/2020/11/07/biden-and-harris-win-2020-election-people-celebrate-streets/6202739002/; Jeremy Herb, "Cities Erupt in Celebration after Biden Named Winner," CNN, November 7, 2020, accessed November 8, 2020, https://www.cnn.com/2020/11/07/politics/biden-celebrations-victory-cities/index.html; Aram Roston and Mark Makela, "Thousands Take to Streets of US in Celebration of Biden Victory," Reuters, November 7, 2020, accessed November 8, 2020, https://www.reuters.com/article/us-usa-election-celebration/celebrations-erupt-in-major-us-cities-after-biden-election-win-idUSKBN27N0OR; Brooke Seipel, "Cities Erupt in Cheers, Church Bells Ring after News of Biden's Projected Win," *The Hill*, November 7, 2020, accessed November 8, 2020, https://thehill.com/homenews/campaign/524939-cities-erupt-in-cheers-church-bells-ring-after-news-of-bidens-projected-win; "US Election 2020: Agony and Ecstasy as Americans React to Biden's Win," BBC News, November 7, 2020, accessed November 8, 2020, https://www.bbc.com/news/world-us-canada-54854986.

8. "Americans Celebrate Joe Biden's Victory."

9. "The Liberty Bell," National Park Service, accessed November 8, 2020, https://www.nps.gov/inde/learn/historyculture/stories-libertybell.htm.

10. Audrey Conklin, "Europe Celebrates Biden Win with Fireworks, Church Bells," Fox News, November 7, 2020, accessed November 8, 2020, https://www.foxnews.com/world/europe-celebrates-biden-win-with-fireworks-church-bells; "Global Leaders React to Joe Biden's Election Win," *US News and World Report*, November 7, 2020, accessed November 8, 2020, https://www.usnews.com/news/top-news/articles/2020-11-07/factbox-global-leaders-react-to-joe-bidens-election-win; Mark Landler,

"Biden Victory Brings Sighs of Relief Overseas," *New York Times*, November 7, 2020, accessed November 8, 2020, https://www.nytimes .com/2020/11/07/world/americas/biden-international-reaction.html; Amanda Macias, "'Welcome Back America!' World Congratulates Joe Biden on US Presidential Election Win," CNBC, November 7, 2020, accessed November 8, 2020, https://www.cnbc.com/2020/11/07/world -congratulates-joe-biden-on-us-presidential-election-win.html; Zamira Rahim and Martin Goillandeau, "World Leaders Congratulate Joe Biden on His Victory," CNN, November 7, 2020, accessed November 8, 2020, https://www.cnn.com/2020/11/07/americas/biden-global-reaction -election-intl/index.html; Paul Scheem and Adam Taylor, "'Good News': America's Allies Celebrate Biden Win, Hope for More Cooperative Relations," *Washington Post*, November 8, 2020, accessed November 8, 2020, https://www.washingtonpost.com/world/2020/11/08/world-reaction-us -election/; Billy Perrigo, Suyin Haynes and Amy Gunia, "How the World Is Reacting to Joe Biden's Election Win," *Time*, November 8, 2020, accessed November 8, 2020, https://time.com/5908777/joe-biden -world-reaction/; Brooke Seipel, "Fireworks in London, Edinburgh as Biden Win Celebrated Abroad," *The Hill*, November 7, 2020, accessed November 8, 2020, https://thehill.com/homenews/campaign/524962 -fireworks-in-london-edinburgh-as-biden-win-celebrated-abroad; Jason Slotkin and Joanna Kakissis, "World Leaders Congratulate Biden on Win, and Some Celebrate Trump's Defeat," NPR, November 7, 2020, accessed November 8, 2020, https://www.npr.org/sections/live-updates -2020-election-results/2020/11/07/932530415/world-leaders-congratulate -biden-on-win-and-some-celebrate-trumps-defeat; "US Election 2020: How the World Reacted to a Biden Win," BBC News, November 8, 2020, accessed November 8, 2020, https://www.bbc.com/news/world-us -canada-54845979.

11. Anne Hidalgo, @Anne_Hidalgo, November 7, 2020, accessed November 8, 2020, https://twitter.com/Anne_Hidalgo/status/1325115 998966607873.

12. Ian Davidson, *The French Revolution: From Enlightenment to Tyranny* (London: Profile Books, 2018); Norman Desmarais, *America's First Ally: France in the Revolutionary War* (Havertown, PA: Casemate, 2019); Susan Dunn, *Sister Revolutions: French Lightning, American Light* (New York: Farrar, Straus, and Giroux, 2000); Larrie D. Ferreiro, *Brothers at*

Arms: American Independence and the Men of France and Spain Who Saved It (New York: Alfred A. Knopf, 2016); Jeremy Popkin, *A New World Begins: The History of the French Revolution* (New York: Basic Books, 2019); Simon Schama, *Citizens: A Chronicle of the French Revolution* (New York: Vintage Books, 1990).

13. Martin Luther King, "I Have a Dream," in *A Testament of Hope: The Essential Writings and Speeches*, ed. James M. Washington (New York: HarperCollins, 1991), 217–20.

14. Michael Meyer, *The Year that Changed the World: The Untold Story Behind the Fall of the Berlin Wall* (New York: Simon & Schuster, 2012); Mary Elise Sarotte, *The Collapse: The Accidental Opening of the Berlin Wall* (New York: Basic Books, 2015); Victor Sebestyen, *Revolution 1989: The Fall of the Soviet Empire* (New York: Vintage Books, 2010).

15. Julia Franck, Heike Geissler, Maxim Leo, Norman Ohler, and Bernhard Schlink, "German Novelists on the Fall of the Berlin Wall: 'It Was a Source of Energy We Lived Off for Years,'" *The Guardian*, November 3, 2019, accessed November 8, 2020, https://www.theguardian.com/world/2019/nov/03/berlin-wall-30-years-on-five-german-writers-assess-bernhard-schlink-franck-geissler-ohler.

16. George Black and Robin Munro, *Black Hands of Beijing: Lives of Defiance in China's Democracy Movement* (Hoboken, NJ: John Wiley & Sons, 1993); Jeremy Brown: *June Fourth: The Tiananmen Protests and Beijing Massacre of 1989* (Cambridge: Cambridge University Press, 2021); Antony Dapiran, *City on Fire: The Fight for Hong Kong* (Melbourne, Australia: Scribe, 2020); Andreas Fulda, *The Struggle for Democracy in Mainland China, Taiwan and Hong Kong: Sharp Power and Its Discontents* (London: Routledge, 2019); Louisa Lim, *The People's Republic of Amnesia: Tiananmen Revisited* (New York: Oxford University Press, 2014); Laikwan Pang, *The Appearing Demos: Hong Kong During and After the Umbrella Movement* (Ann Arbor: University of Michigan Press, 2020).

17. Pamela Constable and Arturo Valenzuela, *A Nation of Enemies: Chile Under Pinochet* (New York: W.W. Norton, 1993); Ariel Dorfman, *Exorcising Terror: The Incredible Unending Trial of Augusto Pinochet* (New York: Seven Stories Press, 2002); Richard E. Feinberg, "Order from Chaos: Chileans Learned the Right Lessons After the Pinochet Era," Brookings Institution, November 18, 2019, accessed November 8, 2020, https://www.brookings.edu/blog/order-from-chaos/2019/11/18/

chileans-learned-the-right-lessons-after-the-pinochet-era/; Heraldo Munoz, *The Dictator's Shadow: Life Under Augusto Pinochet* (New York: Basic Books, 2008); Patricia Politzer, *Fear in Chile: Lives Under Pinochet*, trans. Diane Wachtell (New York: The New Press, 2001).

18. Asaad Alsaleh, *Voices of the Arab Spring: Personal Stories from the Arab Revolutions* (New York: Columbia University Press, 2015); Asef Bayat, *Revolution without Revolutionaries: Making Sense of the Arab Spring* (Stanford, CA: Stanford University Press, 2017); Jason Brownlee, Tarek Masoud, and Andrew Reynolds, *The Arab Spring: Pathways of Repression and Reform* (Oxford: Oxford University Press, 2015); Mark L. Haas and David W. Lesch, eds., *The Arab Spring* (New York: Routledge, 2018).

19. King, "I Have a Dream," in *A Testament of Hope*, 219.

20. *Cicero's Tusculan Disputations: Also Treatises on the Nature of the Gods and on the Commonwealth*, trans. C. D. Yonge (New York: Harper & Brothers, 1890), 437.

21. "Hebrews 11:1," *The Holy Bible*, King James Version (New York: American Bible Society, 1999).

22. Robert Gross, *The Minutemen and Their World* (New York: Hill & Wang, 1976), 11.

23. Thomas S. Kidd, *The Great Awakening: The Roots of Evangelical Christianity in Colonial America* (New Haven, CT: Yale University Press, 2009); Frank Lambert, *Inventing the "Great Awakening"* (Princeton, NJ: Princeton University Press, 1999); John Howard Smith, *The First Great Awakening: Redefining Religion in British America, 1725–1775* (Lanham, MD: Fairleigh Dickinson University Press, 2015).

24. Sam Bass Warner, *The Private City: Philadelphia in Three Stages of Its Growth* (Philadelphia: University of Pennsylvania Press, 1968), chapter 1.

25. A. J. Langguth, *Patriots: The Men Who Started the American Revolution* (New York: Simon & Schuster, 1988); Gordon S. Wood, *The Creation of the American Republic, 1776–1787* (Chapel Hill: University of North Carolina Press, 1969).

26. Locke, *Second Treatises of Government*, 9.

27. Ibid.

28. Thomas Paine, *Common Sense: The Origin and Design of Government*, ed. Coventry House Publishing (Dublin, OH: Coventry House Publishing, 2016), 11.

29. Plato, *Six Great Dialogues: Apology, Crito, Phaedo, Phaedrus, Symposium, The Republic*, trans. Benjamin Jowett (Mineola, NY: Dover, 2007), 293.

30. Norberto Bobbio, *Thomas Hobbes and the Natural Law Tradition*, trans. Daniela Gobetti (Chicago: University of Chicago Press, 1993); Kody W. Cooper, *Thomas Hobbes and the Natural Law* (Notre Dame, IN: University of Notre Dame Press, 2018).

31. Thomas Hobbes, *The Life of Mr. Thomas Hobbes of Malmesbury Written by Himself in a Latine Poem, and Now Translated into English*, Online Text Creation Partnership, 2010, accessed November 10, 2020, https://quod.lib.umich.edu/e/eebo/A44004.0001.001/1:2?rgn=div1;view=fulltext.

32. Thomas Hobbes, *Leviathan: With Selected Variants from the Latin Edition of 1668*, ed. Edwin Curley (New York: Hackett, 1994).

33. Jean-Jacques Rousseau, *The Social Contract, or Principles of Political Right*, trans. H. J. Tozer (Ware, UK: Wordsworth, 1998), 5.

34. Thomas Jefferson to John Adams, October 28, 1813, Founders Online, National Archives, accessed November 11, 2020, https://founders.archives.gov/documents/Jefferson/03-06-02-0446.

35. Charles C. Ware, *1491: New Revelations of the Americas Before Columbus* (New York: Alfred A. Knopf, 2005).

36. Ronald Sanders, *Lost Tribes and Promised Lands: The Origins of American Racism* (Detroit, MI: Dzanc Books, 1978); David E. Stannard, *American Holocaust: The Conquest of the New World* (New York: Oxford University Press, 1992).

37. Lerone Bennett Jr., *Before the Mayflower: A History of the Negro in America, 1619–1962* (Chicago: Johnson Publishing, 1962); Stephen Hanks, *1619—Twenty Africans: Their Story, and Discovery of Their Black, Red, & White Descendants* (Portland, OR: Inkwater Press, 2019); James Horn, *1619: Jamestown and the Forging of American Democracy* (New York: Basic Books, 2018); Ibram X. Kendi, *Stamped from the Beginning: The Definitive History of Racist Ideas in America* (New York: Hachette Books, 2016); Isabel Wilkerson, *Caste: The Origins of Our Discontents* (New York: Random House, 2020).

38. Thucydides, *History of the Peloponnesian War*, revised ed., trans. Rex Warner (New York: Penguin, 1972), 145, 147.

39. Ibid., 402.

40. Declaration of Independence.

41. King, "Letter from Birmingham City Jail," in *A Testament of Hope*, 292.

42. Thomas Jefferson to James Madison, January 30, 1787, Founders Online, National Archives, accessed November 14, 2020, https://founders .archives.gov/documents/Jefferson/01-11-02-0095/.

Chapter Two

1. Quoted in Hunter Styles, "Resist Like It's 1786: Modern Protest Movements Have Echoes of Shays' Rebellion," *Valley Advocate*, March 6, 2019, accessed December 3, 2020, https://valleyadvocate.com/2019/03/06/ resist-like-its-1786-modern-protest-movements-have-echoes-of-shays -rebellion/.

2. Gillian Flaccus and Sara Cline, "Portland Protesters Breach Fence Around Federal Courthouse," *Washington Post*, July 26, 2020, accessed December 3, 2020, https://www.washingtonpost.com/national/ portland-big-protest-crowds-again-over-us-agents-presence/2020/07/26/ 2353b684-cefc-11ea-99b0-8426e26d203b_story.html.

3. "Insurrection at Harper's Ferry," *Valley Spirit*, October 26, 1859, accessed December 3, 2020, http://www2.iath.virginia.edu/jbrown/news .vs/vsbrown7.gif.

4. Tony Horwitz, *Midnight Rising: John Brown and the Raid That Sparked the Civil War* (New York: Henry Holt, 2011); David S. Reynolds, *John Brown, Abolitionist: The Man Who Killed Slavery, Sparked the Civil War, and Seeded Civil Rights* (New York: Vintage Books, 2005).

5. Leonard L. Richards, *Shays's Rebellion: The American Revolution's Final Battle* (Philadelphia: University of Pennsylvania, 2002); David P. Szatmary, *Shays' Rebellion: The Making of an Agrarian Insurrection* (Amherst: University of Massachusetts Press, 1980).

6. Henry Knox to George Washington, October 23, 1786, Founders Online, accessed December 4, 2020, https://founders.archives.gov/ documents/Washington/04-04-02-0274.

7. Akhil Reed Amar, *America's Constitution: A Biography* (New York: Random House, 2005); Catherine Drinker Bowen, *Miracle at Philadelphia: The Story of the Constitutional Convention May–September 1787* (New York: Back Bay Books, 1986); Joseph J. Ellis, *The Quartet: Orchestrating the Second American Revolution, 1783–1789* (New York: Vintage Books,

2015); Michael J. Klarman, *The Framers' Coup: The Making of the United States Constitution* (New York: Oxford University Press, 2016); David O. Stewart, *The Summer of 1787: The Men Who Invented the Constitution* (New York: Simon & Schuster, 2007).

8. Henry Knox to George Washington, October 23, 1786.

9. Barry McGuire, "Eve of Destruction," 1965, RCA-Victor, compact disc.

10. Great Seal, accessed December 4, 2020, https://www.greatseal.com/mottoes/unum.html.

11. John Adams, *The Revolutionary Writings of John Adams*, C. Bradley Thompson, ed. (Indianapolis, IN: Liberty Fund, 2001), 226–27.

12. Declaration of Independence.

13. The Constitution of the United States: A Transcription, America's Founding Documents, National Archives, accessed November 19, 2020, https://www.archives.gov/founding-docs/constitution-transcript.

14. Merrill Jensen, *The Articles of Confederation: An Interpretation of the Social-Constitutional History of the American Revolution, 1774–1781* (Madison: University of Wisconsin Press, 1959); George William Van Clive, *We Have Not a Government: The Articles of Confederation and the Road to the Constitution* (Chicago: University of Chicago Press, 2017).

15. Transcript of Articles of Confederation (1777), Our Documents, accessed November 24, 2020, https://www.ourdocuments.gov/doc.php?flash=false&doc=3&page=transcript.

16. Edward G. Lengel, ed., *This Glorious Struggle: George Washington's Revolutionary War Letters* (New York: HarperCollins, 2007).

17. Declaration of Independence.

18. George Washington to Continental Congress, January 1, 1777, in Lengel, ed., *This Glorious Struggle*, 93.

19. Transcript of President George Washington's Farewell Address, September 19, 1796, Our Documents, accessed December 11, 2020, https://www.ourdocuments.gov/doc.php?flash=false&doc=15&page=transcript.

20. Bernard M. Bass, *Leadership and Performance Beyond Expectations* (New York: The Free Press, 1985); James MacGregor Burns, *Leadership* (New York: Harper & Row, 1978); John W. Gardner, *On Leadership* (New York: The Free Press, 1990).

21. James Madison, "Federalist No. 10," in Clinton Rossiter, ed., *The Federalist Papers* (New York: Signet Classics, 2003), 75.

22. Ibid.

23. Ibid., 73.

24. Articles of Confederation.

25. Ibid.

26. The Federalist Farmer, "Letter VII," December 31, 1787, in Herbert J. Storing and Murray Dry, eds., *The Anti-Federalist: Writings by the Opponents of the Constitution*, abridged ed. (Chicago: University of Chicago Press, 1985), 74.

27. Congressman Earl Blumenauer on Redistricting and Gerrymandering, November 15, 2011, C-SPAN, accessed December 14, 2020, https://www.cspan.org/video/?c4497075/congressman-earl-blumenauer -redistricting-gerrymandering.

28. Barack Obama, "Address Before a Joint Session of the Congress on the State of the Union," January 12, 2016, online by Gerhard Peters and John T. Woolley, The American Presidency Project, accessed December 14, 2020, https://www.presidency.ucsb.edu/node/313186.

29. Ronald Reagan, "Remarks at the Republican Governors Club Annual Dinner," October 15, 1987, online by Gerhard Peters and John T. Woolley, The American Presidency Project, accessed December 14, 2020, https://www.presidency.ucsb.edu/node/251904.

30. "Gerrymandering": Newt Gingrich at GenerationEngage, February 1, 2006, YouTube, accessed December 14, 2020, https://www.youtube .com/watch?v=hTj9aaAizr0.

31. Constitution of the United States.

32. Renée Jacobs, "The Iroquois Great Law of Peace and the United States Constitution: How the Founding Fathers Ignored the Clan Mothers," *American Indian Law Review* 16, no. 2 (January 1991): 497–531.

33. Constitution of the United States.

34. James Madison, *Notes of Debates in the Federal Convention of 1787*, 2nd ed. (New York: W.W. Norton, 1987), 116.

35. Jan Ellen Lewis, "Women and the Constitution: Why the Constitution Includes Women," *Commonplace: The Journal of Early American Life* 2, no. 4 (April 2002), accessed December 14, 2020, http://common place.online/article/women-and-the-constitution-why-the-constitution -includes-women/.

36. Sally McMillen, *Seneca Falls and the Origins of the Women's Rights Movement* (New York: Oxford University Press, 2008); Lisa Tetrault,

The Myth of Seneca Falls: Memory and the Women's Suffrage Movement, 1848–1898 (Chapel Hill: University of North Carolina Press, 2014); Judith Wellman, *The Road to Seneca Falls: Elizabeth Cady Stanton and the First Woman's Rights Convention* (Urbana: University of Illinois Press, 2004).

37. Report of the Woman's Rights Convention, held at Seneca Falls, New York, July 19–20, 1848, Proceedings and Declaration of Sentiments, Library of Congress, accessed December 14, 2020, https://www.loc.gov/resource/rbcmil.scrp4006702/?sp=10.

38. Petition for Universal Suffrage, Signed by Elizabeth Cady Stanton, Susan B. Anthony and Others, National Archives, accessed December 14, 2020, https://www.archives.gov/historical-docs/todays-doc/index.html?dod-date=1112.

39. The Constitution: Amendments 11–27, America's Founding Documents, National Archives, accessed December 14, 2020, https://www.archives.gov/founding-docs/amendments-11-27.

40. Ronald R. Sundstrom, *The Browning of America and the Evasion of Social Justice* (Albany: State University of Albany Press, 2008).

41. Ryan C. Henderson, *Obama at War: Congress and the Imperial Presidency* (Lexington: University Press of Kentucky, 2015); Peter Irons, *War Powers: How the Imperial Presidency Hijacked the Constitution* (New York: Henry Holt, 2006); Andrew Rudalevige, *The New Imperial Presidency: Renewing Presidential Power after Watergate* (Ann Arbor: University of Michigan Press, 2006); Charlie Savage, *Takeover: The Return of the Imperial Presidency and the Subversion of American Democracy* (New York: Little, Brown, 2007); Arthur Schlesinger Jr., *The Imperial Presidency*, reprint ed. (Boston: Mariner Books, 2004); Gary Schmitt, Joseph M. Bessette, and Andrew E. Busch, eds., *The Imperial Presidency and the Constitution* (Lanham, MD: Rowman & Littlefield, 2017).

42. Constitution of the United States.

43. The Bill of Rights: A Transcription, America's Founding Documents, National Archives, accessed December 14, 2020, https://www.archives.gov/founding-docs/bill-of-rights-transcript.

44. The Constitution: Amendments 11–27.

45. Ibid.

46. Herbert A. Simon, *Administrative Behavior: A Study of Decision-Making Processes in Administrative Organizations*, 4th ed. (New York: The Free Press, 1997).

Chapter Three

1. James McHenry, *Papers of Dr. James McHenry on the Federal Convention of 1787*, The Avalon Project, accessed December 25, 2020, https://avalon.law.yale.edu/18th_century/mchenry.asp. Note that punctuation was added to improve readability.

2. Alexis de Tocqueville, *Democracy in America*, trans. Arthur Goldhammer (New York: Library of America, 2004), 275.

3. Edwin L. James, "Mussolini Says Fascism Will Live After He Is Gone," *New York Times*, April 15, 1928, accessed December 25, 2020, https://www.nytimes.com/1928/04/15/archives/mussolini-says-fascism-will-live-after-he-is-gone-he-tells-times.html.

4. Richard Hofstadter, "The Paranoid Style in American Politics," *Harper's Magazine*, November 1964, accessed December 23, 2020, https://harpers.org/archive/1964/11/the-paranoid-style-in-american-politics/; Richard Hofstadter, *The Paranoid Style in American Politics*, first vintage ed. (New York: Vintage Books, 2008), chapter 1.

5. Devan Cole, "John Lewis Urges Attendees of Selma's 'Bloody Sunday' Commemorative March to 'Redeem the Soul of America' by Voting," CNN, March 1, 2020, accessed December 26, 2020, https://www.cnn.com/2020/03/01/politics/john-lewis-bloody-sunday-march-selma/index.html.

6. Thomas Jefferson to James Madison, January 30, 1787.

7. John Lewis, *Across That Bridge: Life Lessons and a Vision for Change* (New York: Hachette Books, 2012), 5.

8. Eric Hoffer, *The True Believer: Thoughts on the Nature of Mass Movements* (New York: Harper & Row, 1951), 12–13.

9. Ibid., 72.

10. Ibid., 11.

11. Timothy Snyder, *On Tyranny: Twenty Lessons from the Twentieth Century* (New York: Tim Duggan Books, 2017), 40–41.

12. President George Washington's Farewell Address.

13. Rüdiger Barth and Hauke Friederichs, *The Last Winter of the Weimar Republic: The Rise of the Third Reich*, trans. Caroline Waight (New York: Pegasus, 2020); Benjamin Carter Hett, *The Death of Democracy: Hitler's Rise to Power and the Downfall of the Weimar Republic* (New York: St.

Martin's Press, 2018); Peter Ross Range, *The Unfathomable Ascent: How Hitler Came to Power* (New York: Hachette Books, 2020).

14. Sinclair Lewis, *It Can't Happen Here* (New York: Signet Classics, 2014), 43.

15. Republican Party Platform of 1860, May 17, 1860, online by Gerhard Peters and John T. Woolley, The American Presidency Project, accessed December 30, 2020, https://www.presidency.ucsb.edu/node/273296.

16. 1860 Democratic Party Platform, June 18, 1860, online by Gerhard Peters and John T. Woolley, The American Presidency Project, accessed December 30, 2020, https://www.presidency.ucsb.edu/node/273172.

17. Democratic Party Platform (Breckinridge Faction) of 1860, June 23, 1860, online by Gerhard Peters and John T. Woolley, The American Presidency Project, accessed December 30, 2020, https://www.presidency.ucsb.edu/node/273278.

18. Constitutional Union Party Platform of 1860, May 9, 1860, online by Gerhard Peters and John T. Woolley, The American Presidency Project, accessed December 30, 2020, https://www.presidency.ucsb.edu/node/273159.

19. 1860 Presidential Election, 270toWin, accessed December 26, 2020, https://www.270towin.com/1860_Election/. For more detail on the election, see Douglas R. Egerton, *Year of Meteors: Stephen Douglas, Abraham Lincoln, and the Election that Brought on the Civil War* (London: Bloomsbury Press, 2010); Michael F. Holt, *The Election of 1860: A Campaign Fraught with Consequences* (Lawrence: University of Kansas Press, 2017); Nathan P. Kalmoe, *With Ballots and Bullets: Partisanship and Violence in the American Civil War* (Cambridge: Cambridge University Press, 2020).

20. Adolf Hitler, *Mein Kampf*, trans. Ralph Manheim (Boston, MA: Mariner Books, 1998), 231.

21. Ibid.

22. "South Carolina: Serenade to Hon. Edmund Ruffin," November 22, 1860, *New York Times*, accessed December 30, 2020, https://www.nytimes.com/1860/11/22/archives/newspaper-indications-south-carolina-serenade-to-hon-edmund-ruffin.html.

23. "Edmund Ruffin, 1794–1865," The Latin Library, accessed January 10, 2021, http://www.thelatinlibrary.com/chron/civilwarnotes/ruffin.html.

24. Frank Brown, "Nixon's 'Southern Strategy' and Forces against Brown," *Journal of Negro Education* 73, no. 3 (Summer 2004): 191–208;

Dean J. Kotlowski, "Nixon's Southern Strategy Revisited," *Journal of Policy History* 10, no. 2 (April 1998): 207–38; Angie Maxwell and Todd Shields, *The Long Southern Strategy: How Chasing White Voters in the South Changed American Politics* (New York: Oxford University Press, 2019); Reg Murphy and Hal Gulliver, *The Southern Strategy* (New York: Scribner, 1971).

25. Randall Balmer, "The Real Origins of the Religious Right," *Politico Magazine*, May 27, 2014, accessed September 8, 2020, https://www.politico.com/magazine/story/2014/05/religious-right-real-origins-107133; Heidi Beirich and Mark Potok, "The Council for National Policy: Behind the Curtain," May 17, 2016, Southern Poverty Law Center, accessed September 15, 2020, https://www.splcenter.org/hatewatch/2016/05/17/council-national-policy-behind-curtain; Andrew Breitbart, *Righteous Indignation: Excuse Me While I Save the World!* (New York: Grand Central Publishing, 2011); "Buying a Movement: Right-Wing Foundations and American Politics," People for the American Way, accessed September 15, 2020, http://files.pfaw.org/pfaw_files/buyingamovement.pdf; Christopher Leonard, *Kochland: The Secret History of Koch Industries and Corporate Power in America* (New York: Simon & Schuster, 2019); Jane Mayer, *Dark Money: The Hidden History of the Billionaires Behind the Rise of the Radical Right* (New York: Anchor, 2017); Anne Nelson, *Shadow Network: Media, Money, and the Secret Hub of the Radical Right* (London: Bloomsbury, 2019); David Schulman, *Sons of Wichita: How the Koch Brothers Became America's Most Powerful and Private Dynasty* (New York: Grand Central Publishing, 2015).

26. Colleen Long and Ed White, "Trump Thought Courts Were Key to Winning. Judges Disagreed," AP, December 8, 2020, accessed January 7, 2021, https://apnews.com/article/donald-trump-courts-election-results-e1297d874f45d2b14bc99c403abd0457; Kadhim Shubber, "Lawsuit Tracker: Donald Trump's Legal Battle Runs into Repeated Dead Ends," *Financial Times*, December 11, 2020, accessed January 7, 2021, https://www.ft.com/content/20b114b5-5419-493b-9923-a918a2527931.

27. "AG Paxton Sues Battleground States for Unconstitutional Changes to 2020 Election Laws," Press Release, December 8, 2020, Office of Ken Paxton, Attorney General of Texas, accessed January 7, 2021, https://www.texasattorneygeneral.gov/news/releases/ag-paxton-sues-battleground-states-unconstitutional-changes-2020-election-laws.

28. Tom Goldstein, "The Supreme Court, Faithless Electors, and Trump's Final, Futile Fight," *Supreme Court of the United States Blog*, November 28, 2020, accessed January 7, 2021, https://www.scotusblog.com/2020/11/the-supreme-court-faithless-electors-and-trumps-final-futile-fight/.

29. Jordan Williams, "Michael Flynn: Trump Could Deploy Military to 'Rerun' Election," *The Hill*, December 18, 2020, accessed January 7, 2021, https://thehill.com/homenews/news/530795-michael-flynn-trump-should-deploy-military-to-rerun-election.

30. Julie Grace Brufke, "Top Republicans Praise Trump's Flynn Pardon," *The Hill*, November 25, 2020, accessed January 7, 2021, https://thehill.com/homenews/house/527643-top-republicans-praise-trumps-flynn-pardon.

31. Dan Berman, "Appeals Court Dismisses Gohmert Case Asking Pence to Interfere in Electoral College Vote Count," CNN, January 3, 2021, accessed January 7, 2021, https://www.cnn.com/2021/01/02/politics/gohmert-pence-electoral-college-case-appeal-dismissed/index.html; Josh Gerstein and Kyle Cheney, "Federal Appeals Court Tosses Gohmert Suit Aimed at Overturning 2020 Election Results," *Politico*, January 1, 2021, accessed January 7, 2021, https://www.politico.com/news/2021/01/01/louie-gohmert-lawsuit-pence-453387.

32. Jack Arnholz,, "Which GOP Members of Congress Plan on Challenging the Electoral College Results?" ABC News, January 4, 2021, accessed January 7, 2021, https://abcnews.go.com/Politics/gop-members-congress-plan-challenging-electoral-college-certification/story?id=75045395.

33. Michael F. Holt, *By One Vote: The Disputed Presidential Election of 1876* (Lawrence: University Press of Kansas, 2008); Roy Morris Jr., *Fraud of the Century: Rutherford B. Hayes, Samuel Tilden, and the Stolen Election of 1876* (New York: Simon & Schuster, 2003); William H. Rehnquist, *Centennial Crisis: The Disputed Election of 1876* (New York: Random House, 2004).

34. Dan Barry and Sheera Frenkel, "'Be There. Will Be Wild!' Trump All but Circled the Date," *New York Times*, January 6, 2021, accessed January 7, 2021, https://www.nytimes.com/2021/01/06/us/politics/capitol-mob-trump-supporters.html.

35. Aaron Blake, "'Let's Have Trial by Combat': How Trump and Allies Egged on the Violent Scenes Wednesday," January 6, 2021, *Washington Post*, accessed January 7, 2021, https://www.washingtonpost.com/

politics/2021/01/06/lets-have-trial-by-combat-how-trump-allies-egged-violent-scenes-wednesday/.

36. Jason Lemon, "Mo Brooks Attacks 'Weakling, Cowering, Wimpy' GOP Congressmen during DC Protest Speech," *Newsweek*, January 6, 2021, accessed January 7, 2021, https://www.newsweek.com/mo-brooks-attacks-weakling-cowering-wimpy-gop-congressmen-during-dc-protest-speech-1559345.

37. Quint Forgey, "'I'm Going to Be in Your Backyard': Trump Sons Threaten Primaries for GOP Lawmakers," *Politico*, January 6, 2021, accessed January 7, 2021, https://www.politico.com/news/2021/01/06/trump-threat-primaries-gop-lawmakers-455366.

38. Donald Trump Speech "Save America" Rally Transcript, January 6, 2021, accessed January 7, 2021, https://www.rev.com/blog/transcripts/donald-trump-speech-save-america-rally-transcript-january-6.

39. "Assault on Democracy: Sen. Josh Hawley Has Blood on His Hands in Capitol Coup Attempt," *Kansas City Star*, January 6, 2021, accessed January 7, 2021, https://www.kansascity.com/opinion/editorials/article248317375.html.

40. "Sen. Hawley's Campaign Sends Fundraising Text at Height of Capitol Siege," KMOV4 News, January 7, 2021, accessed January 7, 2021, https://www.kmov.com/news/sen-hawleys-campaign-sends-fundraising-text-at-height-of-capitol-siege/article_281a7014-507e-11eb-aead-a719246c8e1a.html.

41. Ted Barrett, Manu Raju, and Peter Nickeas, "US Capitol Secured, 4 Dead After Rioters Stormed the Halls of Congress to Block Biden's Win," CNN, January 7, 2021, accessed January 7, 2021, https://www.cnn.com/2021/01/06/politics/us-capitol-lockdown/index.html; "Today's Rampage at the Capitol, as It Happened," *New York Times*, January 6, 2021, accessed January 7, 2021, https://www.nytimes.com/live/2021/01/06/us/washington-dc-protests; "Woman Dies After Shooting in US Capitol; DC National Guard Activated After Mob Breaches Building," *Washington Post*, January 7, 2021, accessed January 7, 2021, https://www.washingtonpost.com/dc-md-va/2021/01/06/dc-protests-trump-rally-live-updates/.

42. Donald J. Trump, @realDonaldTrump, 2021, Twitter, January 6, 2021, accessed January 6, 2021, pic.twitter.com/Pm2PKV0Fp3.

43. Zeke Miller and Jill Colvin, "After Excusing Violence, Trump Acknowledges Biden Transition," Associated Press, January 7, 2021,

accessed January 7, 2021, https://apnews.com/article/f03215c31a400f815 a8f62960a430063.

44. "Mob Attack, Incited by Trump, Delays Election Certification," *New York Times*, January 7, 2021, accessed January 7, 2021, https://www .nytimes.com/live/2021/01/06/us/electoral-vote; John Wagner, Felicia Sonmez, Mike DeBonis, Karoun Demirjian, Amy B. Wang, Colby Itko-witz, and Paulina Firozi, "Pence Declares Biden Winner of the Presidential Election After Congress Finally Counts Electoral Votes," *Washington Post*, January 7, 2021, accessed January 7, 2021, https://www.washingtonpost .com/politics/2021/01/06/congress-electoral-college-vote-live-updates/.

45. Mo Brooks, @RepMoBrooks, Twitter, January 7, 2021, accessed January 7, 2021, https://twitter.com/hashtag/FakeNewsMedia?src=hashtag _click.

46. Nicholas Bogel-Burroughs and Sandra E. Garcia, "What Is Antifa, the Movement Trump Wants to Declare a Terror Group?" *New York Times*, September 28, 2020, accessed January 9, 2021, https://www.nytimes.com/ article/what-antifa-trump.html; "Who Are Antifa?" Anti-Defamation League, accessed January 9, 2021, https://www.adl.org/antifa.

47. The Constitution: Amendments 11–27.

48. Jill Colvin, "Trump Bids Farewell to Washington, Hints of Comeback," Associated Press, January 20, 2021, accessed January 20, 2021, https://apnews.com/article/biden-inauguration-joe-biden-capitol -siege-donald-trump-michael-pence-ad718c0048c341d0044c4709fb23c8 dd; Steven Harper, "Insurrection Timeline: First the Coup and Then the Cover-Up," Moyers on Democracy, January 18, 2021, accessed January 20, 2021, https://billmoyers.com/story/insurrection-timeline -first-the-coup-and-then-the-cover-up-updated/; Neal Katyal, "Trump's Final Pardons Warped Presidential Powers for His Own Benefit," *Washington Post*, January 20, 2021, accessed January 20, 2021, https:// www.washingtonpost.com/outlook/2021/01/20/trump-final-pardons -constitution/; Kevin Liptak, "Trump Departs Washington a Pariah as His Era in Power Ends," CNN, January 20, 2021, accessed January 20, 2021, https://www.cnn.com/2021/01/20/politics/donald-trump-leaves -white-house/index.html; Statement from the Press Secretary Regarding Executive Grants of Clemency, January 20, 2021, White House, accessed January 20, 2021, https://www.whitehouse.gov/briefings-statements/ statement-press-secretary-regarding-executive-grants-clemency-012021/.

49. "Biden Inauguration Live Updates: Speech Emphasizes Unity, Vows to Be 'A President for All Americans,'" *Washington Post*, January 20, 2021, accessed January 20, 2021, https://www.washingtonpost.com/politics/2021/01/20/biden-inauguration-day-live-updates/; Meg Wagner, Melissa Mahtani, Melissa Macaya, Mike Hayes, Veronica Rocha, and Fernando Alfonso, "The Inauguration of Joe Biden," CNN, January 20, 2021, accessed January 20, 2021, https://edition.cnn.com/politics/live-news/biden-harris-inauguration-day-2021.

50. Aaron Blake, "Four Takeaways from Trump's Impeachment Trial," *Washington Post*, February 13, 2021, accessed March 4, 2021, https://www.washingtonpost.com/politics/2021/02/13/takeaways-trump-impeachment-trial-final/; "Impeachment Trial: Trump Is Acquitted by the Senate," *New York Times*, February 17, 2021, accessed March 4, 2021, https://www.nytimes.com/live/2021/02/13/us/impeachment-trial; Meg Wagner, Melissa Mahtani, Melissa Macaya, and Veronica Rocha, "Donald Trump Acquitted in Second Impeachment Trial," CNN, February 13, 2021, accessed March 4, 2021, https://www.cnn.com/politics/live-news/trump-impeachment-trial-02-13-2021/.

51. "State Voting Bills Tracker 2021," February 24, 2021, Brennan Center for Justice, accessed March 4, 2021, https://www.brennancenter.org/our-work/research-reports/state-voting-bills-tracker-2021.

52. Donald Jude and Devan Cole, "Biden Signs Executive Order Expanding Voting Access," CNN, March 7, 2021, accessed March 7, 2021, https://www.cnn.com/2021/03/07/politics/voting-access-executive-order/index.html; Ella Nielsen, "House Democrats' Massive Voting Rights Bill, Explained," *Vox*, March 3, 2021, accessed March 7, 2021, https://www.vox.com/2021/3/3/22309123/house-democrats-pass-voting-rights-bill-hr1; Brett Samuels, "Biden Signs Executive Order Aimed at Increasing Voting Access," *The Hill*, March 7, 2021, accessed March 7, 2021, https://thehill.com/homenews/administration/541968-biden-to-sign-executive-order-to-increase-voting-access; Peter W. Stevenson, "Here's What H.R. 1, the House-Passed Voting Rights Bill, Would Do," *Washington Post*, March 5, 2021, accessed March 7, 2021, https://www.washingtonpost.com/politics/2021/03/05/hr1-bill-what-is-it/.

53. Gillian Brockell, "Why March 4 Matters to QAnon Extremists, Leading to Fears of Another Capitol Attack," *Washington Post*, accessed March 4, 2021; Nicole Narea, "QAnon Believers Think Trump Will Be

Inaugurated Again on March 4," *Vox*, March 3, 2021, accessed March 4, 2021, https://www.vox.com/policy-and-politics/22280323/qanon-march-trump-inaugration-conspiracy-theory-militia.

54. James Charles Cobb, *Away Down South: A History of Southern Identity* (New York: Oxford University Press, 2005); Gaines M. Foster, *Ghosts of the Confederacy: Defeat, the Lost Cause, and the Emergence of the New South, 1865 to 1913* (New York: Oxford University Press, 1987); Gary W. Gallagher and Alan T. Nolan, ed., *The Myth of the Lost Cause and Civil War History* (Bloomington: Indiana University Press, 2010); Charles Reagan Wilson, *Baptized in Blood: The Religion of the Lost Cause, 1865–1920* (Athens: University of Georgia Press, 1980).

55. Constitution of the United States.

56. Andrew B. Hall, Connor Huff, and Shiro Kuriwaki, "Wealth, Slaveownership, and Fighting for the Confederacy: An Empirical Study of the American Civil War," *American Political Science Review* 113, no. 3 (August 2019): 658–73.

57. "Party Affiliation," Gallup, accessed January 3, 2021, https://news.gallup.com/poll/15370/party-affiliation.aspx.

58. Robert Reich, "Amid Talk of Civil War, America Is Already Split—Trump Nation Has Seceded," *The Guardian*, September 27, 2020, accessed January 7, 2021, https://www.theguardian.com/commentisfree/2020/sep/27/donald-trump-american-civil-war-joe-biden-republicans-democrats-robert-reich.

Chapter Four

1. King, "Letter from Birmingham City Jail," in *A Testament of Hope*, 295.

2. Tocqueville, *Democracy in America*, 275.

3. Jefferson's "Original Rough Draught" of the Declaration of Independence, Declaring Independence: Drafting the Documents, Library of Congress, accessed December 27, 2020, https://www.loc.gov/exhibits/declara/ruffdrft.html.

4. "Consciousness of Guilt," Justipedia, accessed December 27, 2020, https://www.justipedia.com/definition/20145/consciousness-of-guilt.

5. Constitution of the United States.

6. Ibid.

7. Simon J. Gilhooley, *The Antebellum Origins of the Modern Constitution: Slavery and the Spirit of the American Founding* (New York: Cambridge University Press, 2020); Elizabeth Varon, *Disunion! The Coming of the American Civil War, 1789–1859* (Chapel Hill: University of North Carolina Press, 2008).

8. Resmaa Menakem, "Healing Your Thousand-Year-Old Trauma," *Medium*, June 7, 2018, accessed March 4, 2021, https://medium.com/@rmenakem/healing-our-thousand-year-old-trauma-d815009ae93; see also Resmaa Menakem, *My Grandmother's Hands: Racialized Trauma and the Pathway to Mending Our Hearts and Bodies* (Las Vegas, NV: Central Recovery Press, 2017), chapter 4.

9. Joy Dugruy, *Post Traumatic Slave Syndrome: America's Legacy of Enduring Injury and Healing* (Portland, OR: Joy Dugruy, 2005), 75.

10. Leon Festinger, *A Theory of Cognitive Dissonance* (Stanford, CA: Stanford University Press, 1957); Eddie Harmon-Jones, *Cognitive Dissonance: Reexamining a Pivotal Theory in Psychology*, 2nd ed. (Washington, DC: American Psychological Association, 1999).

11. Abraham Lincoln to Horace Greeley, Friday, August 22, 1862 (Clipping from August 23, 1862, *Daily National Intelligencer*, Washington, DC), Abraham Lincoln Papers: Series 2. General Correspondence. 1858–1864, Library of Congress, accessed January 3, 2021, https://www.loc.gov/resource/mal.4233400/?st=text.

12. Transcript of the Emancipation Proclamation, January 1, 1863, National Archives, accessed January 3, 2021, https://www.archives.gov/exhibits/featured-documents/emancipation-proclamation/transcript.html.

13. Abraham Lincoln, Address at the Dedication of the National Cemetery at Gettysburg, Pennsylvania [Gettysburg Address], November 19, 1863, online by Gerhard Peters and John T. Woolley, The American Presidency Project, accessed January 3, 2021, https://www.presidency.ucsb.edu/node/201980.

14. Frederick Douglass, *On Slavery and the Civil War: Selections from His Writings*, ed. Philip S. Foner (Mineola, NY: Dover, 2014), 24.

15. Eldridge Cleaver, *Soul on Ice* (New York: McGraw-Hill, 1968), 133.

16. "Text of Eisenhower's Speech at Abilene, Opening His Political Campaign," *New York Times*, June 5, 1952, accessed December 8, 2020, https://www.nytimes.com/1952/06/05/archives/text-of-eisenhowers-speech-at-abilene-opening-his-political.html.

17. Thomas Jefferson to James Madison, January 30, 1787.

18. Cole, "John Lewis Urges Attendees of Selma's 'Bloody Sunday' Commemorative March to 'Redeem the Soul of America' by Voting."

19. Constitution of the United States.

20. William J. Barber II, with Jonathan Wilson-Hargrove, *The Third Reconstruction: How a Moral Movement Is Overcoming the Politics of Division and Fear* (Boston, MA: Beacon Press, 2016), 111.

21. John Adams to Zabdiel Adams, June 21, 1776, Founders Online, accessed December 29, 2020, https://founders.archives.gov/documents/Adams/04-02-02-0011.

22. Susan Friend Harding, *The Book of Jerry Falwell: Fundamentalist Language and Politics* (Princeton, NJ: Princeton University Press, 2000); Dirk Smillie, *Falwell Inc.: Inside a Religious, Political, Educational, and Business Empire* (New York: St. Martin's Press, 2008); Michael Shawn Winters, *God's Right Hand: How Jerry Falwell Made God a Republican and Baptized the American Right* (New York: HarperOne, 2012).

23. Rufus Burrow Jr., *Martin Luther King Jr. and the Theology of Resistance* (Jefferson, NC: McFarland, 2015); Marshall Frady, *Martin Luther King Jr.: A Life* (New York: Penguin, 2002); David J. Garrow, *Bearing the Cross: Martin Luther King Jr., and the Southern Christian Leadership Conference* (New York: Harper Perennial, 1999); Martin Luther King Jr., *The Autobiography of Martin Luther King Jr.*, ed. Clayborne Carson (New York: Grand Central Publishing, 1976); Stephen B. Oates, *Let the Trumpet Sound: A Life of Martin Luther King Jr.* (New York: Harper & Row, 1982); Kevin Shird, with Nelson Malden, *The Colored Waiting Room: Empowering the Original and the New Civil Rights Movements; Conversations Between an MLK Jr. Confidant and a Modern-Day Activist* (New York: Apollo, 2018).

24. King, "Nonviolence and Racial Justice," in *A Testament of Hope*, 8.

25. Ibid., 6.

26. Susan Dunn, *Jefferson's Second Revolution: The Election Crisis of 1800 and the Triumph of Republicanism* (Boston: Houghton Mifflin, 2004); John Ferling, *Adams vs. Jefferson: The Tumultuous Election of 1800* (New York: Oxford University Press, 2004); Edward J. Larson, *A Magnificent Catastrophe: The Tumultuous Election of 1800, America's First Presidential Campaign* (New York: Free Press, 2007); Jeffrey L. Pasley, *The First Presidential Contest: 1796 and the Founding of American Democracy* (Lawrence: University Press of Kansas, 2013); Roger Sharp, *The Deadlocked Election of 1800:*

Jefferson, Burr, and the Union in the Balance (Lawrence: University Press of Kansas, 2010); Bernard Weisberger, *America Afire: Jefferson, Adams, and the Revolutionary Election of 1800* (New York: William Morrow, 2000).

27. Thomas Jefferson, Inaugural Address, March 4, 1801, online by Gerhard Peters and John T. Woolley, accessed January 3, 2021, The American Presidency Project, https://www.presidency.ucsb.edu/node/201948.

28. Egerton, *Year of Meteors*; Holt, *The Election of 1860*; Kalmoe, *With Ballots and Bullets*.

29. King, "Letter from Birmingham City Jail," in *A Testament of Hope*, 294.

30. Abraham Lincoln, "Inaugural Address," online by Gerhard Peters and John T. Woolley, accessed November 22, 2021, The American Presidency Project, https://www.presidency.ucsb.edu/node/202167.

31. Matt Stevens, "Read Joe Biden's President-Elect Acceptance Speech: Full Transcript," *New York Times*, November 9, 2020, accessed January 8, 2021, https://www.nytimes.com/article/biden-speech-transcript .html.

Chapter Five

1. John F. Kennedy, "Address of Senator John F. Kennedy Accepting the Democratic Party Nomination for the Presidency of the United States," July 15, 1960, online by Gerhard Peters and John T. Woolley, The American Presidency Project, accessed February 11, 2021, https://www .presidency.ucsb.edu/node/274679.

2. Quoted in Francis J. Bremer, *John Winthrop: America's Forgotten Founding Father* (Oxford: Oxford University Press, 2003), 218, 385.

3. John L. O'Sullivan, "The Great Nation of Futurity," *United States Democratic Review* 6 (1839): 426–30.

4. John L. O' Sullivan, "Manifest Destiny," editorial, *New York Morning News*, December 27, 1845.

5. Declaration of Independence.

6. John Quincy Adams, *An Address Delivered at the Request of a Commission of Citizens of Washington; on the Occasion of Reading the Declaration of Independence, on the Fourth of July, 1821* (Washington, DC: Davis and Force, 1821), 29.

7. Constitution of the United States.

8. President George Washington's Farewell Address.

9. Constitution of the United States.

10. Ian W. Toll, *Six Frigates: The Epic History of the Founding of the US Navy* (New York: W.W. Norton, 2006).

11. Alexander DeConde, *The Quasi-War: The Politics and Diplomacy of the Undeclared War with France, 1797–1801* (New York: Charles Scribner's Sons, 1966); William J. Phalen, *The First War of United States: The Quasi War with France 1798–1801* (Delhi, IN: Vij Books, 2019).

12. Wendell Bird, *Press and Speech Under Assault: The Early Supreme Court Justices, the Sedition Act of 1798, and the Campaign against Dissent* (New York: Oxford University Press, 2016); John C. Miller, *Crisis in Freedom: The Alien and Sedition Acts* (Boston, MA: Little, Brown, 1951); Charles Slack, *Liberty's First Crisis: Adams, Jefferson, and the Misfits Who Saved Free Speech* (New York: Atlantic Monthly Press, 2015); William Watkins, *Reclaiming the American Revolution: The Kentucky and Virginia Resolutions and Their Legacy* (New York: Palgrave Macmillan, 2004).

13. James Madison, "Political Observations," April 20, 1795, in *Letters and Other Writings of James Madison*, vol. 4 (Philadelphia: J. P. Lippincott and Co., 1865), 491.

14. Brian Brown, *Someone Is Out to Get Us: A Not So Brief History of Cold War Paranoia and Madness* (New York: Grand Central Publishing, 2019); Carey Stacey Smith and Li-Ching Hung, *The Patriot Act: Issues and Controversies* (Springfield, IL: Charles C. Thomas, 2010).

15. Paul Fryer, *Building an American Empire: The Era of Territorial and Political Expansion* (Princeton, NJ: Princeton University Press, 2017).

16. Sam W. Haynes and Christopher Morris, eds., *Manifest Destiny and Empire: American Antebellum Expansionism* (College Station: Texas A&M University Press, 2008); Frederick Merk, *Manifest Destiny and Mission in American History*, reprint ed. (Cambridge, MA: Harvard University Press, 1995); Anders Stephanson, *Manifest Destiny: American Expansion and the Empire of Right* (New York: Hill & Wang, 1995); Steven E. Woodworth, *Manifest Destinies: America's Westward Expansion and the Road to the Civil War* (New York: Alfred A. Knopf, 2010).

17. Stephen E. Ambrose, *Nothing Like It in the World: The Men Who Built the Transcontinental Railroad 1863–1869* (New York: Simon & Schuster, 2000); David Haward Bain, *Empire Express: Building the First Transcontinental Railroad* (New York: Penguin, 1999); Michael A. Hiltzik,

Iron Empires: Robber Barons, Railroads, and the Making of Modern America (Boston, MA: Houghton Mifflin Harcourt, 2020); Richard White, *Railroaded: The Transcontinentals and the Making of Modern America* (New York: W.W. Norton, 2011).

18. "Increasing Urbanization Population Distribution by City Size, 1790 to 1890," US Census Bureau, accessed February 14, 2021, https://www.census.gov/programs-surveys/sis/resources/visualizations/urbanization.html.

19. Gerald D. Nash, "The Census of 1890 and the Closing of the Frontier," *Pacific Northwest Quarterly* 71, no. 3 (July 1980): 98–100.

20. Adams, *An Address Delivered at the Request of a Commission of Citizens of Washington*, 29.

21. John Whiteclay Chambers II, *The Tyranny of Change: America in the Progressive Era, 1890–1920* (New York: St. Martin's Press, 1992); Jackson Lears, *Rebirth of a Nation: The Making of Modern America, 1877–1920* (New York: Harper Perennial, 2010); Michael McGerr, *A Fierce Discontent: The Rise and Fall of the Progressive Movement in America* (New York: Free Press, 2003); Nell Irvin Painter, *Standing at Armageddon: A Grassroots History of the Progressive Era* (New York: W.W. Norton, 1987).

22. Robert C. Bannister, *Social Darwinism: Science and Myth in Anglo-American Social Thought* (Philadelphia, PA: Temple University Press, 1979); Richard Hofstadter, *Social Darwinism in American Thought*, reprint ed. (Boston, MA: Beacon Press, 1992).

23. Suzanne Geissler, *God and Sea Power: The Influence of Religion on Alfred Thayer Mahan* (Annapolis, MD: Naval Institute Press, 2015); A. T. Mahan, *The Influence of Sea Power upon History, 1660–1783* (Boston, MA: Little, Brown, 1905); Warren Zimmermann, *First Great Triumph: How Five Americans Made Their Country a World Power* (New York: Farrar, Straus and Giroux, 2002).

24. Ray A. Billington, *The Genius of the Frontier Thesis: A Study in Historical Creativity* (San Marino, CA: Huntington Library, 1971); Tiziano Bonazzi, "Frederick Jackson Turner's Frontier Thesis and the Self-Consciousness of America," *Journal of American Studies* 27, no. 2 (August 1993): 149–71; Frederick Jackson Turner, *The Significance of the Frontier in American History*, reprint ed. (Eastford, CT: Martino Fine Books, 2014).

25. Walter F. LaFeber, *The New Empire: An Interpretation of American Expansion, 1860–1898*, 35th anniversary ed. (Ithaca, NY: Cornell University Press, 1998); Alfred W. McCoy and Francisco A. Scarano, eds., *Colonial Crucible: Empire in the Making of the Modern American State* (Madison: University of Wisconsin Press, 2009); Whitney T. Perkins, *Denial of Empire: The United States and Its Dependencies* (Leiden, NL: A. W. Sythoff, 1962); Julius William Pratt, *Expansionists of 1898: The Acquisition of Hawaii and the Spanish Islands* (Baltimore, MD: Johns Hopkins Press, 1936); William Appleman Williams, *The Roots of the Modern American Empire: A Study of the Growth and Shaping of Social Consciousness in a Marketplace Society* (New York: Random House, 1969).

26. G. J. A. O'Toole, *The Spanish War: An American Epic 1898* (New York: W.W. Norton, 1984); Evan Thomas, *The War Lovers: Roosevelt, Lodge, Hearst, and the Rush to Empire, 1898* (New York: Back Bay Books, 2010).

27. Greg Jones, *Honor in the Dust: Theodore Roosevelt, War in the Philippines, and the Rise and Fall of America's Imperial Dream* (New York: New American Library, 2012); Lester D. Langley, *The Banana Wars: United States Intervention in the Caribbean, 1898–1934* (Lexington: University Press of Kentucky, 1983); Brian McAllister, *The Philippine War, 1899–1902* (Lawrence: University of Kansas Press, 2000); Stuart Creighton Miller, *Benevolent Assimilation: The American Conquest of the Philippines, 1899–1903* (New Haven, CT: Yale University Press, 1982); David J. Silbey, *The Boxer Rebellion and the Great Game in China: A History* (New York: Hill & Wang, 2012); David J. Silbey, *A War of Frontier and Empire: The Philippine-American War, 1899–1902* (New York: Hill & Wang, 2008).

28. Senator Albert Beveridge, "In Support of an American Empire," January 9, 1900, *Congressional Record*, Fifty-Sixth Congress, First Session, XXXIII (Washington, DC: United States Government Printing Office, 1900), 704–11.

29. Rudyard Kipling, "The White Man's Burden," in Peter Washington, ed., *Kipling: Poems* (New York: Alfred A. Knopf, 2007), 96–98.

30. Circular—Telegram, Department of State, Washington, March 12, 1913, *Papers Relating to the Foreign Relations of the United States, With the Address of the President to Congress, 1913*, accessed January 29, 2021, https://history.state.gov/historicaldocuments/frus1913/d7.

31. Woodrow Wilson to William Tyrrell, November 2, 1913, Wilson Papers, Woodrow Wilson Presidential Library, accessed February 5, 2021, http://presidentwilson.org/items/show/29606.

32. Woodrow Wilson, "Address to a Joint Session of Congress Requesting a Declaration of War Against Germany," April 2, 1917, online by Gerhard Peters and John T. Woolley, The American Presidency Project, accessed February 19, 2021, https://www.presidency.ucsb.edu/node/207620.

33. Woodrow Wilson, "Address to a Joint Session of Congress on the Conditions of Peace," January 8, 1918, online by Gerhard Peters and John T. Woolley, The American Presidency Project, accessed February 19, 2021, https://www.presidency.ucsb.edu/node/206651.

34. John Keegan, *The First World War* (New York: Vintage, 2012); G. J. Meyer, *A World Undone: The Story of the Great War, 1914–1918* (New York: Delacorte Press, 2006); Adam Tooze, *The Deluge: The Great War, America and the Remaking of the Global Order, 1916–1931* (New York: Penguin, 2014).

35. Franklin D. Roosevelt, "Statement on the Atlantic Charter Meeting with Prime Minister Churchill," August 14, 1941, online by Gerhard Peters and John T. Woolley, The American Presidency Project, accessed February 19, 2021, https://www.presidency.ucsb.edu/node/209814.

36. Harry S. Truman, "Special Message to the Congress on Greece and Turkey: The Truman Doctrine," March 12, 1947, online by Gerhard Peters and John T. Woolley, The American Presidency Project, accessed February 5, 2021, https://www.presidency.ucsb.edu/node/232818.

37. Dwight D. Eisenhower, "Special Message to the Congress on the Situation in the Middle East," January 5, 1957, online by Gerhard Peters and John T. Woolley, The American Presidency Project, accessed February 5, 2021, https://www.presidency.ucsb.edu/node/233161.

38. John F. Kennedy, "Inaugural Address," January 20, 1961, online by Gerhard Peters and John T. Woolley, The American Presidency Project, accessed February 5, 2021, https://www.presidency.ucsb.edu/node/234470.

39. Lyndon B. Johnson, "Remarks upon Signing Joint Resolution of the Maintenance of Peace and Security in Southeast Asia," August 10, 1964, online by Gerhard Peters and John T. Woolley, The American Presidency Project, accessed February 19, 2021, https://www.presidency.ucsb.edu/node/242073.

40. Ronald Reagan, "Remarks at the Annual Convention of the National Association of Evangelicals in Orlando, Florida," March 8, 1983, online by Gerhard Peters and John T. Woolley, The American Presidency Project, accessed February 19, 2021, https://www.presidency.ucsb.edu/node/262885.

41. George W. Bush, "Address Before a Joint Session of the Congress on the State of the Union," January 29, 2002, online by Gerhard Peters and John T. Woolley, The American Presidency Project, accessed February 19, 2021, https://www.presidency.ucsb.edu/node/211864.

42. Barack Obama, "Remarks in West Lafayette, Indiana," July 16, 2008, online by Gerhard Peters and John T. Woolley, The American Presidency Project, accessed February 19, 2021, https://www.presidency.ucsb.edu/node/278156.

43. Barack Obama, "Inaugural Address," January 20, 2009, online by Gerhard Peters and John T. Woolley, The American Presidency Project, accessed February 19, 2021, https://www.presidency.ucsb.edu/node/217053.

44. Dwight D. Eisenhower, "Farewell Radio and Television Address to the American People," January 17, 1961, online by Gerhard Peters and John T. Woolley, The American Presidency Project, accessed February 19, 2021, https://www.presidency.ucsb.edu/node/234856.

45. Madison, "Federalist No. 10," in *The Federalist Papers*, 72–73.

46. Walter McDougall, *Promised Land, Crusader State: The American Encounter with the World since 1776* (New York: Houghton Mifflin Harcourt, 1997), 3.

Chapter Six

1. Laurel Thatcher Ulrich, "Vertuous Women Found: New England Ministerial Literature, 1668–1735," *American Quarterly* 28, no. 1 (Spring 1976): 20–40.

2. Ibid., 20.

3. Laurel Thatcher Ulrich, *Well-Behaved Women Seldom Make History* (New York: Vintage Books, 2007), xv.

4. Ibid.

5. Ibid., xix.

6. Ulrich, "Vertuous Women."

7. Ibid., 40.

8. Bremer, *John Winthrop*, 179.

9. King, "I Have a Dream," in *A Testament of Hope*, 219.

10. Thomas Carlyle, *On Heroes, Hero-Worship, and the Heroic in History* (London: Chapman & Hall, 1840), 3.

11. Ibid., 16–17.

12. Ibid., 54.

13. Ibid., 55.

14. Stephen David, Patrick Reams, Keith Palmer, Randy Counsman, Ed Fields, et al., *The Men Who Built America* (Santa Monica, CA: A & E Television Networks, 2012), DVD.

15. *The Men Who Built America*, IMDB, accessed March 7, 2021, https://www.imdb.com/title/tt2167393/.

16. Elliot J. Gorn, *Mother Jones: The Most Dangerous Woman in America* (New York: Hill & Wang, 2001); Mary Harris Jones, *Autobiography of Mother Jones*, ed. Mary Field Parton, reprint ed. (Mineola, NY: Dover, 2004).

17. Jones, *Autobiography of Mother Jones*, 7–8.

18. Ibid., 6–7.

19. Ibid., 20–21.

20. Ibid., 27.

21. Studs Terkel, *Working: People Talk about What They Do All Day and How They Feel about What They Do* (New York: Pantheon, 1974), 2.

22. Rick Atkinson, *The British Are Coming: The War for America, Lexington to Princeton, 1775–1777* (New York: Henry Holt, 2019); Bob Drury and Tom Calvin, *Valley Forge* (New York: Simon & Schuster, 2018); David Hackett Fischer, *Paul Revere's Ride* (New York: Oxford University Press, 1994); Charles Patrick Neimeyer, *America Goes to War: A Social History of the Continental Army* (New York: New York University, 1996).

23. Ricardo A. Herrera, *For Liberty and the Republic: The American Citizen as Soldier, 1775–1861* (New York: New York University, 2015).

24. Emily J. Arendt, "'Ladies Going about for Money': Female Volunteer Associations and Civil Consciousness in the American Revolution," *Journal of the Early Republic* 34, no. 2 (Summer 2014): 157–86; Carol Berkin, *Revolutionary Mothers: Women in the Struggle for America's Independence* (New York: Vintage Books, 2006); Susan Casey, *Women Heroes of the American Revolution: 20 Stories of Espionage, Sabotage, Defiance, and*

Rescue (Chicago: Chicago Review Press, 2017); Barbara B. Oberg, ed., *Women in the American Revolution: Gender, Politics, and the Domestic World* (Charlottesville: University of Virginia Press, 2019); Sudie Doggett Wike, *Women in the American Revolution* (Jefferson, NC: McFarland, 2018).

25. Douglas R. Egerton, *Death or Liberty: African Americans and Revolutionary America* (New York: Oxford University Press, 2009); Alan Gilbert, *Black Patriots and Loyalists: Fighting for Emancipation in the War for Independence* (Chicago: University of Chicago Press, 2012); John U. Rees, *"They Were Good Soldiers": African-Americans Serving in the Continental Army, 1775–1783* (Warwick, UK: Helion, 2019); Judith L. Van Buskirk, *Standing in Their Own Light: African American Patriots in the American Revolution* (Norman: University of Oklahoma Press, 2017).

26. Wilson, "Address to a Joint Session of Congress Requesting a Declaration of War Against Germany."

27. D-day Statement to Soldiers, Sailors, and Airmen of the Allied Expeditionary Force, 6/44, Collection DDE-EPRE: Eisenhower, Dwight D: Papers, Pre-Presidential, 1916–1952; Dwight D. Eisenhower Library; National Archives and Records Administration, accessed April 24, 2021, https://www.ourdocuments.gov/doc.php?flash=false&doc=75#.

28. The Vietnam Veterans Memorial, The Wall-USA, accessed March 27, 2021, http://thewall-usa.com/.

29. Michel Eugene Santos, The Vietnam Veterans Memorial, The Wall-USA, accessed March 27, 2021, http://thewall-usa.com/guest.asp?recid=45564.

30. James Ferro, The Vietnam Veterans Memorial, The Wall-USA, accessed March 27, 2021, http://thewall-usa.com/guest.asp?recid=15986.

31. Leonard Picanso, The Vietnam Veterans Memorial, The Wall-USA, accessed March 27, 2021, http://thewall-usa.com/guest.asp?recid=40707.

32. The Vietnam Veterans Memorial, The Wall-USA, accessed March 27, 2021, http://thewall-usa.com/search.asp?1=1&name=&lname=&hometown=&homestate=&service=&age=&ssn=&ranknum=&dobmonth=12&dobday=3&dobyear=&casmonth=&casday=&casyear=&searchpanel=&casualtiesdate=&birthdaydate=12%2F3%2F&searchwoman=&casmonthfrom=&casdayfrom=&casyearfrom=&casmonthto=&casdayto=&casyearto=.

Chapter Seven

1. James Bryce, *The American Commonwealth*, vol. 1, *The National Government* (London: Macmillan, 1888), 14.

2. James Bryce, *The American Commonwealth*, vol. 3, *Public Opinion— Illustrations and Reflections Social Institutions* (London: Macmillan, 1888), 118.

3. Ibid., 328.

4. Rosa Parks, with Jim Haskins, *Rosa Parks: My Story* (New York: Dial Books, 1992), 2.

5. Ibid., 2–3.

6. Ibid., 2.

7. Roxanne Dunbar-Ortiz, *An Indigenous Peoples' History of the United States* (Boston, MA: Beacon Press, 2014); Charles C. Mann, *1491: New Revelations of the Americas Before Columbus*, 2nd ed. (New York: Vintage Books, 2006); Jake Page, *In the Hands of the Great Spirit: The 20,000-Year History of American Indians* (New York: Free Press, 2004).

8. William M. Fenton, *The Great Law and the Longhouse: A Political History of the Iroquois Confederacy* (Norman: University of Oklahoma Press, 1998); Jacobs, "The Iroquois Great Law of Peace and the United States Constitution"; Christopher Vecsey, "The Story and Structure of the Iroquois Confederacy," *Journal of the American Academy of Religion* 54, no. 1 (Spring 1986): 79–106.

9. Donald A. Grinde Jr. and Bruce E. Johansen, *Exemplar of Liberty: Native America and the Evolution of Democracy* (Los Angeles, CA: American Indian Studies Center, 1991); Donald A. Grinde Jr. and Bruce E. Johansen, "Sauce for the Goose: Demand and Definitions for 'Proof' Regarding the Iroquois and Democracy," *William and Mary Quarterly* 53, no. 3 (July 1996): 621–36; Kirke Kickingbird and Lynn Kickingbird, *Indians and the US Constitution: A Forgotten Legacy* (Washington, DC: Institute for the Development of Indian Law, 1987); Philip A. Levy, "Exemplars of Taking Liberties: The Iroquois Influence Thesis and the Problem of Evidence," *William and Mary Quarterly* 53, no. 3 (July 1996): 588–604; Donald S. Lutz, "The Iroquois Confederation Constitution: An Analysis," *Publius: The Journal of Federalism* 28, no. 2 (Spring 1998): 99–127; Samuel B. Payne Jr., "The Iroquois League, the Articles of Confederation, and the Constitution," *William and Mary Quarterly* 53, no. 3 (July 1996): 605–20;

William A. Starna and George R. Hamell, "History and the Burden of Proof: The Case of Iroquois Influence on the U.S. Constitution," *New York History* 77, no. 4 (October 1996): 427–52; Jerry D. Stubben, "The Indigenous Influence Theory of American Democracy," *Social Science Quarterly* 81, no. 3 (September 2000): 716–31; Elisabeth Tooker, "The United States Constitution and the Iroquois League," *Ethnohistory* 35, no. 4 (Autumn 1988): 305–36.

10. US Congress, *A Concurrent Resolution to Acknowledge the Contribution of the Iroquois Confederacy of Nations to the Development of the United States Constitution and to Reaffirm the Continuing Government-to-Government Relationship between Indian Tribes and the United States Established in the Constitution*, 100th Cong. 2nd sess., 1988, H. Con. Res. 331.

11. Peter Cozzens, *Tecumseh and the Prophet: The Shawnee Brothers Who Defied a Nation* (New York: Knopf, 2020); Allan W. Eckert, *A Sorrow in Our Heart: The Life of Tecumseh* (New York: Bantam, 1992); John Sugden, *Tecumseh: A Life* (New York: Holt, 1999).

12. Stephen E. Ambrose, *Crazy Horse and Custer: The Parallel Lives of Two American Warriors* (New York: Anchor Books, 2014); Bob Drury and Tom Clavin, *The Heart of Everything That Is: The Untold Story of Red Cloud, an American Legend*, revised ed. (New York: Simon & Schuster, 2013); Wilbur R. Jacobs, "The Indian and the Frontier in American History—A Need for Revision," *Western Historical Quarterly* 4, no. 1 (January 1973): 43–56; Alvin M. Josephy, *The Patriot Chiefs: A Chronicle of American Indian Resistance*, revised ed. (New York: Penguin, 1993); Kent Nerburn, *Chief Joseph and the Flight of the Nez Perce: The Untold Story of an American Tragedy* (New York: HarperOne, 2009); Jeffrey Ostler, *Surviving Genocide: Native Nations and the United States from the American Revolution to Bleeding Kansas* (New Haven, CT: Yale University Press, 2020); Edward R. Sweeney, *From Cochise to Geronimo: The Chiricahua Apaches, 1874–1886* (Norman: University of Oklahoma Press, 2012); Robert Utley, *Sitting Bull: The Life and Times of an American Patriot* (New York: Holt, 2008).

13. Patricia Nelson Limerick, *The Legacy of Conquest: The Unbroken Past of the American West* (New York: W.W. Norton, 2011); Merk, *Manifest Destiny and Mission in American History;* Anders Stephanson, *Manifest Destiny: American Expansion and the Empire of Right* (New York: Hill & Wang, 1995); Claudio Saunt, *Unworthy Republic: The Dispossession of Native Americans and the Road to Indian Territory* (New York: W.W. Norton, 2020).

14. Dennis Banks, with Richard Erdoes, *Ojibwa Warrior: Dennis Banks and the Rise of the American Indian Movement* (Norman: University of Oklahoma Press, 2011); Richard A. Grounds, George E. Tinker, and David E. Wilkins, eds., *Native Voices: American Indian Identity and Resistance* (Lawrence: University Press of Kansas, 2003); Peter Matthiessen, *In the Spirit of Crazy Horse: The Story of Leonard Peltier and the FBI's War on the American Indian Movement* (New York: Penguin, 1992).

15. Resolution Adopted by the General Assembly, September 13, 2007 [without reference to a Main Committee (A/61/L.67 and Add.1)], 61/295 United Nations Declaration on the Rights of Indigenous Peoples, accessed May 5, 2021, https://www.un.org/development/desa/indigenouspeoples/wp-content/uploads/sites/19/2018/11/UNDRIP_E_web.pdf.

16. United Nations Department of Economic and Social Affairs, Indigenous Peoples, *United Nations Declaration on the Rights of Indigenous Peoples*, accessed May 5, 2021, https://www.un.org/development/desa/indigenouspeoples/declaration-on-the-rights-of-indigenous-peoples.html.

17. Nick Estes, *Our History Is the Future: Standing Rock versus the Dakota Access Pipeline, and the Long Tradition of Indigenous Resistance* (New York: Verso, 2019); Nick Estes, *Standing with Standing Rock: Voices from the #NoDAPL Movement* (Minneapolis: University of Minnesota Press, 2019); Leanne Betasamosake Simpson, *As We Have Always Done: Indigenous Freedom through Radical Resistance* (Minneapolis: University of Minnesota Press, 2020).

18. Kristen Holmes and Gregory Wallace, "Biden Administration Will Not Shut Down Dakota Access Pipeline during Environmental Review, DOJ Lawyer Tells Court," CNN, April 9, 2021, accessed May 12, 2021, https://www.cnn.com/2021/04/09/politics/dakota-access-pipeline-biden-administration/index.html; Stephanie Kelly and Devika Kumar, "Explainer: The Dakota Access Pipeline Faces Possible Closure," Reuters, May 4, 2021, accessed May 12, 2021, https://www.reuters.com/business/energy/dakota-access-pipeline-faces-possible-closure-2021-05-04/; "US Won't Shut Dakota Access Pipe amid New Environmental Review," *Bloomberg Law*, April 9, 2021, accessed May 12, 2021, https://news.bloomberglaw.com/environment-and-energy/u-s-wont-announce-dakota-access-shutdown-tribal-advocate-says.

19. William Shakespeare, *Hamlet*, eds. Barbara A. Mowat and Paul Werstine (New York: Washington Square Press, 1992), 127.

20. Dylan Thomas, *Selected Poems, 1934–1952* (New York: New Directions, 2003), 122.

21. Yolanda Sangweni, "Toni Morrison Breaks Down Racism on 'Colbert,' Admits She Recently Read 'Beloved' for the First Time," *Essence,* November 21, 2014, accessed April 30, 2021, https://www.essence.com/news/toni-morrison-colbert-recently-read-beloved-first-time/.

22. Dorothy Sue Coble, Linda Gordon, and Astrid Henry, *Feminism Unfinished: A Short, Surprising History of American Women's Movements* (New York: W.W. Norton, 2014); Dorothy Sue Coble, *For the Many: American Feminists and the Global Fight for Democratic Equality* (Princeton, NJ: Princeton University Press, 2021); Annelise Orleck, *Rethinking American Women's Activism* (New York: Routledge, 2015); Tetrault, *The Myth of Seneca Falls.*

23. Carl Wittman, *The Gay Manifesto* (New York: The Red Butterfly, 1969), 4, accessed May 21, 2021, http://www.againstequality.org/files/refugees_from_amerika_a_gay_manifesto_1969.pdf.

24. Ibid., 5.

25. Michael Bronski, *A Queer History of the United States* (Boston, MA: Beacon Press, 2011); Eric Cervini, *The Deviant's War: The Homosexual vs. the United States of America* (New York: Farrar, Straus, and Giroux, 2020); Lillian Faderman, *The Gay Revolution: The Story of the Struggle* (New York: Simon & Schuster, 2015); Eric Marcus, *Making Gay History: The Half Century Fight for Lesbian and Gay Equal Rights* (New York: Harper Perennial, 2002); Susan Stryker, *Transgender History: The Roots of Today's Revolution,* 2nd ed. (New York: Seal Press, 2017); Matthew Todd, *Pride: The Story of the LGBTQ Equality Movement* (Richmond, CA: Weldon Owen, 2020).

26. Susan M. Schweik, *The Ugly Laws: Disability in Public* (New York: New York University Press, 2009), 55–56.

27. Laurann Figg and Jane Ferrell-Beck, "Amputation in the Civil War: Physical and Social Dimensions," *Journal of the History of Medicine and Allied Sciences* 48, no. 4 (October 1993): 454–75.

28. Edwin Black, *War Against the Weak: Eugenics and America's Campaign to Create a Master Race* (Washington, DC: Dialog Press, 2003); Thomas C. Leonard, *Illiberal Reformers: Race, Eugenics, and American Economics in the Progressive Era,* reprint ed. (Princeton, NJ: Princeton University Press, 2017); Daniel Okrent, *The Guarded Gate: Bigotry, Eugenics and the Law That Kept Two Generations of Jews, Italians, and Other European*

Immigrants Out of America (New York: Scribner, 2019); Christine Rosen, *Preaching Eugenics: Religious Leaders and the American Eugenics Movement* (New York: Oxford University Press, 2004).

29. Elizabeth Catte, *Pure America: Eugenics and the Making of Modern Virginia* (Cleveland, OH: Belt Publishing, 2021); Adam Cohen, *Imbeciles: The Supreme Court, American Eugenics, and the Sterilization of Carrie Buck* (New York: Penguin, 2016); Stefan Kuhl, *The Nazi Connection: Eugenics, American Racism, and German National Socialism* (New York: Oxford University Press, 1994); Paul A. Lombardo, *Three Generations, No Imbeciles: Eugenics, the Supreme Court, and Buck v. Bell* (Baltimore, MD: Johns Hopkins University Press, 2010); James Q. Whitman, *Hitler's American Model: The United States and the Making of Nazi Race Law* (Princeton, NJ: Princeton University Press, 2017).

30. Allan Brinkley, *Franklin Delano Roosevelt* (New York: Oxford University Press, 2009); Robert Dallek, *Franklin D. Roosevelt: A Political Life*, reprint ed. (New York: Penguin, 2017); Hugh Gregory Gallagher, *FDR's Splendid Deception: The Moving Story of Roosevelt's Massive Disability—And the Intense Efforts to Conceal It from the Public*, 3rd ed. (St. Petersburg, FL: Vandamere Press, 1999); Jean Edward Smith, *FDR* (New York: Random House, 2007); James Tobin, *The Man He Became: How FDR Defied Polio to Win the Presidency* (New York: Simon & Schuster, 2013).

31. David Oshinsky, *Polio: An American Story* (New York: Oxford University Press, 2005).

32. Dorothy Herman, *Helen Keller: A Life* (Chicago: University of Chicago Press, 1999); Helen Keller, *The Complete Story of My Life* (Orinda, CA: SeaWolf Press, 2020); Helen Keller, *The World I Live In*, Roger Shattuck, ed. (New York: New York Review Books, 2003); Kim E. Nielsen, *The Radical Lives of Helen Keller* (New York: New York University Press, 2004).

33. Lennard J. Davis, *Enabling Acts: The Hidden Story of How the Americans with Disabilities Act Gave the Largest US Minority Its Rights* (Boston, MA: Beacon Press, 2015); Paul K. Longmore and Lauri Umansky, eds., *The New Disability History: American Perspectives* (New York: New York University Press, 2001); Kim E. Nielsen, *A Disability History of the United States* (Boston, MA: Beacon Press, 2012).

34. Lerone Bennett Jr., "What's in a Name? Negro vs. Afro-American vs. Black," *Ebony* 23 (November 1967): 54.

35. William Shakespeare, *Romeo and Juliet*, ed. Cederic Watts (Hertfordshire, UK: Wordsworth, 2000), 59.

36. Declaration of Independence; Report of the Woman's Rights Convention, held at Seneca Falls, New York.

37. Emma Lazarus, "The New Colossus," November 2, 1883, National Park Service, accessed May 6, 2021, https://www.nps.gov/stli/learn/history culture/colossus.htm.

38. Ibram X. Kendi, *How to Be an Antiracist* (New York: One World, 2019); Erika Lee, *America for Americans: A History of Xenophobia in the United States* (New York: Basic Books, 2019).

39. Richard Bushman, Neil Harris, David Rothman, Barbara Miller Solomon, and Stephan Thernstrom, eds., *Uprooted Americans: Essays to Honor Oscar Handlin* (Boston, MA: Little, Brown, 1979); Donna R. Gabaccia and Vicki L. Ruiz, "Migrations and Destinations: Reflections on the Histories of US Immigrant Women," *Journal of American Ethnic History* 26, no. 1 (Fall 2006): 3–19; Oscar Handlin, *The Uprooted: The Epic Story of the Great Migrations That Made the American People*, 2nd ed. (Philadelphia: University of Philadelphia Press, 2002); Paul Spickard, *Race and Immigration in the United States: New Histories* (London: Routledge, 2011); Ronald Takaki, *Different Mirror: A History of Multicultural America* (New York: Back Bay Books, 2008).

40. Sarah Coleman, *The Walls Within: The Politics of Immigration in Modern America* (Princeton, NJ: Princeton University Press, 2021); Debra L. DeLaet, *US Immigration Policy in an Age of Rights* (Westport, CT: Praeger, 2000); Louis DeSipio and Rodolfe O. De La Garza, *US Immigration in the Twenty-First Century: Making Americans, Remaking America* (London: Routledge, 2015); Michael C. LeMay, *US Immigration Policy, Ethnicity, and Religion in American History* (Westport, CT: Praeger, 2018).

41. David Dinkins, with Peter Knobler, *A Mayor's Life: Governing New York's Gorgeous Mosaic* (New York: Public Affairs, 2013).

Chapter Eight

1. *To Tell the Truth* on the Web, accessed June 6, 2021, http://www.ttt-tontheweb.com/; *To Tell the Truth*, US Game Shows Wiki, accessed June 6, 2021, https://gameshows.fandom.com/wiki/To_Tell_the_Truth.

2. King, "I Have a Dream," in *A Testament of Hope*, 219.

3. Constitution of the United States.

4. Richard Langworth, ed., *Churchill by Himself: The Definitive Collection of Quotations* (London: Ebury Press, 2008), 574.

5. The *Economist* Intelligence Unit, *Democracy Index 2006* (London: The *Economist* Intelligence Unit, 2006); The *Economist* Intelligence Unit, *Democracy Index 2008* (London: The *Economist* Intelligence Unit, 2008); The *Economist* Intelligence Unit, *Democracy Index 2010: Democracy in Retreat* (London: The *Economist* Intelligence Unit, 2010); The *Economist* Intelligence Unit, *Democracy Index 2012: Democracy at a Standstill* (London: The *Economist* Intelligence Unit, 2013); *Democracy Index 2014: Democracy and Its Discontents* (London: The *Economist* Intelligence Unit, 2015); The *Economist* Intelligence Unit, *Democracy Index 2016: Revenge of the "Deplorables"* (London: The *Economist* Intelligence Unit, 2017); The *Economist* Intelligence Unit, *Democracy Index 2018: Me Too? Political Participation, Protest and Democracy* (London: The *Economist* Intelligence Unit, 2019); The *Economist* Intelligence Unit, *Democracy Index 2020: In Sickness and in Health?* (London: The *Economist* Intelligence Unit, 2021).

6. Rachel Bade, Ryan Lizza, Eugene Daniels, and Tara Palmer, "*Politico* Playbook: McConnell Takes on the 1619 Project," *Politico*, April 30, 2021, accessed June 7, 2021, https://www.politico.com/newsletters/playbook/2021/04/30/mcconnell-takes-on-the-1619-project-492664; Catie Edmondson, "McConnell Attacks Biden Rule's Antiracism Focus, Calling It 'Divisive,'" *New York Times*, April 30, 2021, accessed June 7, 2021, https://www.nytimes.com/2021/04/30/us/politics/mitch-mcconnell-1619-project.html; Tripp Gabriel and Dana Goldstein, "Disputing Racism's Reach, Republicans Rattle American Schools," *New York Times*, June 1, 2021, accessed June 7, 2021, https://www.nytimes.com/2021/06/01/us/politics/critical-race-theory.html; Thomas Moore, "UNC–Chapel Hill Denies Tenure to 1619 Project Author Nikole Hannah-Jones," *The Hill*, May 19, 2021, accessed June 7, 2021, https://thehill.com/homenews/media/554439-unc-chapel-hill-denies-tenure-to-1619-project-author-nikole-hannah-jones; Sean Murphy, "Oklahoma Governor Signs Ban on Teaching Critical Race Theory," ABC News, May 7, 2021, accessed June 7, 2021, https://abcnews.go.com/US/wireStory/oklahoma-governor-signs-ban-teaching-critical-race-theory-77564832; Juan Perez Jr., "Antiracism Teaching Ban Divides Oklahoma Ahead of Tulsa Massacre Centennial," *Politico*, May 5, 2021, accessed June 7, 2021, https://www.politico

.com/news/2021/05/25/antiracism-teaching-ban-oklahoma-490159; Katie
Robertson, "Nikole Hannah-Jones Denied Tenure at University of North
Carolina," *New York Times*, May 19, 2021, accessed June 7, 2021, https://
www.nytimes.com/2021/05/19/business/media/nikole-hannah-jones-unc
.html; Kathryn Schumaker, "What Is Critical Race Theory and Why Did
Oklahoma Just Ban It? *Washington Post*, May 19, 2021, accessed June
7, 2021, https://www.washingtonpost.com/outlook/2021/05/19/what-
is-critical-race-theory-why-did-oklahoma-just-ban-it/; Valerie Strauss,
"Why Republican Efforts to Ban the 1619 Project from Classrooms Are So
Misguided," *Washington Post*, April 7, 2021, accessed June 7, 2021, https://
www.washingtonpost.com/education/2021/04/07/why-republican-efforts
-to-ban-1619-project-classrooms-are-so-misguided/.

SUGGESTED READINGS

Adams, John. *The Revolutionary Writings of John Adams.* Ed. C. Bradley Thompson. Indianapolis, IN: Liberty Fund, 2001.

Amar, Akhil Reed. *America's Constitution: A Biography.* New York: Random House, 2005.

Ambrose, Stephen E. *Crazy Horse and Custer: The Parallel Lives of Two American Warriors.* New York: Anchor Books, 2014.

———. *Nothing Like It in the World: The Men Who Built the Transcontinental Railroad 1863–1869.* New York: Simon & Schuster, 2000.

Armitage, David. *The Declaration of Independence: A Global History.* Cambridge, MA: Harvard University Press, 2007.

Atkinson, Rick. *The British Are Coming: The War for America, Lexington to Princeton, 1775–1777.* New York: Henry Holt, 2019.

Bain, David Haward. *Empire Express: Building the First Transcontinental Railroad.* New York: Penguin, 1999.

Banks, Dennis, with Richard Erdoes. *Ojibwa Warrior: Dennis Banks and the Rise of the American Indian Movement.* Norman: University of Oklahoma Press, 2011.

Bannister, Robert C. *Social Darwinism: Science and Myth in Anglo-American Social Thought.* Philadelphia, PA: Temple University Press, 1979.

Barber, William J., II, with Jonathan Wilson-Hargrove. *The Third Reconstruction: How a Moral Movement Is Overcoming the Politics of Division and Fear.* Boston, MA: Beacon Press, 2016.

Bass, Bernard M. *Leadership and Performance Beyond Expectations.* New York: The Free Press, 1985.

Bennett, Lerone, Jr. *Before the Mayflower: A History of the Negro in America, 1619–1962.* Chicago: Johnson Publishing, 1962.

Berkin, Carol. *Revolutionary Mothers: Women in the Struggle for America's Independence.* New York: Vintage Books, 2006.

Billington, Ray A. *The Genius of the Frontier Thesis: A Study in Historical Creativity.* San Marino, CA: Huntington Library, 1971.

Bird, Wendell. *Press and Speech Under Assault: The Early Supreme Court Justices, the Sedition Act of 1798, and the Campaign against Dissent.* New York: Oxford University Press, 2016.

Black, Edwin. *War Against the Weak: Eugenics and America's Campaign to Create a Master Race.* Washington, DC: Dialog Press, 2003.

Bobbio, Norberto. *Thomas Hobbes and the Natural Law Tradition.* Trans. Daniela Gobetti. Chicago: University of Chicago Press, 1993.

Bowen, Catherine Drinker. *Miracle at Philadelphia: The Story of the Constitutional Convention, May–September 1787.* New York: Back Bay Books, 1986.

Brands, H.W. *The First American: The Life and Times of Benjamin Franklin.* New York: Anchor Books, 2002.

Bremer, Francis J. *John Winthrop: America's Forgotten Founding Father.* Oxford: Oxford University Press, 2003.

Brinkley, Allan. *Franklin Delano Roosevelt.* New York: Oxford University Press, 2009.

Bronski, Michael. *A Queer History of the United States.* Boston, MA: Beacon Press, 2011.

Brown, Brian. *Someone Is Out to Get Us: A Not So Brief History of Cold War Paranoia and Madness.* New York: Grand Central Publishing, 2019.

Bryce, James. *The American Commonwealth.* 3 vols. London: Macmillan, 1888.

Burns, James MacGregor. *Leadership.* New York: Harper & Row, 1978.

Burrow, Rufus, Jr. *Martin Luther King, Jr., and the Theology of Resistance.* Jefferson, NC: McFarland, 2015.

Bushman, Richard, Neil Harris, David Rothman, Barbara Miller Solomon, and Stephan Thernstrom, eds. *Uprooted Americans: Essays to Honor Oscar Handlin.* Boston, MA: Little, Brown, 1979.

Casey, Susan. *Women Heroes of the American Revolution: 20 Stories of Espionage, Sabotage, Defiance, and Rescue.* Chicago: Chicago Review Press, 2017.

Catte, Elizabeth. *Pure America: Eugenics and the Making of Modern Virginia.* Cleveland, OH: Belt Publishing, 2021.

Cervini, Eric. *The Deviant's War: The Homosexual vs. the United States of America.* New York: Farrar, Straus and Giroux, 2020.

Chambers, John Whiteclay, II. *The Tyranny of Change: America in the Progressive Era, 1890-1920.* New York: St. Martin's Press, 1992.

Chernnow, Ron. *Washington: A Life.* New York: Penguin Books, 2010.

Coates, Ta-Nehisi. *We Were Eight Years in Power: An American Tragedy.* New York: BCP Literary, 2017.

Cobb, James Charles. *Away Down South: A History of Southern Identity.* New York: Oxford University Press, 2005.

Coble, Dorothy Sue, Linda Gordon, and Astrid Henry. *Feminism Unfinished: A Short, Surprising History of American Women's Movements.* New York: W.W. Norton, 2014.

Coble, Dorothy Sue. *For the Many: American Feminists and the Global Fight for Democratic Equality.* Princeton, NJ: Princeton University Press, 2021.

Cohen, Adam. *Imbeciles: The Supreme Court, American Eugenics, and the Sterilization of Carrie Buck.* New York: Penguin, 2016.

Coleman, Sarah. *The Walls Within: The Politics of Immigration in Modern America.* Princeton, NJ: Princeton University Press, 2021.

Cooper, Kody W. *Thomas Hobbes and the Natural Law.* Notre Dame, IN: University of Notre Dame Press, 2018.

Cozzens, Peter. *Tecumseh and the Prophet: The Shawnee Brothers Who Defied a Nation.* New York: Knopf, 2020.

Cranston, Maurice. *The Solitary Self: Jean-Jacques Rousseau in Exile and Adversity.* Chicago: University of Chicago Press, 1997.

Dallek, Robert. *Franklin D. Roosevelt: A Political Life.* Reprint ed. New York: Penguin, 2017.

Damrosch, Leopold. *Jean-Jacques Rousseau: Restless Genius.* Boston, MA: Houghton Mifflin, 2005.

Davis, Lennard J. *Enabling Acts: The Hidden Story of How the Americans with Disabilities Act Gave the Largest US Minority Its Rights.* Boston, MA: Beacon Press, 2015.

DeConde, Alexander. *The Quasi-War: The Politics and Diplomacy of the Undeclared War with France, 1797–1801*. New York: Charles Scribner's Sons, 1966.

DeLaet, Debra L. *US Immigration Policy in an Age of Rights*. Westport, CT: Praeger, 2000.

DeSipio, Louis, and Rodolfe O. De La Garza. *US Immigration in the Twenty-First Century: Making Americans, Remaking America*. London: Routledge, 2015.

Desmarais, Norman. *America's First Ally: France in the Revolutionary War*. Havertown, PA: Casemate, 2019.

Dinkins, David, with Peter Knobler. *A Mayor's Life: Governing New York's Gorgeous Mosaic*. New York: Public Affairs, 2013.

Douglass, Frederick. *On Slavery and the Civil War: Selections from His Writings*. Ed. Philip S. Foner. Mineola, NY: Dover, 2014.

Drury, Bob, and Tom Clavin. *The Heart of Everything That Is: The Untold Story of Red Cloud, an American Legend*. Revised ed. New York: Simon & Schuster, 2013.

———. *Valley Forge*. New York: Simon & Schuster, 2018.

Dugruy, Joy. *Post Traumatic Slave Syndrome: America's Legacy of Enduring Injury and Healing*. Portland, OR: Joy Dugruy, 2005.

Dunbar-Ortiz, Roxanne. *An Indigenous Peoples' History of the United States*. Boston, MA: Beacon Press, 2014.

Dunn, Susan. *Jefferson's Second Revolution: The Election Crisis of 1800 and the Triumph of Republicanism*. Boston: Houghton Mifflin, 2004.

———. *Sister Revolutions: French Lightning, American Light*. New York: Farrar, Straus and Giroux, 2000.

Eckert, Allan W. *A Sorrow in Our Heart: The Life of Tecumseh*. New York: Bantam, 1992.

Egerton, Douglas R. *Death or Liberty: African Americans and Revolutionary America*. New York: Oxford University Press, 2009.

———. *Year of Meteors: Stephen Douglas, Abraham Lincoln, and the Election that Brought on the Civil War*. London: Bloomsbury Press, 2010.

Ellis, Joseph L. *American Creation: Triumphs and Tragedies at the Founding of the Republic*. New York: Alfred A. Knopf, 2007.

———. *American Sphinx: The Character of Thomas Jefferson*. New York: Vintage Books, 1996.

———. *Founding Brothers: The Revolutionary Generation.* New York: Vintage Books, 2002.

———. *His Excellency: George Washington.* New York: Vintage Books, 2004.

———. *The Quartet: Orchestrating the Second American Revolution, 1783–1789.* New York: Vintage Books, 2015.

Estes, Nick. *Our History Is the Future: Standing Rock versus the Dakota Access Pipeline, and the Long Tradition of Indigenous Resistance.* New York: Verso, 2019.

———. *Standing with Standing Rock: Voices from the #NoDAPL Movement.* Minneapolis: University of Minnesota Press, 2019.

Faderman, Lillian. *The Gay Revolution: The Story of the Struggle.* New York: Simon & Schuster, 2015.

Fenton, William M. *The Great Law and the Longhouse: A Political History of the Iroquois Confederacy.* Norman: University of Oklahoma Press, 1998.

Ferling, John. *John Adams: A Life.* New York: Oxford University Press, 1992.

———. *Adams vs. Jefferson: The Tumultuous Election of 1800.* New York: Oxford University Press, 2004.

Ferreiro, Larrie D. *Brothers at Arms: American Independence and the Men of France and Spain Who Saved It.* New York: Alfred A. Knopf, 2016.

Fischer, David Hackett. *Paul Revere's Ride.* New York: Oxford University Press, 1994.

Foster, Gaines M. *Ghosts of the Confederacy: Defeat, the Lost Cause, and the Emergence of the New South, 1865 to 1913.* New York: Oxford University Press, 1987.

Frady, Marshall. *Martin Luther King Jr.: A Life.* New York: Penguin, 2002.

Fryer, Paul. *Building an American Empire: The Era of Territorial and Political Expansion.* Princeton, NJ: Princeton University Press, 2017.

Gallagher Gary W., and Alan T. Nolan, eds. *The Myth of the Lost Cause and Civil War History.* Bloomington: Indiana University Press, 2010.

Gallagher, Hugh Gregory. *FDR's Splendid Deception: The Moving Story of Roosevelt's Massive Disability—And the Intense Efforts to Conceal It from the Public.* 3rd ed. St. Petersburg, FL: Vandamere Press, 1999.

Gardner, John W. *On Leadership.* New York: The Free Press, 1990.

Garrow, David. *Bearing the Cross: Martin Luther King Jr., and the Southern Christian Leadership Conference.* New York: HarperCollins, 1986.

Geissler, Suzanne. *God and Sea Power: The Influence of Religion on Alfred Thayer Mahan*. Annapolis, MD: Naval Institute Press, 2015.

Gilbert, Alan. *Black Patriots and Loyalists: Fighting for Emancipation in the War for Independence*. Chicago: University of Chicago Press, 2012.

Gilhooley, Simon J. *The Antebellum Origins of the Modern Constitution: Slavery and the Spirit of the American Founding*. New York: Cambridge University Press, 2020.

Goodwin, Doris Kearns. *Team of Rivals: The Political Genius of Abraham Lincoln*. New York: Simon & Schuster, 2005.

Gorn, Elliot J. *Mother Jones: The Most Dangerous Woman in America*. New York: Hill & Wang, 2001.

Gross, Robert. *The Minutemen and Their World*. New York: Hill & Wang, 1976.

Grounds, Richard A., George E. Tinker, and David E. Wilkins, eds. *Native Voices: American Indian Identity and Resistance*. Lawrence: University Press of Kansas, 2003.

Handlin, Oscar. *The Uprooted: The Epic Story of the Great Migrations That Made the American People*. 2nd ed. Philadelphia: University of Philadelphia Press, 2002.

Hanks, Stephen. *1619—Twenty Africans: Their Story, and Discovery of Their Black, Red, and White Descendants*. Portland, OR: Inkwater Press, 2019.

Haynes, Sam W., and Christopher Morris, eds. *Manifest Destiny and Empire: American Antebellum Expansionism*. College Station: Texas A&M University Press, 2008.

Henderson, Ryan C. *Obama at War: Congress and the Imperial Presidency*. Lexington: University Press of Kentucky, 2015.

Herman, Dorothy. *Helen Keller: A Life*. Chicago: University of Chicago Press, 1999.

Herrera, Ricardo. A. *For Liberty and the Republic: The American Citizen as Soldier, 1775–1861*. New York: New York University, 2015.

Hiltzik, Michael A. *Iron Empires: Robber Barons, Railroads, and the Making of Modern America*. Boston, MA: Houghton Mifflin Harcourt, 2020.

Hobbes, Thomas. *Leviathan: With Selected Variants from the Latin Edition of 1668*. Ed. Edwin Curley. New York: Hackett, 1994.

Hoffer, Eric. *The True Believer: Thoughts on the Nature of Mass Movements*. New York: Harper & Row, 1951.

Hofstadter, Richard. *The Paranoid Style in American Politics*. First Vintage ed. New York: Vintage Books, 2008.

———. *Social Darwinism in American Thought*. Reprint ed. Boston, MA: Beacon Press, 1992.

Holt, Michael F. *The Election of 1860: A Campaign Fraught with Consequences*. Lawrence: University of Kansas Press, 2017.

———. *By One Vote: The Disputed Presidential Election of 1876*. Lawrence: University Press of Kansas, 2008.

Holt, Thomas C. *The Movement: The African American Struggle for Civil Rights*. New York: Oxford University Press, 2021.

Horn, James. *1619: Jamestown and the Forging of American Democracy*. New York: Basic Books, 2018.

Horwitz, Tony. *Midnight Rising: John Brown and the Raid That Sparked the Civil War*. New York: Henry Holt, 2011.

Irons, Peter. *War Powers: How the Imperial Presidency Hijacked the Constitution*. New York: Henry Holt, 2006.

Isaacson, Walter. *Benjamin Franklin: An American Life*. New York: Simon & Schuster, 2003.

Jacobs, Renée. "The Iroquois Great Law of Peace and the United States Constitution: How the Founding Fathers Ignored the Clan Mothers." *American Indian Law Review* 16, no. 2 (January 1991): 497–531.

Jensen, Merrill. *The Articles of Confederation: An Interpretation of the Social-Constitutional History of the American Revolution, 1774–1781*. Madison: University of Wisconsin Press, 1959.

Jones, Greg. *Honor in the Dust: Theodore Roosevelt, War in the Philippines, and the Rise and Fall of America's Imperial Dream*. New York: New American Library, 2012.

Jones, Mary Harris. *Autobiography of Mother Jones*. Reprint ed. Ed. Mary Field. Mineola, NY: Dover, 2004.

Josephy, Alvin M. *The Patriot Chiefs: A Chronicle of American Indian Resistance*. Revised ed. New York: Penguin, 1993.

Kalmoe, Nathan P. *With Ballots and Bullets: Partisanship and Violence in the American Civil War*. Cambridge: Cambridge University Press, 2020.

Kaye, Harvey J. *Thomas Paine and the Promise of America: A History & Biography*. New York: Hill & Wang, 2007.

Klarman, Michael J. *The Framers' Coup: The Making of the United States Constitution*. New York: Oxford University Press, 2016.

Keegan, John. *The First World War*. New York: Vintage, 2012.

Keller, Helen. *The Complete Story of My Life*. Orinda, CA: SeaWolf Press, 2020.

———. *The World I Live In*. Ed. Roger Shattuck. New York: New York Review Books, 2003.

Kendi, Ibram X. *How to Be an Antiracist*. New York: One World, 2019.

———. *Stamped from the Beginning: The Definitive History of Racist Ideas in America*. New York: Hachette Books, 2016.

Kidd, Thomas S. *The Great Awakening: The Roots of Evangelical Christianity in Colonial America*. New Haven, CT: Yale University Press, 2009.

King, Martin Luther, Jr. *A Testament of Hope: The Essential Writings and Speeches*. Ed. James M. Washington. New York: HarperCollins, 1991.

———. *The Autobiography of Martin Luther King Jr*. Ed. Clayborne Carson. New York: Grand Central Publishing, 1976.

Kuhl, Stefan. *The Nazi Connection: Eugenics, American Racism, and German National Socialism*. New York: Oxford University Press, 1994.

LaFeber, Walter F. *The New Empire: An Interpretation of American Expansion, 1860–1898*. 35th anniversary ed. Ithaca, NY: Cornell University Press, 1998.

Lambert, Frank. *Inventing the "Great Awakening."* Princeton, NJ: Princeton University Press, 1999.

Langguth, A. J. *Patriots: The Men Who Started the American Revolution*. New York: Simon & Schuster, 1988.

Langley, Lester D. *The Banana Wars: United States Intervention in the Caribbean, 1898–1934*. Lexington: University Press of Kentucky, 1983.

Larson, Edward J. *A Magnificent Catastrophe: The Tumultuous Election of 1800, America's First Presidential Campaign*. New York: Free Press, 2007.

Lears, Jackson. *Rebirth of a Nation: The Making of Modern America, 1877–1920*. New York: Harper Perennial, 2010.

Lee, Erika. *America for Americans: A History of Xenophobia in the United States*. New York: Basic Books, 2019.

LeMay, Michael C. *US Immigration Policy, Ethnicity, and Religion in American History*. Westport, CT: Praeger, 2018.

Lengel, Edward G., ed. *This Glorious Struggle: George Washington's Revolutionary War Letters*. New York: HarperCollins, 2007.

Leonard, Thomas C. *Illiberal Reformers: Race, Eugenics, and American Economics in the Progressive Era.* Reprint ed. Princeton, NJ: Princeton University Press, 2017.

Lewis, Jan Ellen. "Women and the Constitution: Why the Constitution Includes Women," *Commonplace: The Journal of Early American Life* 2, no. 4 (April 2002), http://commonplace.online/article/women-and-the-constitution-why-the-constitution includes-women/.

Lewis, John. *Across That Bridge: Life Lessons and a Vision for Change.* New York: Hachette Books, 2012.

Lewis, Sinclair. *It Can't Happen Here.* New York: Signet Classics, 2014.

Limerick, Patricia Nelson. *The Legacy of Conquest: The Unbroken Past of the American West.* New York: W.W. Norton, 2011.

Locke, John. *Second Treatise of Government.* Ed. C. B. Macpherson. Indianapolis, IN: Hackett, 1980.

Lombardo, Paul A., *Three Generations, No Imbeciles: Eugenics, the Supreme Court, and Buck v. Bell.* Baltimore, MD: Johns Hopkins University Press, 2010.

Longmore, Paul K., and Lauri Umansky, eds. *The New Disability History: American Perspectives.* New York: New York University Press, 2001.

Madison, James. *Notes of Debates in the Federal Convention of 1787.* 2nd ed. New York: W.W. Norton, 1987.

Mahan, A. T. *The Influence of Sea Power upon History, 1660–1783.* Boston, MA: Little, Brown, 1905.

Mann, Charles C. *1491: New Revelations of the Americas Before Columbus.* 2nd ed. New York: Vintage Books, 2006.

Marcus, Eric. *Making Gay History: The Half Century Fight for Lesbian and Gay Equal Rights.* New York: Harper Perennial, 2002.

Matthiessen, Peter. *In the Spirit of Crazy Horse: The Story of Leonard Peltier and the FBI's War on the American Indian Movement.* New York: Penguin, 1992.

Maxwell, Angie, and Todd Shields. *The Long Southern Strategy: How Chasing White Voters in the South Changed American Politics.* New York: Oxford University Press, 2019.

McCoy, Alfred W., and Francisco A. Scarano, eds. *Colonial Crucible: Empire in the Making of the Modern American State.* Madison: University of Wisconsin Press, 2009.

McDougall, Walter. *Promised Land, Crusader State: The American Encounter with the World since 1776*. New York: Houghton Mifflin Harcourt, 1997.

McGerr, Michael. *A Fierce Discontent: The Rise and Fall of the Progressive Movement in America*. New York: Free Press, 2003.

McAllister, Brian. *The Philippine War, 1899–1902*. Lawrence: University of Kansas Press, 2000.

McMillen, Sally. *Seneca Falls and the Origins of the Women's Rights Movement*. New York: Oxford University Press, 2008.

McPherson, James M. *Battle Cry of Freedom: The Civil War Era*. New York: Oxford University Press, 1988.

———. *The War That Forged a Nation: Why the Civil War Still Matters*. New York: Oxford University Press, 2015.

Meacham, Jon. *The Soul of America: The Battle for Our Better Angels*. New York: Random House, 2018.

———. *Thomas Jefferson: The Art of Power*. New York: Random House, 2012.

Menakem, Resmaa. *My Grandmother's Hands: Racialized Trauma and the Pathway to Mending Our Hearts and Bodies*. Las Vegas, NV: Central Recovery Press, 2017.

Merk, Frederick. *Manifest Destiny and Mission in American History*. Reprint ed. Cambridge, MA: Harvard University Press, 1995.

Meyer, G. J. *A World Undone: The Story of the Great War, 1914–1918*. New York: Delacorte Press, 2006.

Miller, John C. *Crisis in Freedom: The Alien and Sedition Acts*. Boston, MA: Little, Brown, 1951.

Miller, Stuart Creighton. *Benevolent Assimilation: The American Conquest of the Philippines, 1899–1903*. New Haven, CT: Yale University Press, 1982.

Morris, Roy, Jr. *Fraud of the Century: Rutherford B. Hayes, Samuel Tilden, and the Stolen Election of 1876*. New York: Simon & Schuster, 2003.

Murphy, Reg, and Hal Gulliver. *The Southern Strategy*. New York: Scribner, 1971.

Nash, Gary B. *Red, White, and Black: The Peoples of Early North America*. 6th ed. London: Pearson, 2009.

Neimeyer, Charles Patrick. *America Goes to War: A Social History of the Continental Army*. New York: New York University, 1996.

Nelson, Anne. *Shadow Network: Media, Money, and the Secret Hub of the Radical Right.* London: Bloomsbury, 2019.

Nerburn, Kent. *Chief Joseph and the Flight of the Nez Perce: The Untold Story of an American Tragedy.* New York: HarperOne, 2009.

Nielsen, Kim E. *A Disability History of the United States.* Boston, MA: Beacon Press, 2012.

———. *The Radical Lives of Helen Keller.* New York: New York University Press, 2004.

Oates, Stephen B. *Let the Trumpet Sound: A Life of Martin Luther King Jr.* New York: Harper & Row, 1982.

Oberg, Barbara B., ed. *Women in the American Revolution: Gender, Politics, and the Domestic World.* Charlottesville: University of Virginia Press, 2019.

Okrent, Daniel. *The Guarded Gate: Bigotry, Eugenics and the Law That Kept Two Generations of Jews, Italians, and Other European Immigrants Out of America.* New York: Scribner, 2019.

Orleck, Annelise. *Rethinking American Women's Activism.* New York: Routledge, 2015.

Oshinsky, David. *Polio: An American Story.* New York: Oxford University Press, 2005.

Ostler, Jeffrey. *Surviving Genocide: Native Nations and the United States from the American Revolution to Bleeding Kansas.* New Haven, CT: Yale University Press, 2020.

O'Toole, G. J. A. *The Spanish War: An American Epic 1898.* New York: W.W. Norton, 1984.

Page, Jake. *In the Hands of the Great Spirit: The 20,000-Year History of American Indians.* New York: Free Press, 2004.

Paine, Thomas. *Common Sense: The Origin and Design of Government.* Ed. Coventry House Publishing. Dublin, OH: Coventry House Publishing, 2016.

Painter, Nell Irvin *Standing at Armageddon: A Grassroots History of the Progressive Era.* New York: W.W. Norton, 1987.

Parks, Rosa, with Jim Haskins. *Rosa Parks: My Story.* New York: Dial Books, 1992.

Pasley, Jeffrey L. *The First Presidential Contest: 1796 and the Founding of American Democracy.* Lawrence: University Press of Kansas, 2013.

Perkins, Whitney T. *Denial of Empire: The United States and Its Dependencies*. Leiden, NL: A. W. Sythoff, 1962.

Phalen, William J. *The First War of United States: The Quasi War with France 1798–1801*. Delhi, IN: Vij Books, 2019.

Pratt, Julius William. *Expansionists of 1898: The Acquisition of Hawaii and the Spanish Islands*. Baltimore, MD: Johns Hopkins Press, 1936.

Rees, John U. *"They Were Good Soldiers": African-Americans Serving in the Continental Army, 1775–1783*. Warwick, UK: Helion, 2019.

Rehnquist, William H. *Centennial Crisis: The Disputed Election of 1876*. New York: Random House, 2004.

Reynolds, David S. *Abe: Abraham Lincoln in His Times*. New York: Penguin Press, 2020.

———. *John Brown, Abolitionist: The Man Who Killed Slavery, Sparked the Civil War, and Seeded Civil Rights*. New York: Vintage Books, 2005.

Richards, Leonard L. *Shays's Rebellion: The American Revolution's Final Battle*. Philadelphia: University of Pennsylvania, 2002.

Rosen, Christine. *Preaching Eugenics: Religious Leaders and the American Eugenics Movement*. New York: Oxford University Press, 2004.

Rossiter, Clinton, ed. *The Federalist Papers*. New York: Signet Classics, 2003.

Rousseau, Jean-Jacques. *The Social Contract, or Principles of Political Right*. Trans. H. J. Tozer. Ware, UK: Wordsworth, 1998.

Rudalevige, Andrew. *The New Imperial Presidency: Renewing Presidential Power after Watergate*. Ann Arbor: University of Michigan Press, 2006.

Sanders, Ronald. *Lost Tribes and Promised Lands: The Origins of American Racism*. Detroit, MI: Dzanc Books, 1978.

Saunt, Claudio. *Unworthy Republic: The Dispossession of Native Americans and the Road to Indian Territory*. New York: W.W. Norton, 2020.

Savage, Charlie. *Takeover: The Return of the Imperial Presidency and the Subversion of American Democracy*. New York: Little, Brown, 2007.

Schlesinger, Arthur, Jr. *The Imperial Presidency*. Reprint ed. Boston: Mariner Books, 2004.

Schmitt, Gary, Joseph M. Bessette, and Andrew E. Busch, eds. *The Imperial Presidency and the Constitution*. Lanham, MD: Rowman & Littlefield, 2017.

Schweik, Susan M. *The Ugly Laws: Disability in Public*. New York: New York University Press, 2009.

Sellers, Bakari. *My Vanishing Country: A Memoir*. New York: Amistad, 2020.

Sharp, Roger. *The Deadlocked Election of 1800: Jefferson, Burr, and the Union in the Balance*. Lawrence: University Press of Kansas, 2010.

Shird, Kevin, with Nelson Malden. *The Colored Waiting Room: Empowering the Original and the New Civil Rights Movements; Conversations Between an MLK Jr. Confidant and a Modern-Day Activist*. New York: Apollo, 2018.

Silbey, David J. *The Boxer Rebellion and the Great Game in China: A History*. New York: Hill & Wang, 2012.

———. *A War of Frontier and Empire: The Philippine-American War, 1899–1902*. New York: Hill & Wang, 2008.

Simon, Herbert A. *Administrative Behavior: A Study of Decision-Making Processes in Administrative Organizations*. 4th ed. New York: The Free Press, 1997.

Simpson, Leanne Betsamosake. *As We Have Always Done: Indigenous Freedom through Radical Resistance*. Minneapolis: University of Minnesota Press, 2020.

Slack, Charles. *Liberty's First Crisis: Adams, Jefferson, and the Misfits Who Saved Free Speech*. New York: Atlantic Monthly Press, 2015.

Smith, Carey Stacey, and Li-Ching Hung. *The Patriot Act: Issues and Controversies*. Springfield, IL: Charles C. Thomas, 2010.

Smith, Jean Edward. *FDR*. New York: Random House, 2007.

Smith, John Howard. *The First Great Awakening: Redefining Religion in British America, 1725–1775*. Lanham, MD: Fairleigh Dickinson University Press, 2015.

Snyder, Timothy. *On Tyranny: Twenty Lessons from the Twentieth Century*. New York: Tim Duggan Books, 2017.

———. *Our Malady: Lessons in Liberty and Solidarity*. New York: Crown, 2020.

———. *The Road to Unfreedom: Russia, Europe*. New York: Tim Duggan Books, 2017.

Spickard, Paul. *Race and Immigration in the United States: New Histories*. London: Routledge, 2011.

Stannard, David E. *American Holocaust: The Conquest of the New World*. New York: Oxford University Press, 1992.

SUGGESTED READINGS

Stephanson, Anders. *Manifest Destiny: American Expansion and the Empire of Right*. New York: Hill & Wang, 1995.

Stewart, David O. *The Summer of 1787: The Men Who Invented the Constitution*. New York: Simon & Schuster, 2007.

Storing, Herbert J., and Murray Dry, eds. *The Anti-Federalist: Writings by the Opponents of the Constitution*. Abridged ed. Chicago: University of Chicago Press, 1985.

Stryker, Susan. *Transgender History: The Roots of Today's Revolution*. 2nd ed. New York: Seal Press, 2017.

Sugden, John. *Tecumseh: A Life*. New York: Holt, 1999.

Sundstrom, Ronald R. *The Browning of America and the Evasion of Social Justice*. Albany: State University of New York Press, 2008.

Sweeney, Edward R. *From Cochise to Geronimo: The Chiricahua Apaches, 1874–1886*. Norman: University of Oklahoma Press, 2012.

Szatmary, David P. *Shays' Rebellion: The Making of an Agrarian Insurrection*. Amherst: University of Massachusetts Press, 1980.

Takaki, Ronald. *Different Mirror: A History of Multicultural America*. New York: Back Bay Books, 2008.

Terkel, Studs. *Working: People Talk about What They Do All Day and How They Feel about What They Do*. New York: Pantheon, 1974.

Tetrault, Lisa. *The Myth of Seneca Falls: Memory and the Women's Suffrage Movement, 1848–1898*. Chapel Hill: University of North Carolina Press, 2014.

Thomas, Evan. *The War Lovers: Roosevelt, Lodge, Hearst, and the Rush to Empire, 1898*. New York: Back Bay Books, 2010.

Tobin, James. *The Man He Became: How FDR Defied Polio to Win the Presidency*. New York: Simon & Schuster, 2013.

Tocqueville, Alexis de. *Democracy in America*. Trans. Arthur Goldhammer. New York: Library of America, 2004.

Todd, Matthew. *Pride: The Story of the LGBTQ Equality Movement*. Richmond, CA: Weldon Owen, 2020.

Toll, Ian W. *Six Frigates: The Epic History of the Founding of the US Navy*. New York: W.W. Norton, 2006.

Tooze, Adam. *The Deluge: The Great War, America and the Remaking of the Global Order, 1916–1931*. New York: Penguin, 2014.

Turner, Frederick Jackson. *The Significance of the Frontier in American History*. Reprint ed. Eastford, CT: Martino Fine Books, 2014.

Ulrich, Laurel Thatcher. *Well-Behaved Women Seldom Make History*. New York: Vintage Books, 2007.

Unger, Harlow Giles. *Thomas Paine and the Clarion Call for American Independence*. New York: Hachette Books, 2019.

Utley, Robert. *Sitting Bull: The Life and Times of an American Patriot*. New York: Holt, 2008.

Van Buskirk, Judith L. *Standing in Their Own Light: African American Patriots in the American Revolution*. Norman: University of Oklahoma Press, 2017.

Van Clive, George William. *We Have Not a Government: The Articles of Confederation and the Road to the Constitution*. Chicago: University of Chicago Press, 2017.

Varon, Elizabeth. *Disunion! The Coming of the American Civil War, 1789–1859*. Chapel Hill: University of North Carolina Press, 2008.

Ware, Charles C. *1491: New Revelations of the Americas Before Columbus*. New York: Alfred A. Knopf, 2005.

Warner, Sam Bass. *The Private City: Philadelphia in Three Stages of Its Growth*. Philadelphia: University of Pennsylvania Press, 1968.

Watkins, William. *Reclaiming the American Revolution: The Kentucky and Virginia Resolutions and Their Legacy*. New York: Palgrave Macmillan, 2004.

Weisberger, Bernard. *America Afire: Jefferson, Adams, and the Revolutionary Election of 1800*. New York: William Morrow, 2000.

Wellman, Judith. *The Road to Seneca Falls: Elizabeth Cady Stanton and the First Woman's Rights Convention*. Urbana: University of Illinois Press, 2004.

White, Richard. *Railroaded: The Transcontinentals and the Making of Modern America*. New York: W.W. Norton, 2011.

Whitman, James Q. *Hitler's American Model: The United States and the Making of Nazi Race Law*. Princeton, NJ: Princeton University Press, 2017.

Wike, Sudie Doggett. *Women in the American Revolution*. Jefferson, NC: McFarland, 2018.

Wilkerson, Isabel. *Caste: The Origins of Our Discontents*. New York: Random House, 2020.

SUGGESTED READINGS

Williams, William Appleman. *The Roots of the Modern American Empire: A Study of the Growth and Shaping of Social Consciousness in a Marketplace Society.* New York: Random House, 1969.

Wilson, Charles Reagan. *Baptized in Blood: The Religion of the Lost Cause, 1865–1920.* Athens: University of Georgia Press, 1980.

Woodworth, Steven E. *Manifest Destinies: America's Westward Expansion and the Road to the Civil War.* New York: Alfred A. Knopf, 2010.

Woolhouse, Roger. *Locke: A Biography.* New York: Cambridge University Press, 2007.

Wood, Gordon S. *The Creation of the American Republic, 1776–1787.* Chapel Hill: University of North Carolina Press, 1969.

Zimmermann, Warren. *First Great Triumph: How Five Americans Made Their Country a World Power.* New York: Farrar, Straus and Giroux, 2002.

Zinn, Howard. *A People's History of the United States.* Reissue ed. New York: Harper Perennial, 2015.

INDEX

Picanso, Leonard, 133
Pinckney, Charles C., 86
Pinochet, Augusto, 6
Plato, 12
Porter, Robert, 100
Portland, Oregon, protests (2020), 19–20
Powel, Elizabeth Willing, 43, 50
Priddy, Albert, 151, 152

QAnon, 68–69
Quasi-War, 97

Radical Republicans, 79
Reagan, Ronald, 33, 108–9
Reciprocity Treaty (1875), 101
Reconstruction. *See* Lincoln, Abraham, Civil War and Reconstruction
Red Cloud, 140
Reed, Deborah, 127
Reed, Esther de Berdt, 126–27, 128, 146
Reed, Joseph, 126
Refugee Relief Act (1953), 161–62
Rehabilitation Act, 156–58
The Republic. See Plato
Revere, Paul, 126
Robertson, Pat, 84
Rockefeller, John D., 121
Rolfe, John, 15
Roosevelt, Franklin D., 39–40, 107, 152–55, 171
Roosevelt, Theodore, 39, 101, 124, 152, 161
Ross, Eugene, 161
Rousseau, Jean-Jacques, 13

Ruffin, Edwin, 55–56, 65

same-sex marriage. *See* gay rights movement
Santos, Michael, 132–33
Scalise, Steve, 58
Schwab, Charles, 121
Scientific-Humanitarian Committee. *See* gay rights movement
Second Treatise on Government. See Locke, John
Section 504. *See* Rehabilitation Act
Seneca Falls Convention (1848), 36, 158–59
"The Sentiments of an American Woman." *See* Reed, Esther de Berdt
Seward, William, 101
Shakespeare, William, 145, 158
Shays's Rebellion, 19–21, 22
Sherman, Roger, 2
Simon, Herbert, 41
Sitting Bull, 140
Smith, Adam, 94
Smith, Al, 153
Snyder, Timothy, 47, 48
Snyder Act (1924), 38
Social Contract. See Rousseau, Jean-Jacques
Social Darwinism, 101, 103
Social Gospel, 101, 103
Society for Human Rights. *See* gay rights movement
Sons of Liberty, 10
Spanish-American War, 102
Spencer, Charles, 101

Stanton, Elizabeth Cady, 37, 146
Statue of Liberty, 159, 160
Steinem, Gloria, 146
Stonewall Riots. *See* gay rights
　movement
Strode, Aubrey, 151
Sullivan, Anne, 155
Sumner, William Graham, 101
Sussex Pledge, 104–5

Taft, William Howard, 104
Tecumseh, 138–40
Ten Percent Plan, 79
Tenskwatawa, 138–39
Terkel, Studs, 125
Thälmann, Ernst, 49
Thomas, Dylan, 146
Thomas Road Baptist Church, 83
Thucydides, 16
Tiananmen Square, 6
Tilden, Samuel, 59
Tocqueville, Alexis de, 43–44, 45,
　48, 73
To Tell the Truth, 165
transcontinental railroad, 99, 160
Treaty of Fort Wayne, 139
Treaty of Greenville, 138
Treaty of Versailles, 106–7
Truman Doctrine, 108
Trump, Don, Jr., 61–62
Trump, Donald J., ix–x, 121;
　election of 2020, 3–4, 17, 40,
　50, 57–58; impeachments, 28,
　39; insurrection, 61–62, 64,
　65–67; as president, 110, 145,
　161. *See also* elections, 2020
Trump, Ivanka, 66

Trump, Melania, 66
Turner, Frederick Jackson, 101
Tyrrell, William, 104

ugly laws, 150–51
Ulrich, Laurel Thatcher, 115–16,
　117, 118, 128, 146

Vanderbilt, Cornelius, 121
Vietnam War Memorial, 132–33
Virginia and Kentucky Resolutions,
　97
Virginia Eugenical Sterilization
　Act, 151
Virginia State Colony for
　Epileptics and Feeble Minded,
　151–52

Walker, Quock, 130
Wallace, George, 83
Warm Springs Foundation, 154
War of 1812, 139–40
Washington, George, 21, 29, 88,
　98, 127; as general, 27, 30; as
　president, 27–28, 48
Watts, John W., 60
Weimar Republic. *See* Germany
　and rise of Nazism
Weininger, Al, 148
*Well-Behaved Women Seldom Make
　History. See* Ulrich, Laurel
　Thatcher
Weyrich, Paul, 84
"White Man's Burden." *See*
　Kipling, Rudyard
Wilhelm II (kaiser), 49
Wilson, Dick, 142

ABOUT THE AUTHOR

Michael Wayne Santos lives in Lynchburg, Virginia, where he is professor of history at the University of Lynchburg. He has taught a variety of courses in American history, world history, foreign policy, social and cultural history, and local history, and he has been responsible for helping to initiate a variety of programs at the university. Santos was the founding director of the institution's Symposium Readings Program, helped organize the campus chapter of Habitat for Humanity, and established the Center for the History and Culture of Central Virginia. He is the author of multiple books and articles on American history and liberal arts education, and he has presented at regional and national conferences. Santos has received the Shirley Rosser Excellence in Teaching Award and the T. A. Abbott Award for Faculty Excellence.